Confidence-building in South-East Asia

Bradford Arms Register Studies

The Bradford Arms Register Studies (BARS) series, published in cooperation with Westview Press, is the result of an on-going research project based at the Department of Peace Studies, University of Bradford and supported by Ford Foundation. Studies published so far include:

1. Malcolm Chalmers and Owen Greene, *Implementing and Developing the UN Register of Conventional Arms*, May 1993.

2. Malcolm Chalmers and Owen Greene, *The United Nations Register of Conventional Arms: An Initial Examination of the First Report*, October 1993.

3. Malcolm Chalmers and Owen Greene, *Background Information: an analysis of information provided to the UN on military holdings and procurement through national production in the first year of the Register of Conventional Arms*, March 1994 (reprinted April 1995).

4. Malcolm Chalmers, Owen Greene, Edward J. Laurance, and Herbert Wulf (eds), *Developing the UN Register of Conventional Arms*, May 1994.

5. Malcolm Chalmers and Owen Greene, *Taking Stock: the UN Register After Two Years*, June 1995.

Confidence-Building

in South-East Asia

Malcolm Chalmers

Bradford Arms Register Studies No. 6

1996

Westview Press

ISSN 1360-8622

ISBN 1-85143-116-0

Printed in Great Britain on acid-free paper

by Redwood Books, Trowbridge, Wiltshire

Distributed by Westview Press

For Christine, Jenny and Paul

Contents

1. Introduction...1

2. The ASEAN Way 13

3. China and South-East Asia..41

4. The ASEAN Arms Build-Up...61

5. The ASEANization of Australia......................................121

6. The regional security dialogue.......................................137

7. The UN Register and South-East Asia............................171

8. Confidence-building measures..221

9. Beyond confidence-building measures..............................243

Appendix 1: Information provided to the UN Register on
imports into Australasia and South-East Asia, 1992-1994...............269

CHAPTER 1

Introduction

This book forms part of a larger project designed to examine the role and effectiveness of the United Nations Register of Conventional Arms and associated measures. Previous volumes in the Bradford Arms Register Studies series have focused on the development of the UN Register as a global regime. Perhaps the most important test of the relevance and utility of the Register, however, is whether it can make a contribution to security at a regional level. This volume addresses this question through an examination of the role of the UN Register, and other transparency and confidence-building measures, in South-East Asia.

Recent developments in South-East Asia are of more than regional significance. As support for confidence-building measures in the region grows, it strengthens in turn the support for confidence-building measures at a global level. Ideas generated from the regional security dialogue find their way into global policy agendas. And the creation of distinct Asia-Pacific processes - the Asia-Pacific Economic Cooperation (APEC) and the ASEAN Regional Forum (ARF) - have the potential to provide as significant a building block in global society as their Atlantic counterparts, the G7, the OSCE and NATO.

The focus of this volume is on conventional arms. Yet, as will become apparent, confidence-building and transparency are instruments for increasing political stability as much as they are about stability at a purely military level. If such measures are to play a useful role, it will be more through increasing mutual understanding of what is driving policies for the use of weapons than through increasing technical knowledge of the characteristics of the weapons themselves.

I   Transparency and confidence-building

Military transparency has been defined as

> 'the systematic provision of information on specific aspects of activities in the military field under informal or formal international arrangements.'[1]

Transparency measures include the exchange of information on aspects of military capabilities, budgets, operations, and policies, as well as governments talking with each other about their respective military concerns. Transparency measures are not a replacement for the balance of power. Indeed they are relevant precisely because the distribution and nature of military power still matters to states. Yet they are also possible because states recognise that, although they have conflicting interests, they also have common ones (not least in avoiding the destruction of war). At least in the absence of a fully-fledged 'security community', transparency measures, and confidence-building measures more generally, are best seen as one part of a total effort to manage the balance of power system in a benign way.

In many regions of the world, including Asia, efforts to create and sustain a balance of power between major powers (so that no single state is in a position of dominance) play a central role in efforts to pursue these common and conflicting interests simultaneously.[2] But the form which this balance takes can vary considerably, depending on a range of political, geographical and institutional factors. The balance can be sustained at high or low levels of military spending. It can involve defence policies based primarily on deterrence by denial or on deterrence by retaliation, or more commonly by some combination of the two. It can involve a balance based primarily on active military forces or with more emphasis on a broader appreciation of national power potential. Finally, states can seek to manage their relationships through a series of bilateral discussions, or they can seek to develop rules and institutional arrangements in multilateral fora. Transparency measures provide one of the possible mechanisms through which this management, whether bilateral or multilateral, takes place.

The confidence-building argument for transparency in armaments emerges from a consideration of a contradiction at the heart of national attitudes towards military secrecy. On the one hand, armed forces are aware of the critical role that uncertainty and deception play in warfare. In order to protect this potential advantage, they therefore seek to minimise how much other states know about them. Moreover, in order to protect against leakage, access to information within their own bureaucracies is strictly controlled, and often restricted on the basis of a narrowly-conceived 'need to know' principle.

On the other hand, states also devote considerable resources to finding out what others are doing. Massive resources are expended towards this end, ranging from routine legal activities (maintaining embassies, monitoring the specialist press and keeping in close contact with commercial sources) to more covert activities such as signals intelligence and straightforward spying. The result of this activity is that armed forces usually know much more about technical aspects of each others' military activities than is publicly available. With major states in particular, not least in Asia, devoting a great deal of effort to improving their national intelligence capabilities, transparency measures may thus add relatively little knowledge at a military-operational level.[3]

In a climate of excessive secrecy, intelligence activity can have a stabilising effect by reducing the potential for misunderstanding. Yet, for obvious reasons, there are real political costs in a reliance on covert methods for data collection. Indeed, in some cases - for example the 1989 dispute over alleged Singaporean espionage activity in Malaysia - such methods can contribute to a marked deterioration in mutual confidence.

While military secrecy is a legitimate element of self-defence, an obsession with total secrecy can create problems. It can generate mistrust between states, thus contributing to arms races, increasing the risk of conflict, and raising the economic burden of defence spending. Not least, excessive military secrecy can reduce trust between states more generally, in ways that undermine prospects for co-operation in a wide range of non-military fields.

In the 1980s such arguments began to have an impact on thinking in the governments of both NATO and Warsaw Pact countries. An influential group of thinkers within the Soviet Union began to take up arguments for 'common security', already being developed by Western analysts and, to some extent, governments. The process culminated in the process of 'glasnost' adopted by the Soviet Union from 1985 onwards.

In the context of the intense confrontation of conventional forces in Central Europe at the time, a key concern in this debate was to reduce the military incentives for pre-emption created by high levels of secrecy. Accordingly, the transparency measures agreed in the 1986 Stockholm agreement - the first concrete result of the new Soviet policy - focused on providing prior notification of large scale military exercises, together with modest steps towards some verification processes. The Stockholm agreement had a significant impact in making it more difficult for the Warsaw Pact to mobilise for war without setting off various 'tripwires.' It was hoped that the result would be to reduce the danger that war would result - as arguably it may have done in 1914 - from the extreme pressure during a crisis to mobilise first and strike first.

As well as performing this tripwire role in future crises, a role which may have contemporary relevance in the Korean peninsula, the transparency measures undertaken during this period also had a broader function. They began the process of developing states' understanding of each others' concerns and priorities. It is a principle of human interaction in general, by no means confined to the military field, that trust is enhanced by openness. The willingness to be honest with each other, therefore, can have a confidence-building effect far beyond the specific stabilising effect of the data provided. No realistic amount of standardised information exchange is likely to reveal more than a fraction of the data required for a full appraisal of military capability. As important as data exchange, therefore, are opportunities to discuss the fears and concerns which drive states' policies, and which provide the rationale for military forces. The confidence-building process as a whole provides a means through which states can bring their own concerns out into the open, while also having to justify their own policies to others. Its real value lies in providing countries with greater understanding of each others' policies, strategies and long term ambitions and, where possible, encouraging them to take greater account of other countries' concerns in their own policies.

If carefully applied, confidence-building and transparency measures can have a role in making a balance of power system more benign by helping to provide states with a greater understanding of what others are doing and why they are doing it. It can help to reduce the risk of war by reducing the extent to which arms procurement is driven by worst case assumptions. Beyond survival concerns, it can encourage states to moderate their policy objectives in ways that take account of the interest of others. Over time, by creating greater mutual understanding, it can perhaps facilitate the trend towards a 'mature anarchy.' As Barry Buzan suggests

> 'The international anarchy does not constitute a single form with relatively fixed features, but rather a single condition within which many variations can be arranged. ... In a very mature anarchy, all states would have to be strong as states ... on this basis, a strong international society could be built on the foundations of mutual recognition and acceptance.'[4]

Transparency cannot always be reassuring in a world in which some states remain prepared to use force in pursuit of interests beyond self-defence.

While security planners have a tendency to 'worst case' planning, new information on the capabilities of others can heighten concerns further. Governments use the release of information on their capabilities not only to reassure others, but also to deter, and in some cases intimidate, them. In these circumstances, and in the absence of reassurance at a policy level, increased transparency can sometimes contribute to an intensification of military competition, with states able to use early warning of developing threats in order to prepare a more timely response of their own.

The effects of transparency measures are also complicated by the fact that the blunt acknowledgement of national concerns about possible future threats, as part of a process of transparency, can cause offence in circumstances where previous diplomatic platitudes have been more customary. This was seen in the late 1980's when Indonesian government officials took offence at the increasingly explicit orientation of Australian defence policy towards defending against an attack coming from Indonesian territory. To some extent, the expression of concerns can be softened by using convenient stories, for example that countries need to make contingency plans in case circumstances in neighbouring countries take a turn for the worse, for example as a result of invasion of a neighbour by a third party. But, even by the use of such devices, military transparency and dialogue cannot avoid contention and vigorous debate altogether if it is to be of value.

The end of the Cold War has seen a marked increase in interest in transparency and confidence-building measures at both a global and regional level. Measures for verification and information exchange have been adopted, both for weapons of mass destruction and for conventional forces, that would have been unthinkable a decade ago. In the case of conventional arms, the Gulf War increased political pressure for something to be done to prevent destabilising accumulations of arms in regions of tension. Not least because of the economic pressures on major arms producers to offset declining domestic orders by increased exports, no progress was possible in efforts to limit arms transfers. But there was agreement that there was a role for transparency measures. As a result, in December 1991, the UN General Assembly voted to establish the United Nations Register of Conventional Arms. Only about half of UN members participate in the Register on a regular basis, although this does include virtually all major exporting states. As we shall discuss in Chapter 7, however, the UN Register has been relatively more successful in South-East Asia.

II   South-East Asia

South-East Asia is of particular interest for several reasons. Not least is the increasing importance of Asia to the world as a whole. Recent estimates suggest that, by 2000, Asian economic output will exceed that of either Europe or North America.[5] Partly as a result of the increased resources available from rapid growth, Asian defence expenditure is already roughly equivalent to that of NATO-Europe, and is likely to exceed it substantially if recent trends continue. As a result of continuing increases in defence budgets, a recent Pentagon report suggests that East Asia's share of world demand for arms imports will increase from 11% in 1981-90 to 30% in 1994-2000, in contrast to falls in the Middle East (from 37% to 30%) and the rest of the world (from 52% to 40%).[6]

Asia is a massive region, and the decision has therefore been taken to examine North-East Asia and South-East Asia separately. A book-length study of North-East Asia, authored by my colleague Owen Greene, will be published in summer 1996.[7] It will focus on the potential role of confidence-building measures, including the UN Register, in addressing the security concerns of Japan, China, Taiwan and the two Koreas.

The primary concern of this book is with the seven members of ASEAN (Brunei, Indonesia, Malaysia, the Philippines, Singapore, Thailand, and Vietnam), together with Australia. Although these eight states are at the heart of the South-East Asia security complex, others are also of importance and will be discussed briefly. Myanmar is a potential member of ASEAN, and the implications of political development there are of importance to Thailand in particular. The South Pacific states, Papua New Guinea and New Zealand have close ties to Australia, with Papua New Guinea also sharing a land border with Irian Jaya in Indonesia.

South-East Asia has specific characteristics that distinguish it clearly from North-East Asia. It is less militarised (no state within the region possesses weapons of mass destruction). With the end of the Cold War and the accommodation of Vietnam, it lacks the intense fixed conflict that characterises both North-East Asia (China/Taiwan and North Korea/South Korea) and South Asia (India/Pakistan). At the same time, South-East Asia is far from becoming a 'zone of peace.' In a time of uncertainty and rapid change, strategic planners are inclined to prepare for the worst even while they hope for the best. The economic miracle in the region has allowed most governments to fund ambitious arms acquisition programmes without increased burdens on their economies. But there is continuing concern that a faltering of the process of economic success in one or more country could lead to the re-emergence of destabilising tendencies and dormant disputes. South-East Asia appears to be managing the transition towards a security community more successfully than did Western Europe during its own industrial revolution. But it is early days, and the stresses of economic and political change in a diverse region could yet destroy what has, in recent years, been lauded as the Third World's biggest success story.

South-East Asia is made up of states which, at least in Asian terms, are all small or medium powers. They constitute a very diverse group in terms of population size, culture and political system. But their common vulnerability to outside pressure and events has led to a level of interest in multilateralism and the development of clear norms for inter-state activity that is largely absent from North-East Asia. The role of ASEAN during the 1970s and 1980s, and its continuing importance after the Cold War, is of particular interest for this study.

All regional divisions will, to some extent, be arbitrary. In the case of South-East Asia, no understanding is possible without taking account of the central importance of China. All states in South-East Asia are concerned, to a lesser or greater extent, by the growing power of China, and relations between China and South-East Asia are therefore a recurring theme of the analysis.

III   The book

The book begins, in Chapter 2, by showing that the idea of confidence-building is not new in the region. Since 1967, the Association of South-East Nations (ASEAN) has developed a series of norms of inter-state behaviour that have in turn played an important role in building confidence between its members. In the process, ASEAN has helped to create the environment in which the 'economic miracle' of the last twenty years has been possible.

The 'ASEAN Way' of confidence-building has been characterised by a high degree of informality, especially in relation to security matters. Although its members have developed a network of bilateral military relationships, there is no overall multilateral framework in existence. No attempt has been made to establish the sort of formal confidence-building measures that are characteristic of European security. Finally, although its greatest successes have been in the area of conflict prevention, ASEAN did not have a formally recognised role in security matters until 1992.

Since the end of the Cold War, South-East Asia has experienced a period of rapid strategic change, much of it to the benefit of the region. But the reduction in the American military presence in the region has heightened concerns about China's long term intentions. Chapter 3 examines these concerns, which for South-East Asia nations means most of all the issue of China's claims of sovereignty over the Spratly Islands. The desire for a more open dialogue with China, on this and other questions, is at the heart of ASEAN's support for extending the process of confidence-building to encompass East Asia as a whole.

Chapter 4 examines recent trends in arms purchases in each ASEAN member. Since 1990, defence spending has grown rapidly in most ASEAN states, with the bulk of the additional resources being used to buy new weapons systems. Part of the explanation for this growth is the availability of additional financial resources as a result of high levels of economic growth. In addition, some ASEAN states have felt it necessary to spend more in order to defend their maritime resources against piracy, illegal fishing, and other sub-state threats. Yet the growth in arms spending has also raised concerns about a possible arms race that could, if unchecked, divert scarce resources from economic development and contribute to regional tension. These concerns have helped convince ASEAN leaders of the need for new confidence-building measures.

Chapter 5 requires some explanation. Australia is not in South-East Asia, and it is not an Asian country. But its long-standing military relationship with Singapore and Malaysia (through the Five Powers' Defence Arrangements), together with its growing military ties with Indonesia (symbolised in the December 1995 treaty between the two countries), is evidence that it is an integral part of the region's security landscape. For the purposes of this book, it will be particularly important to examine the key role that Australia has played in the development of regional dialogue and confidence-building measures.

Since the Vietnamese withdrawal from Cambodia, there have been rapid developments in the security architecture of the region, and these changes are outlined in Chapter 6. ASEAN has expanded to include Vietnam, and

Cambodia, Laos and Myanmar are all due to become members by 2000. A new body - the ASEAN Regional Forum (ARF) - has been established, bringing together countries from the Asia-Pacific region as a whole. Regional processes have been established, both in ARF and at an unofficial 'second track' level, to carry forward the development of specific confidence-building measures.

One of the most important confidence-building measures specifically endorsed by ARF is the UN Register. The Register has been in existence since 1993, and has already led to a significant increase in levels of transparency in the region with regard to conventional arms transfers. After discussing the experience of the Register in the region over this period, together with the reasons for its endorsement by ARF, Chapter 7 goes on to discuss ways in which the countries of the region might seek to integrate the UN Register more fully into regional dialogue processes.

Greater use of the UN Register is only one of several confidence-building measures under discussion. Chapter 8 examines other proposals, including the suggested production of national defence policy statements, possible measures to observe and notify military activities, and the creation of a Regional Arms Register.

Finally, Chapter 9 puts the book's discussion of confidence-building measures in a wider context. The long term prospects for peace in the region are cautiously positive. But it will be many years before South-East Asia, far less East Asia as a whole, can be considered free from the possibility of inter-state conflict. Until then, transparency and confidence-building measures have an important part to play in preventing conflict and encouraging the development of cooperative security attitudes.

IV   Acknowledgements

In my research for this book, I have been fortunate in having been able to draw on the expertise and assistance of a wide range of people.

I am grateful to the staff of the Australian National University's Peace Research Centre in Canberra for their generous hospitality during the winter months of July and August 1994. My particular appreciation goes to Kevin Clements, Brahma Chellaney, Betts Fetherston (now at Bradford University), Jan Preston-Stanley, Carol Staples, and Christine Wilson. For their help during my visit to Canberra, I would also like to thank Gillian

Bird, Gary Brown, Graeme Cheeseman, Paul Dibb, Rosemary Greaves, Ron Huisken, Pauline Kerr, Andrew Mack, and Carlyle Thayer for their help and insights. Particular thanks go to Desmond Ball for the considerable assistance he was able to provide.

I would like to express my gratitude to Cao Xiaobing, Xie Zhiqiong and their colleagues at the Chinese People's Association for Peace and Disarmament for their hospitality in hosting my visits to China in 1992 and 1993. I would also like to thank Fu Cong, Guan Yuofei, Jiang Zhenxi, Luo Renshi, Niu Qiang, Pan Zhenqiang, Qian Wenrong, and Xu Weidi for their help in understanding Chinese policy.

My thanks go to B. A. Hamzah and Joon Num Mak of the Malaysian Institute for Maritime Affairs for allowing me the opportunity to spend a week with them in Kuala Lumpur in February 1995. I would also like to thank: (in Malaysia) Mohamed Jawhar Hassan and his colleagues at ISIS-Malaysia, Abdul Razak Abdullah Baginda, Siti Aziz Abod, Mohamed Zain Abu Bakar, Abdul Wahid; (in Singapore) Derek da Cunha, Chandran Jeshurun, Chan Kwong Lok, Yap Ong Heng, Yeo Kok Phuang; (in Thailand) Kusuma Snitwongse, Panitan Wattanayagorn, Morakot Sriswasdi and Rushda Thavaravej; and (in Vietnam) Nguyen Phuong Binh, Nguyen Ngoc Dien, Pham Thi Mien, Nguyen Tien Minh, Bui Thanh Son, Nguyen Ngoc Truong, Hoang Anh Tuan, Pham Quang Vinh, and Vu Xuan Vinh.

Thanks are also due to: Ralph Cossa and Gerry Segal, for inviting me to take part (as the CSCAP-Europe representative) in the CSCAP working group on confidence-building measures; Tim Huxley and Sue Willett for inviting me to their seminar series on Asia-Pacific security; Provoslav Davinic, Hannelore Hoppe, Eiko Ikegaya and their colleagues in the UN Centre for Disarmament Affairs for their assistance in facilitating access to information contained in the Register; Sue Miller at Westview Press for her enthusiasm for the project, assistance with publicity, and unstinting support; Doris Coombs and Lionel Parker at Redwood Books for their efficiency and advice; Jenny Braithwaite, Chris Bowers and Simon Coley for their work on the cover design; and Judith Anstee in the Department of Peace Studies for her continuing help in administering our project.

This book would not have been possible without the financial support of the Ford Foundation. Particular thanks go to Geoffrey Wiseman and Marion Pendleton for their advice and assistance.

Finally, I would like to express my heartfelt thanks to my colleague, and friend, Owen Greene. Owen is writing his own study, about confidence-building in North-East Asia, and the two volumes are intended to complement each other. Owen has provided me with ideas and detailed comments at every stage of the book's drafting and, although I bear sole responsibility for any errors, Owen must share much of the credit for the final product.

Notes

1.   UN Panel of Technical Experts, *Study on ways and means of promoting transparency in international transfers of conventional arms,* UN General Assembly Document A/46/301, September 1991, p. 13.

2.   For an extended discussion of the application of the balance of power concept to Asia, see Paul Dibb, *Towards a New Balance of Power in Asia*, Adelphi Paper Number 295, International Institute for Strategic Studies, Oxford University Press, 1995.

3.   For a detailed discussion of developments, see Desmond Ball, *Signals Intelligence in the Post-Cold War Era: Developments in the Asia-Pacific Region*, Institute of South-East Asian Studies, 1993.

4.   Barry Buzan, *People, States and Fear*, 2nd edition, Harvester-Wheatsheaf, 1991, p. 176.

5.   Paul Dibb, op cit, p. 19.

6.   Department of Defense, *World-wide Conventional Arms Trade (1994-2000)*, December 1994, pp. 18-24.

7.   Owen Greene, *Confidence-building in North-East Asia*, Bradford Arms Register Studies Number 7, Westview Press, 1996.

CHAPTER 2

The ASEAN Way

... 'The rules of procedure are Western; English is the only language spoken at meetings of officials; golf, a game with Scottish origins, is the one game they all play; but the behavioural culture within the organisation is heavily influenced by Asia. Direct confrontation is avoided - 'face' must not be lost. Everybody must feel 'comfortable'.'[1]

I   A Success Story

South-East Asia has been the setting for a remarkable success story. The countries of the region have benefited from an economic 'take-off' that is, even by the standards of previous 'economic miracles', remarkably rapid.

The exit from the vicious cycle of underdevelopment and conflict began with Singapore in the 1960s, which was joined by Indonesia, Malaysia and Thailand in the 1970s and 1980s. The 1990s saw Vietnam and the Philippines, after a long period during which economic growth barely kept ahead of population growth, begin to join in their neighbours' success. Some countries with poor growth performance remain, notably Burma and Cambodia. Yet the overall trend is impressive. The take-off to self-sustaining growth is no longer confined to city-states or to close US Cold War allies. Rather it is a region-wide phenomenon that is increasingly self-generating and in which the region's economic leaders - Singapore, Malaysia and Thailand - are playing an important role (through private investment) in the development of the rest of the region.

Much remains to be done if recent progress is to be sustained, and the process of rapid development has created many tensions, not least due to the considerable human and environmental costs involved. Yet there is widespread confidence that the countries of the region have the capacity to address these problems, and that the success of recent years can be sustained into the next century.

South-East Asia has not always been viewed in this way. In the early 1960s, shortly before the final stages of decolonisation were completed, the portents for the region's future were not at all auspicious. In economic terms, the countries of the region were amongst the poorest of the world, with national incomes per head comparable to those in sub-Saharan Africa.

Rapid population growth threatened to consume most of the growth of economies that remained trapped in dependence on the production of raw materials for export to Northern markets.

Nor did the political conditions for development appear to be present. Conflict was widely viewed as endemic, in much the same way that it is sometimes seen as intractable in much of sub-Saharan Africa today. The division of Vietnam in 1954 had led to a protracted period of conflict, culminating in one of the most costly wars of the post-1945 period. Independent Indonesia was wracked by internal conflict, which culminated in the killing of more than 300,000 suspected government opponents in 1965-66. Profound internal ethnic divisions were often exacerbated by territorial disputes, most notably in the case of conflict between Indonesia, Malaysia and the Philippines for control of the island of Borneo. Burma, Malaysia, the Philippines and Thailand all faced serious insurgencies, often fuelled by external support.

This is not the place to discuss the reasons for the economic take-off in detail.[2] What is of relevance to this study is that one of the key factors in the economic success of the region has undoubtedly been its ability to contain and reduce the extent of armed conflict. Economic growth would not have been possible without some degree of political and international stability. South-East Asia is not yet a 'security community' like Western Europe, since war between its states is not yet unthinkable. But it has moved a long way towards that ultimate goal.

It is generally recognised that one of the keys to the security of South-East Asia has been the improvement in the 'resilience' of the states in the region. Most states in South-East Asia (with the exceptions of Thailand and Vietnam) are creations of colonialism, and a central task of their leaders has been to develop workable political structures for states in which national loyalty is often weak. There are few stable democracies, and elections when they occur are often rigged or heavily controlled. The armed forces often have a significant political role, dominant in Indonesia and Burma, still powerful in (currently) democratic Thailand.

Barry Buzan defines weak states as those with 'low levels of socio-political cohesion' and argues that

> 'the creation of stronger states is a necessary condition for both individual and national security ... Both national security and international security for the system as a whole will

remain problematic as long as the structure of anarchy is flawed by the presence of so many weak states.'[3]

Certainly the early post-colonial period in South-East Asia bears out these fears. The biggest security problem of most of the new states was internal, with armed insurgency and inter-ethnic disputes widespread. These disputes in turn led to a virtual state of war between Indonesia and Malaysia - the *'konfrontasi'* - and to severe tensions between the Philippines and Malaysia over competing claims to Sabah.

Tim Huxley argues that ASEAN member states continue to have severe problems in maintaining national unity:

> 'Perhaps the most fundamental problem in relation to the widely-recognised need to improve the 'national resilience' of the four largest ASEAN countries is that the very nature of their regimes has often tended to impede the implementation of policies which are clearly necessary in order to ameliorate tensions between classes and between regions. In very broad terms, these regimes' rather narrow power bases have been located principally in the military, business, landowning, bureaucratic and technocratic elites.
>
> ... Perhaps there should be some concern over the long-term viability of ... Indonesia and Malaysia, in view of their multiple problems of geographical extensiveness, ethnic and religious complexity, and emerging economically-based centre-periphery strains ....'[4]

This pessimistic view is, however, contested by other authors, who argue that growing economic resources have given ASEAN governments more opportunities to consolidate the extent to which they are able to draw on a wide measure of popular consent. Singapore is the most stable politically, with the ruling party enjoying widespread popular support, periodically tested in elections, for its particular brand of guided democracy. Malaysia has developed a political system based on a sophisticated balancing of the interests of the two main ethnic groups in the country, and has so far managed to prevent a repeat of the riots of the late 1960s. The ruling coalition was returned to power with an increased majority in the 1995 elections. Both Thailand and the Philippines are at present multi-party democracies. Although concerns remain as to the willingness of the armed forces to refrain from political involvement, the growing middle class produced by rapid economic growth (especially in Thailand) is making this more difficult than in the past. As one recent survey suggests:

> 'Greater maturity and confidence is beginning to characterise the domestic and international situations of many of these countries (which) ... are in the process of change from their earlier preoccupation with traditional security to broader concerns with greater emphasis on economic growth and development.'[5]

The one exception to this generalisation is, however, ASEAN's biggest state. Indonesia is now the only country in the region - apart from Myanmar - whose government is still dominated by the armed forces. There is little opportunity for open dissent even within the dominant Javanese community, with many former political prisoners still subject to systematic surveillance and discrimination. Disaffected minorities - including movements for independence in Aceh in Northern Sumatra, in Irian Jaya, and in East Timor - continue to resist the government's control, and are crushed with little regard to human rights.

Indonesia has made considerable progress in the thirty years of Suharto's one-person rule, both in terms of economic and social development, and in its ability to contribute to the overall stability of a region. Indonesian democrats hope that his eventual retirement will lead to political liberalisation and to a resolution of the East Timor dispute. But a smooth transition to a more pluralist polity may not be the most likely next step. There is widespread concern that the struggle for succession to Suharto could be extremely bloody, with the eventual outcome far from clear.[6]

In addition to worries over the internal resilience of South-East Asian regimes, concern has also been expressed at the strength of regional organisations, especially if compared with the European experience. This concern was particularly widespread in the immediate aftermath of the end of the Cold War. For example:

> 'What is so striking about discussions of building better security in the Asia/Pacific region is the virtual absence of any multilateral mechanism. Europeans are blanketed by NATO, the Western European Union (WEU), the CSCE, and now perhaps even a security role for the European Community. These structures have helped limit the spread of conflict in Yugoslavia, manage the transition in Central Europe, and

prevent panic as the Soviet Union disintegrates. No similar schemes exist to moderate the uncertainties in the Asia/Pacific region.'[7]

'Next to Europe, Asia appears strikingly under-institutionalised. The rich 'alphabet soup' of international agencies that has helped to nurture peaceful relations among the European powers is, in Asia, a very thin gruel indeed.'[8]

Asia is clearly 'under-institutionalised' in comparison with Western Europe, where both NATO and the European Union provide significant checks on individual states' ability to undertake unilateral action. Once the comparison moves to consideration of 'Europe' as a whole, however, it is rather less convincing. Bodies such as the Organisation for Security and Cooperation in Europe and the Council for Europe have played significant roles in conflict prevention and mediation in both Eastern Europe and the former Soviet Union. But the experience of former Yugoslavia suggests that the value or strength of European organisations should not be overstated.

There is also a danger, especially in wide-ranging surveys of 'Asia-Pacific security,' of failing to differentiate sufficiently between different parts of this vast area. In North-East Asia, 'under-institutionalisation' is a reasonably accurate description of the state of international relations. In South-East Asia, by contrast, there is a much richer experience of multilateral dialogue, focusing since 1967 on ASEAN (the Association of South-East Asian Nations). Indeed ASEAN's success is such that some analysts have suggested that it is one of the world's most successful regional organisations outside Western Europe.[9]

Certainly in terms of its record in avoiding armed conflict between its members, or indeed between its members and any third party, ASEAN's record since its formation in 1967 compares quite favourably with those of the Organisation of African Unity (OAU), the Organisation of Arab States (OAS) or even the Conference (now Organisation) for Security and Cooperation in Europe (OSCE).[10] It is not a European Union in embryo, nor is it yet a security community. But its achievements are nevertheless considerable.

II   Origins

ASEAN was founded in August 1967. It was not the first attempt to form a regional association: Thailand, Malaysia and the Philippines had belonged to the Association of Southeast Asia since 1961. Unlike this attempt, however, all the major non-communist states of the region (Indonesia, Malaysia, Philippines, Thailand and Singapore) were founding members. Brunei joined the organisation in 1985, and Vietnam in 1995.

The critical ingredient that made the formation of ASEAN possible was a fundamental shift in Indonesian policy. Under President Sukarno, Indonesia had pursued an increasingly assertive regional role, culminating in the 'Crush Malaysia' campaign - or *konfrontasi* - launched in 1963, a walkout from the UN, and an increase in military spending to almost 10% of GNP.[11] Increasingly close to the Indonesian Communist Party, Sukarno announced the formation of a 'Djakarta - Phnom Penh - Hanoi - Peking - Pyongyang' axis, and is reported to have suggested that

> 'Communist China would "strike a blow against the American troops in Vietnam from the north while Indonesia would strike from the south." '[12]

The Indonesian armed forces had never been happy with the increasingly radical turn in Sukarno's policy. In October 1965, in response to what was claimed to be a communist coup attempt, the Army took control. There followed what was described by the American Central Intelligence Agency as 'one of the worst mass murders of the century', as the Army moved to eliminate the power of what had been one of the world's largest Communist Parties.[13] An estimated 300,000-400,000 were killed, and many more interned. Over the next few months, Suharto moved to consolidate the Army's power, and in March 1966 most of Sukarno's power were effectively transferred to the 'New Order' government.

The New Order government adopted an approach to foreign and security policy that was different in almost every respect from that of the Sukarno regime. The highly rhetorical and confrontational approach of Sukarno was replaced by a policy that placed top priority on economic development. The new government still sought non-alignment and regional influence. But its approach to attaining these objectives was much more low key and pragmatic, and took more account of the constraints that Indonesia's poverty imposed on its international position. Above all, the new government realised that achieving these objectives would require cooperation with neighbouring states. Accordingly, in its first major foreign policy initiatives, it ended the policy of 'konfrontasi', normalised relations with Malaysia and Singapore, and took a leading role in the process of discussions that was to lead to the formation of ASEAN in August 1967. A former Foreign Minister of Malaysia, and a participant in ASEAN's formation, described it as:

'a development out of the pains of konfrontasi.'[14]

The members of the new organisation shared a common fear of communism, and a growing concern that they could not rely solely on external support to defend against it. The UK took the opportunity of the end of konfrontasi to pull its forces out of the region. The US was forced to withdraw from South Vietnam, suffering humiliation at the hands of communist North Vietnam in the process. The threat of a communist take-over in Indonesia had been crushed. But Malaysia, Thailand and the Philippines still faced serious communist insurgencies, backed to varying degrees by China.

In addition to these concerns, regional leaders found common ground in the belief that cooperation would help them address the urgent need for economic development, widely seen as the only guarantor of national security in the long term. As one commentator has suggested:

'although reducing external threats among past regional adversaries and new found regional partners was a dominant purpose in itself for forming ASEAN, an important collateral reason was to prevent a diversion of national energies and resources from security-relevant economic development.'[15]

III   Norms

The agreements on which ASEAN was based during the Cold War (the 1967 Bangkok declaration and the 1976 Treaty of Amity and Cooperation) were general and overarching in nature. Yet they provided the basis for the development of distinct norms of behaviour. From the beginning, the leaders involved saw that strengthening the authority of national governments - making them 'strong states' - was a necessary condition for regional security. Central to ASEAN, therefore, has been a common commitment to norms of:

• strict non-interference in the internal affairs of fellow members;

- pacific settlement of conflicts between members;

- solidarity towards the outside world.

Together, these norms contributed, and continue to contribute, to the development of strong states and a strong region. No state has found itself able to conform to each of these norms without deviation. Yet their existence has significantly altered the behaviour of member states in ways that could not reasonably have been anticipated in the absence of cooperation.

Non-interference

The central norm underpinning ASEAN has been a mutual commitment by governments to refrain from intervening in the internal politics of other member states. With the exception of Singapore (highly vulnerable itself because of its size), all member states have faced serious armed opposition movements from within their borders, and these have often been supported by sympathisers in neighbouring states. The norm of non-interference was designed to strengthen the hand of ASEAN governments against these movements, even if the governments in question abused human rights or ignored reasonable demands for autonomy. It is a norm that continues to be criticised in Western countries, where respect for human rights, and democratisation more generally, is seen as a means towards achieving security, not an alternative to it. Given the fragility of their own states and the real dangers of further conflict, however, ASEAN governments were far from convinced of the applicability of these arguments to their own specific circumstances. 'Turning a blind eye' to abuses in neighbouring countries was a price that had to be paid, it was argued, in order to achieve regional stability.

Cooperation with respect to internal threats sometimes went beyond the negative norm of non-interference to encompass mutual assistance. For example, Indonesia made clear its support for the Philippines government in its battle with Muslim insurgents in Moro, carrying out joint military exercises with the Manila government from 1972 onwards. Despite some internal criticism, the Indonesian government made it clear that its commitment to oppose any separatist movements in ASEAN was more important than responding to calls for Islamic solidarity.[16] Malaysia and Thailand co-operated with each other in order to defeat cross-border movements of insurgents, despite strong local sympathies for some of the movements in question. And all five other heads of government decided to attend the Third ASEAN summit in December 1987 despite the fact that

President Aquino had just survived a coup attempt. Their full attendance was widely seen as a much needed vote of confidence.[17]

Indonesia probably gained more than any other ASEAN member state from the 'non-interference' norm. In the period in question, its armed forces were involved in attempts to suppress opposition groups in East Timor, Aceh, Irian Jaya, southern Sulawesi and central and western Sumatra.[18] External sympathy with these rebellions was considerable, especially in the case of the annexation of Irian Jaya in 1969 and the invasion of East Timor in 1975, and it grew further following reports of extreme brutality and human rights abuses. But the norm of non-interference ensured that, while fellow ASEAN governments condemned the Vietnamese occupation of Cambodia and the Soviet invasion of Afghanistan, they supported Indonesia on the question of East Timor.[19] Faced with a united regional front, solidarity groups in other countries found it more difficult to make headway in their campaign.

The non-interference norm continues to come under periodic strain within member states. There is unhappiness, for example, as to the impact of Indonesia's inflexible approach in East Timor on the image of ASEAN as a whole. But, over time, ASEAN governments have learnt that their mutual vulnerability requires cooperation. As long as they continue to believe this to be the case, they are likely to believe it to be in their interests to abide by the norm.

Conflict Resolution

The second norm - a commitment not to use force in order to settle disputes - is also a vital requirement for regional peace. Non-intervention is not enough when states do not agree where their territories begin and end. Six of the boundary disputes in the South China Sea are between ASEAN members, with Malaysia involved in disputes with every other ASEAN member.[20] The Malacca Straits, for example, has proven a source of considerable tension in the past, given differences between the three ASEAN states concerned (Indonesia, Malaysia and Singapore) on controls over international transit, as well as the strong interest of extra-regional powers such as Japan and the Soviet Union. British withdrawal from East of Suez, together with the first appearance of a Soviet naval flotilla in the Indian Ocean in 1968 and the proclamation of the Nixon doctrine in 1969, had raised concerns in Japan about the security of the straits, prompting the deployment of four Japanese destroyers in the strait on a training mission in October 1969, together with Japanese pressure for inclusion in a four-power straits council. Common ASEAN membership played a positive role in defusing tension between the three local powers concerned by helping to transform it from a military/ strategic issue to one of safety and environment.[21] It also helped them to rebuff the suggestion of external involvement in traffic management, which was established as the Tripartite Council (consisting of Singapore, Malaysia and Indonesia) in 1971.[22]

Other issues - such as Singapore's draconian penal policy - also provide a source of periodic disputes. In each such case so far, however, governments' long-standing commitment to ASEAN has helped to cool tempers and limit the extent to which domestic pressure is allowed to develop out of control.

Solidarity

The commitment of ASEAN governments to each other is also reflected in their support for each other in wider discussions. In general, the commitment to solidarity has meant that ASEAN governments will seek, if at all possible, to reach a consensus on specific foreign policy issues, as well as striving for a convergence of outlook on global matters. By grouping together, ASEAN members can increase their room for movement in a region dominated by larger powers. By helping each other face external concerns, they can reduce the extent to which members feel the need to turn outside the region for support.

The degree of success of ASEAN in this regard is illustrated by a study of voting behaviour at the UN which showed that, in the 1970s, ASEAN members voted together 85% of the time. For comparison, West European states achieved a rate of concordance 79% of the time, NATO 55% of the time, and the Muslim group of countries 44%.[23] Although ASEAN's comparative position is inflated by the greater ease of achieving consensus amongst a small group compared to a large one, it nevertheless illustrates the extent to which policies, in the UN at least, had converged.

The most impressive, and widely known, example of ASEAN solidarity was its response to Vietnam's invasion of Kampuchea in December 1978. Throughout the 1980s, ASEAN took the lead in the UN in sponsoring an annual resolution calling for Vietnam to withdraw. The resolution attracted increasing majorities each year, and ASEAN's efforts are widely recognised as having played an important role in isolating Vietnam and the Soviet Union on the issue and eventually laying the basis for a settlement.[24]

This show of ASEAN unity was not achieved without difficulty, and concealed a pronounced difference in emphasis within the Association. While Thailand saw the invasion as a direct threat to its own security, and was prepared to take any means necessary (including support for the Khmer Rouge) in order to force Vietnam to withdraw, the main security concern of Malaysia and Indonesia during this period was China, with whom they had no diplomatic relations until 1990. They viewed Vietnam as an important buffer against Chinese expansion, were concerned at Beijing's alliance with the Khmer Rouge government in Cambodia, and were opposed to the policy of 'bleeding Vietnam dry' supported by Thailand, Singapore and China. In 1981, for example, Indonesia opposed a Singaporean proposal that ASEAN supply arms to the opposition forces in Cambodia, although it was agreed that the association would not object if individual ASEAN members did so.[25]

Despite these divisions within its ranks, ASEAN's members proved willing to compromise in order to maintain a united position. Indonesia and Malaysia supported the ASEAN campaign to deny recognition to the Phnom Penh government at the UN, despite misgivings about the wisdom of alliance with China. They sought to moderate ASEAN's position from within, but were also aware of the need to defer to the fellow member (Thailand) that had most at stake. At the same time, other members were prepared to support Indonesia taking a leading role in diplomatic efforts to resolve the conflict from 1987 onwards. The 1991 Paris peace agreement, and the subsequent 1993 election, could not have been achieved without the active participation of extra-regional powers. But ASEAN's important role was recognised by the appointment of Indonesian Foreign Minister Ali Altas as co-chair of the International Conference.[26]

ASEAN also played an important role as a negotiating block on economic matters with individual extra-regional powers. ASEAN members collectively expressed their concerns over Japanese plans for producing synthetic rubber in the early 1970s, successfully supported Singapore in its civil aviation dispute with Australia in the late 1970s, and acted as a block in trade negotiations with the EU. In a model that was unique amongst Third World organisations, ASEAN also set up a system of 'dialogue partners' in order to institutionalise their relationships with important trading partners: the EEC, Japan, Australia, New Zealand, the US and Canada. In 1991, in a reflection of its growing economic importance, South Korea also became a full Dialogue Partner.[27]

Like any group of countries that is based on voluntary cooperation, ASEAN has not always been successful in maintaining unity in action. But the experience since its formation is that its existence has created a strong presumption of consultation, and where possible consensus, between its members. In return for respect for each others' interests, and a strong sense of mutual obligation, ASEAN members have found that other countries are increasingly willing to treat the Association as an actor in the Asian equation on a par with some of the larger powers of the region. As Paul Dibb has suggested:

> 'the ASEAN group, which acts together as a united bloc on key issues, has already accrued to itself significant political influence out of all proportion to any objective measure of its economic, military or political power.'[28]

IV   Equality

Some highly successful voluntary international groupings - such as NATO - have been based on the clear leadership of a single state. But this is not been the case with ASEAN. As by far the largest state in terms of population, Indonesia is often seen as *primus inter pares*. Although there are no formal voting procedures, it is widely accepted that Indonesia exerts an effective veto on collective decisions in a way that, for example, Brunei does not. But Indonesia has often been happy to leave the initiative on particular issues to others, and its leaders are acutely aware that it would be counter-productive for it to attempt to throw its weight around. Indonesia has thus been willing to accept the principle of equality between member states: reflected, for example, in the practices of sharing organisational costs and the hosting of meetings equally between all members.[29]

In direct contradiction to the 'hegemonic stability' model of institutional success, which posits that international organisations only succeed if they are dominated by a single dominant state,[30] the ASEAN experience suggests that success is also possible when this is not the case. Indeed, ASEAN's success may have depended upon a balance of power between its members such that no one state can hope to achieve dominance over its neighbours.

Such a proposition at first seems counter-intuitive, given the fact that Indonesia's population of 190 million is a third greater than those of all other (pre-1995) ASEAN member states combined, and eight times as great as the combined populations of Malaysia and Singapore. But it reflects the fact that ASEAN's smallest states (in terms of population) have also been its richest and have grown most rapidly. As a consequence, despite the fact that Singapore has a population that is only 5% of that of Thailand and a mere 1.5% of that of Indonesia, its defence budget in absolute terms is around the same. Indeed, as Table 2.1 shows, both Singapore and Malaysia have been able to use their relative wealth to maintain a rough military parity (measured on the crude indicator of military budgets) with their two larger neighbours, as well as with each other. Indeed, if anything, these figures underestimate Singapore's military potential compared with that of its neighbours. Free of the need to devote a large part of its defence resources to counter-insurgency warfare (in the way that Indonesia does), Singapore's armed forces are clearly ahead of those of their neighbours in terms of both their operational readiness and technological sophistication.[31] And one recent analysis has suggested that Singapore's air force plans on the precept that it should deploy as many front-line combat aircraft as Malaysia and Indonesia combined.[32] Preoccupied with its internal problems, Indonesia simply does not have the military resources needed to overrun its neighbours: an important confidence-building reality in its own right.

Table 2.1: The Balance of Power within ASEAN

Country	Population	1994 Defence Budget	Combat aircraft
Brunei	0.3 million	$0.2 billion	2
Indonesia	192.5 million	$2.3 billion	73
Malaysia	19.9 million	$2.1 billion	120
Philippines	69.2 million	$0.9 billion	43
Singapore	2.9 million	$2.9 billion	155
Thailand	60.5 million	$3.6 billion	197
Vietnam	74.1 million	$0.9 billion	190

Source: International Institute for Strategic Studies, *The Military Balance 1995-96*, London, Oxford University Press, 1995.

As important as the balance of military capability in underpinning ASEAN is the balance of vulnerability. Even if no explicit trade-offs are made, each member state is aware, when being asked to help its fellow members, that it too has its security problems. Singapore is well aware of its economic dependence on Malaysia, as well as the difficulties that being a Chinese city-state in a predominantly Malay subregion can create. Thailand has, until recently, set great store on ASEAN's ability to provide unified support for its opposition to Vietnam's occupation of Cambodia. For Indonesia, ASEAN has fulfilled the invaluable function of providing 'cover' for its continuing inability to resolve its problems in East Timor, Irian Jaya and Aceh. And Brunei, whose very existence had been a matter of considerable dispute with Malaysia and Indonesia, has benefited from the recognition of its status that ASEAN membership has provided.[33]

An approximate balance of capabilities and concerns was not a sufficient condition in itself for ASEAN's success. A multipolar balance of power is not necessarily a stabilising state of affairs, leading as it can to arms racing, shifting tactical alliances, and dangerous incentives for military pre-emption. The great achievement of ASEAN was to ensure that the balance of power has been accepted and managed in such a way that these malign effects have, on the whole, not been evident.

V   Processes

ASEAN is often seen as being institutionally fragile. Although the Treaty of Amity and Cooperation provides for an official conflict resolution mechanism, consisting of representatives from all member states, it has never met.[34] ASEAN held no summit meeting at all between 1977 and 1987, because the Malaysian prime minister refused to meet in Manila (the next venue on the basis of rotation) while the Philippines continued to claim Sabah as part of its territory. It was not until the Bali summit in 1976 that a minimal ASEAN organisational structure was established, based in Jakarta. Even then, it was made clear that its head would have minimal authority (as Secretary-General of the ASEAN Secretariat, not of ASEAN), and could not attend meetings at which political issues were discussed.[35]

Yet these organisational weaknesses did not prevent ASEAN achieving a significant degree of success in generating support for cooperative norms of behaviour amongst its members. These norms have not been codified in detail: indeed it is hard to see how they could have been. Rather, a deliberate decision was taken to adopt a more informal approach. More progress, it was argued, could be made if the public airing of conflict was minimised. Tan Sri Ghazali Shafie, former Foreign Minister of Malaysia, has suggested that this was one of the reasons for ASEAN's success:

> 'The purpose has been not to puff the diplomatic pimples in public to make them look like big boils. Without the blare and glare of publicity, the foreign ministers have been able to examine difficult political issues with thoroughness and cool heads. Thus many sharp edges of conflict were blunted and the first 25 years became a period of confidence-building.'[36]

Moreover, in contrast with the relative infrequency of summit meetings, but very much in keeping with the preference for dialogue away from the glare of publicity, the establishment of ASEAN was followed by a mushrooming of lower-level multilateral dialogue, across the range of government activities. By 1975, five permanent committees had grown to twelve plus eight special committees, each meeting on a rotational meeting between ASEAN member states, and co-ordinated by the work of the Senior Officials' Meeting (SOM) and permanent ASEAN Secretariats in each member state.[37] By 1995, ASEAN was holding an estimated 220 meetings each year,[38] and this official ASEAN network was complemented by a number of parallel intergovernmental organisations that drew their inspiration (and often their name) from ASEAN.[39] Not least, the ASEAN Secretariat has reported the existence of 41 non-governmental organisations using the name ASEAN, bringing together businesspeople, journalists, educators, doctors, footballers, and many others.[40]

The concrete output of all this activity is hard to measure. But it is widely regarded as having a powerful, and cumulative, confidence-building effect. Before the formation of ASEAN, the elites of the region had little knowledge of each other or of their cultures, and 'getting to know each other' has therefore been an important element in the process of developing mutual trust. The density of intra-ASEAN networks may also have helped to 'ASEANize' the self-image of members of the elite groups involved: further helping to develop a broader constituency in support of ASEAN cooperation.

The development of ASEAN 'family feeling' may have been aided by the continuity in leadership in ASEAN's three 'central' states. There has been considerable turnover in government in both Thailand and the Philippines. But Suharto of Indonesia was in power when ASEAN was founded 28 years ago. Mahathir, the Prime Minister of Malaysia, has been in power since 1981, and has just been returned to power with a huge majority. Although Lee Kuan Yew has retired as Singapore's leaders, he remains influential and the new government is following closely in his footsteps. One day - perhaps quite soon - new generations will assume power in all three countries. In both Singapore and Malaysia, the process of elite 'ASEANization', together with the machinery already in place for an orderly leadership succession, should mean that the commitment to ASEAN will emerge essentially unaltered. In the more uncertain circumstances of Indonesia, however, it remains to be seen whether a new leadership will be tempted to pursue a more independent foreign policy path.

VI   Defence cooperation

Whenever the issue has been raised, ASEAN has clearly rejected the idea of using its framework for the purposes of defence cooperation. Yet this has not prevented its members seeing ASEAN as an informal 'umbrella' within which a 'spider-web' of bilateral arrangements can be established. Ever since ASEAN's formation, member states have taken part in bilateral military exercises, and these have tended to grow in number and scale over the years. Military cooperation in turn seems to have helped build broader confidence between ASEAN members, and thus contributed to the overall goals of the organisation.

The Five Power Defence Arrangements

The most formal defence arrangement involving ASEAN members is the Five Powers Defence Arrangements (FPDA). In the aftermath of *konfrontasi,* and in response to the imminent prospect of British withdrawal, Singapore and Malaysia persuaded Britain, Australia and New Zealand to agree to the Arrangements, which were designed to provide for a continuing external contribution to their defence. As a result of the Arrangements, Australia based two squadrons of around 40 Mirage fighter aircraft at Butterworth in northern Malaysia until 1988, and it continues to base P3C maritime patrol aircraft and an infantry company in this location. The level of UK involvement in FPDA exercises has increased in recent years, due in part to the prospect of withdrawal of British forces from Hong Kong, as well as the perceived need to support arms sales. Tornado fighters, together with an aircraft carrier, took part in exercise 'Lima Bersatu' in 1988, in which a total of one hundred aircraft exercised against a hypothetical aggression from 'Pengavia', a leftist government east of Malaysia and Singapore, which had sought to secure territory from the two in order to further its position in a dispute over resources in the South China Sea.[41] All three UK services took part in FPDA exercises in 1993 (including Royal Navy deployment in the South China Sea).[42] A recent report suggests that the new Malaysian special forces base at Mershing will include accommodation for three battalions of British special forces, along with submarine docking facilities and reinforced hangers for Hercules aircraft.[43]

FPDA is not an alliance and does not include a security guarantee. But it does have as its central assumption the 'indivisibility' of the defence of Singapore and Malaysia, and it obliges participants to consult each other for the purpose of deciding what actions should be taken in the event of a threat or potential threat to Malaysia or Singapore.[44] Singapore in particular has emphasised that the presence of Australian forces could have a significant deterrent effect.

As a result of the modernisation of the armed forces of Singapore and Malaysia over the last 25 years, they now constitute the bulk of forces involved in FPDA activities. Yet the FPDA process continues to be viewed as being of value by both Singapore and Malaysia. Its continuing relevance may, in part, be a result of the fact that it is consistent with the 'ASEAN Way': weakly institutionalised, able to adapt to changing circumstances, and achieving its objectives indirectly through processes of working together.[45] Not least, it still has an important confidence-building role between Singapore and Malaysia, the bilateral relations between whom are perhaps the most problematic in ASEAN. It allows the armed forces of the two countries to understand better what their counterparts are thinking and doing, even when bilateral channels have been closed. It also helps to emphasise the concerns they have in common, even while some of their objectives are competing.

While FPDA may help to improve relations between Singapore and Malaysia, however, it has at times exacerbated relations with Indonesia, which sees it as a direct descendant of the alliance involved in the *konfrontasi* of the 1960s. Indonesian criticism of the Arrangements is usually muted, but it resurfaced in 1989/90 in the form of concerns expressed that Australia might be seeking to become the dominant Western-aligned nation in South-East Asia through the projection of military power.[46] It remains to be seen what the effects of the security treaty between Australia and Indonesia, signed in December 1995, will be on these perceptions.

FPDA would not be created today if it did not already exist. But it is now an established part of the complex 'spiderweb' of defence arrangements in the region, helping to reassure two of ASEAN's smaller member states without unduly offending their larger neighbour, and providing a role in the region for Australia without requiring it to make unrealistic, and potentially provocative, commitments.

Bilateral Defence Cooperation

Although ASEAN has no formal role in military affairs, the political cooperation between its members has made possible the development of a network of close, and highly significant, bilateral defence relationships: a pattern termed a 'defence spiderweb' by General Try Sutrisno, chief of the Indonesian armed forces. This 'spiderweb' involves an intensive programme of joint exercises, participation in each others' training programmes, and (of particular benefit to Singapore) the provision of training facilities to each other. In ASEAN's earlier years, the main focus of this cooperation was joint counter-insurgency operations, for example between Malaysia and Thailand and (after *konfrontasi*) between Indonesia and Malaysia.[47] But bilateral cooperation has also increasingly taken the form of intelligence sharing, joint exercises (especially focused on maritime and air-space concerns), provision of training facilities, and attendance of personnel at each others' staff command schools.[48]

As with the development of ASEAN's political dialogue, this extensive network of military cooperation has taken many years to reach its current level. But it is now arguably one of the most significant aspects of the intra-ASEAN confidence-building process, with the frequency and sophistication of the exercises growing over time.

All ASEAN members have been involved to some extent in military cooperation with their ASEAN partners, but some are more involved than others. The most active participant in joint exercises has been Indonesia, which has undertaken joint exercises with all other ASEAN members except Brunei.[49] As important, however, is cooperation in the provision of training facilities. In this area, because of its limited size, Singapore is the main beneficiary, using facilities made available to it by fellow ASEAN members Thailand, Brunei, Indonesia, and the Philippines, in addition to its use of facilities in Australia, Taiwan and the US.[50]

The growing scale of bilateral military cooperation is in part a consequence of the increased capability of ASEAN armed forces for larger-scale and more sophisticated activities. Yet common ASEAN membership, and the experience of dialogue and confidence-building within ASEAN over a wide range of policy issues, has provided the essential context within which military cooperation has in turn flourished. Given the degree of mutual suspicion between ASEAN armed forces, the development of military cooperation has been a gradual process, and there remains considerable potential for further development. In the initial years, there were fears that joint exercises would provide foreign troops with an opportunity for territorial familiarisation with the host country.[51] Over time, however, fears that transparency might compromise security - whilst never entirely dissipated - have been increasingly offset by an awareness of what might be gained, in terms of both possible joint activity and confidence-building. As the cancellation of Singaporean exercises in the Philippines in May 1995 in response to the crisis over the execution of a Filipino maid in Singapore illustrated most recently, bilateral defence relationships remain dependent on the state of broader relationships. Despite this, however, the ASEAN 'spiderweb' of defence cooperation remains a good example of the confidence-building effects of military transparency in practice.

Within ASEAN, the discriminatory nature of bilateralism is moderated by the existence of a number of cross-cutting relationships. The closeness of the Malaysia/ Indonesia military relationship tends to contribute to historic Singaporean fears of being squeezed by the two predominantly Malay states that surround it. But the intimidatory character of this axis is diluted by the existence of the FPDA, from which Indonesia is excluded, and by the continuing strength of Singapore/Indonesia military cooperation (seen most recently in the provision of extensive training facilities in Sumatra to the Singaporean Air Force).[52] In addition, the close military relationship between ASEAN's two smallest states - Singapore and Brunei - acts as a further counterweight to Malaysia and Indonesia, helping to reassure Brunei that its military weakness will not tempt Malaysia to intervene. It has even been speculated that, in the event of open conflict, Brunei territory could be used by Singapore as a base for opening a 'second front' against Malaysia.[53]

The 'spiderweb' is, however, noticeably thinner in some relationships than in others, a result, amongst other factors, of lingering difficulties in some bilateral relationships, most notably between Malaysia and the Philippines over Sabah and between Malaysia and Singapore.

The latter case cautions us not to put too much emphasis on transparency and confidence-building measures as an easy solution to distrust between states. Malaysia and Singapore have the longest standing bilateral military relationship in ASEAN, dating back to their common ancestry in a single Malaysian state and continued ever since in the FPDA. Yet the legacy of Singapore's expulsion from Malaysia in August 1965 remains difficult to overcome. For many years, FPDA provided the main forum through which military cooperation between the two states took place. In early 1989, the military relationship appeared at last to be improving, with a major bilateral land exercise being held for the first time in Malaysia in October 1989.[54] But this trend towards greater cooperation was brought to a sudden halt by the arrest in Malaysia in late 1989 of nine alleged spies (including five Malaysian military personnel, two civil servants and two Singaporeans) accused of selling military plans for the defence of Johor (the part of Malaysia nearest to Singapore).[55] This event was particularly sensitive in the light of the strong preference of the Singaporean armed forces for compensating for their lack of strategic depth by a policy of 'forward defence' in southern peninsular Malaysia. It resulted in the suspension of what had begun to seem a promising development of the bilateral military exercise programme between the two countries. In addition, in February 1990, the Malaysian government barred the Singapore Flying College and the Singapore Flying Club from using Malaysian air space, alleging that they had been conducting photographic reconnaissance.[56]

In April 1990, in the immediate aftermath of the spy scandal, Singapore's Prime Minister Lee Kuan Yew proposed that the two countries should allow mutual inspection of each other's military bases.[57] In the suspicious circumstances of the time, however, the offer was rejected by Malaysia, whose armed forces feared further exposure of the details of their weak state of readiness.[58] Bilateral military exercises between the two countries did not resume until early 1992, and the relationship between the two states remains guarded.

The Singapore-Malaysia relationship may be a classic example of a situation in which further transparency may be unable to make a contribution to security unless undertaken alongside measures to address the other causes of mistrust. The two countries already know each other, and their respective defence postures, extremely well, having been bound together in a web of 'complex interdependence' since they were separated in 1965. Singapore relies on Malaysia for supplies of food and water, and Malaysia relies on Singapore's pivotal position in the regional economy. Yet Malaysia is aware that, if its large Chinese minority should become disaffected, it might be tempted to seek help from their Chinese neighbours: an insecurity that is reflected in the tiny number of ethnic Chinese in the Malaysian armed forces. Mutual suspicion is further enhanced by Singapore's 'forward defence' posture, which Malaysians often interpret as a Singaporean attempt to retain a 'droit de regard' over (mainly Chinese) Johor province. So far, these mutual suspicions have been ameliorated by common prosperity, internal stability, ASEAN membership, and a continuing bilateral dialogue. If the danger of conflict is to be removed, however, more will need to be done.

VII Not an Alliance

One of the strongest motivations for states to reveal more military information to each other is the possibility of joint action. Cooperation between states, with a view to future joint military operations, requires states to share information with each other and to understand each others' military doctrines if it is to be effective. Even if it is not described as being part of confidence-building and transparency, therefore, it may indirectly fulfil these roles.

Thus defence cooperation within ASEAN is not motivated solely by a desire to improve trust between participating countries. It is also driven by the possibility of future joint operations against a third party, and by a political desire to send signals to potential aggressors. For example, Amitav Acharya suggests how bilateral cooperation programmes might have the dual functions of intra-ASEAN confidence-building and preparing to meet an external threat:

> 'The proliferation of such exercises is partly explained by their value in confidence-building. Fears that joint exercises would provide foreign troops an opportunity for territorial familiarisation with the host country have gradually given way to recognition that they can help build links with neighbours, overcome suspicions and promote cooperation. Bilateral exercises also help develop common operating procedures and tactics, standardise modes of command and control, and

enhance inter-operability between the armed forces of the
ASEAN states, thereby creating the basis for mutual help
against a common security threat. This consideration is
especially noteworthy in the case of the Malaysia-Indonesia
agreement to use the latter's Natuna Island as a base for joint
exercises. The accord has been officially explained as a
measure to meet maritime threats from the South China Sea,
especially that hypothetically posed by the escalating naval
competition between Vietnam and China.'[59]

As the network of bilateral defence cooperation has grown in
sophistication, and as ASEAN's ability to act as a coherent negotiating
block has increased, there have been periodic calls for defence cooperation
to take on a more multilateral form. These arguments have, however, been
consistently rejected in the past by ASEAN members.

First, it was felt that, with considerable lingering distrust between some
member states, governments would find a gradual development of bilateral
military cooperation easier to pursue than the more uniform commitments
that a multilateral organisation might involve. The formation of a
multilateral defence organisation was seen as reducing the ability of
individual states to control the extent of their own transparency. Armed
forces in particular remained wary of revealing their weaknesses to
potential foes in joint activities. In order to keep them supportive of the
process of confidence-building, therefore, progress had to be incremental.

Second, for most of this period, the main threat faced by most ASEAN
armed forces was internal. As we have seen, there was a considerable
degree of bilateral cooperation in countering these threats (particularly
between Indonesia and Malaysia, and between Malaysia and Thailand). It
was unclear how a multilateral alliance could improve on these
arrangements.

Third, in part because of their internal orientation and in part because of
their overall weakness, ASEAN armed forces had little actual capability for
coming to each others' assistance in the event of external attack. For
example if Vietnam had attacked Thailand in the 1980s in order to cut off
supplies to the Khmer Rouge resistance in Cambodia - probably the
external threat of most concern during this period - the main burden of
external support to Thailand would have had to come from the US and/or
China. ASEAN diplomatic efforts to rally opposition to the Vietnamese
invasion of Cambodia were effective. But ASEAN military commitments

would have had little credibility without its forming a much closer military relationship with external powers: a move that would have been unacceptable to those member states (most notably Indonesia) that saw ASEAN as an expression of regional self-reliance.[60]

Finally, but perhaps most significantly, ASEAN members did not form a military alliance because it was believed that such a step would be counter-productive. By refraining from forming an anti-Communist alliance, ASEAN members helped to reassure Vietnam of their peaceful intentions, thus complementing the continuing efforts of Indonesia, in particular, to keep channels of dialogue open. At the same time, the processes of military modernisation and increased bilateral cooperation within ASEAN acted as a longer term insurance policy, keeping the alliance option open should a clearer external threat emerge.

Notes

1. Kishore Mahbubani, 'The Pacific Impulse', *Survival*, 37, 1, Spring 1995, pp. 117-118.

2. For discussions of these issues, see World Bank, *The East Asian Miracle: Economic Growth and Public Policy*, 1993, Oxford University Press; Steve Chan, *East Asian Dynamism: Growth, Order and Security in the Pacific Region*, 2nd edition, Westview Press, 1993.

3. Barry Buzan, *People, States and Fear*, Harvester-Wheatsheaf, 1991, p. 106. Also see Barry Buzan and Gerald Segal, 'Rethinking East Asian Security', *Survival*, 36, 2, Summer 1994, pp. 15-17.

4. Tim Huxley, *Insecurity in the ASEAN Region*, Royal United Services Institute for Defence Studies, London, 1993, pp. 7-10.

5. Muthiah Alagappa, 'The Dynamics of International Security in South-East Asia: Change and Continuity', *Australian Journal of International Affairs*, 45, 1, May 1991, p. 1. Paul Dibb agrees, noting that, in the case of middle powers such as Vietnam, Indonesia and Thailand, "Far from being 'weak states', they are marked by a growing sense of confidence and resilience." Paul Dibb, *Towards a New Balance of Power in Asia*, Adelphi Paper Number 295, International Institute for Strategic Studies, Oxford University Press, 1995, p. 72.

Notes continued

6.   For a discussion of Indonesian politics, see Adam Schwarz, *A Nation in Waiting: Indonesia in the 1990s*, Allen and Unwin, 1994.

7.   Gerald Segal, 'Managing New Arms Races in the Asia/Pacific', *Washington Quarterly*, 16, 2, Summer 1992, pp. 97-98. Also see Barry Buzan and Gerald Segal, 'Rethinking East Asian Security', *Survival*, 36, 2, Summer 1994, pp. 15-16; Aaron Friedberg, 'Ripe for Rivalry: Prospects for Peace in a Multipolar Asia', *International Security*, 18, 3, Winter 1993/4.

8.   Aaron Friedberg, ibid, p. 22.

9.   For a particularly favourable account, see Michael Hass, *The Asian Way to Peace: A Story of Regional Cooperation*, Praeger, 1989. Also see: Michael Leifer, *ASEAN and the Security of South-East Asia*, Routledge, 1989; Miles Kahler, 'Institution-Building in the Pacific' in Andrew Mack and John Ravenhill (eds), *Pacific Cooperation: Building Economic and Security Regimes in the Asia-Pacific*, Allen and Unwin, 1994, pp. 16-39.

10.   For a perceptive discussion of the lessons of the CSCE experience for Asia, see Trevor Findlay, 'The European Cooperative Security Regime: New Lessons for the Asia-Pacific', in Andrew Mack and John Ravenhill, ibid, pp. 209-232.

11.   Muthiah Alagappa, op cit, p. 18; Dewi Fortuna Anwar, *Indonesia in ASEAN*, Institute of South-East Asian Studies, 1994, pp. 23-31.

12.   quoted in John Mueller, *Retreat from Doomsday: The Obsolescence of Major War*, Basic Books, 1989, p. 171.

13.   Adam Schwarz, op cit, p. 20.

14.   quoted in Michael Leifer, op cit, p. 2.

15.   Ibid, p. 2.

16.   Ibid, pp. 266-267.

17.   Bilson Kurus, 'Understanding ASEAN', *Asian Survey*, XXXIII, 8, August 1993, p. 825. In order to ensure the success of the summit, President Aquino formally renounced the Philippines claim to Sabah, which is part of Malaysia. Her decision was, however, not ratified by the Philippine congress.

18.   Amitav Acharya, *A New Regional Order in South-East Asia: ASEAN in the Post Cold War Era*, Adelphi Paper Number 279, International Institute for Strategic Studies, August 1993, p. 19.

Notes continued

19. Dewi Fortuna Anwar, op cit, p. 205.

20. Amitav Acharya, op cit, pp. 30-33.

21. Muthiah Alagappa, op cit, pp. 22-23. Also see Yaacov Vertzberger, *The Malacca-Singapore Straits: the Suez of South-East Asia*, Institute for the Study of Conflict, London, 1982.

22. Michael Haas, op cit, pp. 171-175.

23. quoted in Dewi Fortuna Anwar, op cit, pp. 215-216.

24. Bilson Kurus, op cit, pp. 821-823.

25. Dewi Fortuna Anwar, op cit, pp. 186-187.

26. Ibid, p. 307.

27. Ibid, pp 64-65; Bilson Kurus, op cit, pp. 823-824.

28. Paul Dibb, op cit, p. 41.

29. Michael Hass, op cit, pp. 132-134.

30. For example, see Robert Gilpin, *War and Change in World Politics*, Cambridge University Press, 1981. For a powerful critique, see Isabella Grunberg, 'Exploring the 'myth' of hegemonic stability', *International Organisation*, 44, 4, Autumn 1990, pp. 431-477.

31. J. N. Mak, 'Armed but Ready? ASEAN Conventional Warfare Capabilities', *Harvard International Review*, Spring 1994, pp. 20-24.

32. Tim Huxley, 'The ASEAN States' Defence Policies: Influences and Outcomes', in Colin McInnes and Mark Rolls, (eds), *Post-Cold War Security Issues in the Asia-Pacific Region*, Frank Cass, 1994, p. 144.

33. On Brunei, see Michael Leifer, op cit, pp. 46-48.

34. Amitav Acharya, op cit, p. 32.

35. Dewi Fortuna Anwar, op cit, p. 312.

36. Quoted in Desmond Ball, *Strategic Culture in the Asia-Pacific Region (with some implications for regional security cooperation)*, Strategic and Defence Studies Centre, Working Paper Number 270, Australian National University, 1993, p. 12.

Notes continued

37.   Dewi Fortuna Anwar, op cit, p. 62.

38.   'Mahathir's high hopes', *The Economist*, July 8, 1995, p. 66.

39.   For example, the ASEAN Inter-Parliamentary Organisation (AIPO) and the Meeting of Chiefs of National Police of ASEAN Countries (ASEANAPOL). Michael Haas, op cit, pp. 140-148.

40.   As of 1984. Dewi Fortuna Anwar, op cit, p. 242.

41.   Philip Methven, *The Five Powers Defence Arrangements and Military Cooperation Among the ASEAN States*, Canberra Papers on Strategy and Defence Number 92, Strategic and Defence Studies Centre, 1992, p. 113.

42.   Ministry of Defence (UK), *Statement on the Defence Estimates 1994*, 1994, p. 49.

43.   *The Age* (Melbourne), 28 January 1994.

44.   Chin Kin Wah, 'The Five Powers Defence Arrangements: Twenty Years After', *Pacific Review*, 4, 3, 1991, pp. 193-203.

45.   Miles Kahler, op cit, p. 24.

46.   Philip Methven, op cit, pp. 126-134.

47.   Amitav Acharya, 'The Association of Southeast Asian Nations: "Security Community" or "Defence Community"', *Pacific Affairs*, 64, Summer 1991, p. 164.

48.   For details of exercises held in recent years, see ibid, pp. 164-168; Dewi Fortuna Anwar, op cit, pp. 139-151; Desmond Ball, *Building Blocks for Regional Security: An Australian Perspective on Confidence and Security Building Measures (CSBMs) in the Asia/Pacific Region*, Canberra Papers on Strategy and Defence Number 83, Strategic and Defence Studies Centre, Australian National University, 1991, p. 36; Amitav Acharya, 'A New Regional Order', op cit, pp. 70-71. Amitav Acharya reports that, from the mid 1970s, intelligence agencies of all the ASEAN countries held secret annual meetings, with countries taking turn to host the meetings. Amitav Acharya, 'The Association of Southeast Asian Nations: "Security Community" or "Defence Community"', op cit, p. 166. He suggests that 'multilateral (intelligence) meetings provide a rare precedent for other forms of ASEAN wide military cooperation, such as defence ministers' meetings, which the ASEAN states have so far resisted.' On relations between ASEAN and Australian intelligence agencies, also see Desmond Ball, *Building Blocks,* op cit, pp. 32-35.

Notes continued

49.   Dewi Fortuna Anwar, op cit, p. 139.

50.   Amitav Acharya, 'The Association', op cit, pp. 167-168.

51.   Ibid, p. 167.

52.   Ministry of Defence, *Defence of Singapore 1994-95*, 1995, p. 77.

53.   Tim Huxley, 'Singapore and Malaysia: A Precarious Balance?', *Pacific Review*, 4, 3, 1991, pp. 209-210.

54.   Philip Methven, op cit, p. 98.

55.   Tim Huxley, *Singapore and Malaysia,* op cit, p. 207. Richard Stubbs reports that ten were arrested. Richard Stubbs, 'Malaysian Defence Policy: Strategy versus Structure', *Contemporary Southeast Asia*, 13, 1, June 1991, p. 54.

56.   Tim Huxley, ibid, p. 207; Chin Kin Wah, op cit, p. 200.

57.   Chin Kin Wah, ibid, p. 200.

58.   Interview.

59.   Ibid, p. 167.

60.   See comments by Noordin Sopiee quoted in Amitav Acharya, 'Regional Military- Security Cooperation in the Third World: A Conceptual Analysis of the Relevance and Limitations of ASEAN', *Journal of Peace Research*, 29, 1, 1992, pp. 12-13.

CHAPTER 3

China and South-East Asia

I   Introduction

The end of the Cold War seemed to vindicate the 'ASEAN Way', both in terms of economics and politics. When ASEAN was founded in 1967, many believed it was only a matter of time before Soviet-style communism swept the region. By 1990, however, the dominoes were falling in the other direction. One country after another in the region - most recently Vietnam and Myanmar - adopted market reforms, eager to emulate the success of the ASEAN 'tiger' economies. Communist rebellions in both Thailand and Malaysia, previously backed by China, came to an end. And the retreat of Soviet power led directly to the Vietnamese agreement to withdraw from Cambodia, followed by the UN-organised elections in that country in May 1993 and the subsequent application by Vietnam for ASEAN membership.

Yet the end of the Cold War has not led to the end of concerns regarding Great Power designs on the region. For ASEAN, the Cold War was about the containment of two great communist powers, not only one. China had played a key role in supporting communist plans for a take-over in Indonesia in the 1960s, and it continued to support insurgent communist movements in Malaysia and Thailand, which drew their main support from ethnic Chinese, well into the 1980s. Indeed, suspicion remained so deep-rooted that Indonesia did not open formal diplomatic relations with Beijing until 1990.

Moreover, the precipitate decline in Soviet power, while welcome in its own right, also removed some of the constraints on Chinese action. Free of the danger on its northern border, China was able to divert more of its limited military resources to improving its capabilities for maritime operations, thus strengthening its ability to pursue territorial claims in the South China Sea and against Taiwan. The withdrawal of the Soviet Navy from Vietnam removed a longstanding obstacle to Chinese action in the region. Most of all, there was a concern that, with the end of the Cold War, US commitment to the security of the region would be further curtailed, increasing the possibility of a power vacuum which China might be tempted to fill.

II   The relative decline of US power

The US is likely to be the world's largest power, measured in terms of total GNP, for many decades to come. It will also remain the only military superpower, with an unrivalled ability to project its military power worldwide. Yet there is a common perception in Asia that the US is preoccupied with its own internal problems, resentful at the supposed 'free-riding' of longstanding allies such as Japan, and increasingly reluctant to risk the lives of its service personnel in overseas interventions.

Nor is this perceived trend simply a short term by-product of the end of the Cold War. If it were, it might be expected to have run its course by the mid 1990s. Rather, it is seen as the continuation of a more long-established trend that has been under way for many years as a delayed result of decolonisation. Ever since the promulgation of the Nixon doctrine in 1971, and the subsequent withdrawal of troops from Vietnam, the US commitment to the security of South-East Asia has always been noticeably less strong than to Western Europe, Japan or South Korea. The US maintained large naval forces in the region in order to offset the power of the growing Soviet Pacific Fleet. But it also made clear that it would not allow its forces to become embroiled in a protracted war in a region of only secondary importance to its own interests. As Douglas Stuart and William Tow argued in 1995:

> 'America's collective memory of the Vietnam War and the attentuated US military presence in the region all but rules out direct US involvement in another South-east Asian conflict unless US lives and property are threatened.'[1]

Where they perceive possible threats to their security, therefore, ASEAN members are increasingly inclined to assume, at least for planning purposes, that they may be on their own. As a 1993 study suggested:

> 'the continuing American military role in South-East Asia has the extremely useful side-effect of preventing Japan from feeling the need to become directly involved in protecting its security interests in the region. But it is also true that the US is unlikely to become directly involved in defending ASEAN members' territorial claims in the South China Sea against (for example) Chinese aggression. In 1992, the Philippine foreign secretary claimed that the US was obligated under the Mutual Defence Treaty to defend the Philippine Navy if it was attacked in the Spratleys. But the US Ambassador to the

Philippines said that while Washington would oppose the use
of force by any party to impose its claim in the Spratleys, there
were limits to what it could do if fighting broke out.'[2]

The US withdrawal from its Clark and Subic Bay bases in the Philippines,
completed in 1992, helped prompt other ASEAN states - including
Indonesia, Malaysia and Singapore - to offer alternative repair facilities.[3]
As well as naval logistics facilities, the US is now reported to have a
rotating fighter squadron in Singapore.[4] There are reports of the possibility
of the US returning to Cam Ranh Bay in Vietnam.[5] Perhaps of greatest
significance, US assistant defense secretary Joseph Nye indicated on June
16 1995 that, if military action occured in the Spratlys and this interfered

'with freedom of the seas, then we would be prepared to escort
and make sure that free navigation continues.'[6]

Yet ASEAN concerns about the wisdom of relying on a US security
umbrella relate not only to fears as to the US's reliability. There is also a
concern that an excessive reliance on the US may make ASEAN members
hostage to wider trends in US-China relations, thus reducing their ability to
play an independent role in shaping the regional security agenda. While
ASEAN members have made clear their desire for the US to be actively
involved in the region, therefore, they remain ambivalent about the extent
to which they want a demonstrable US presence in order to balance China,
not least because of the danger that such a presence may be counter-
productive, provoking rather than restraining. They are also reluctant to
endorse moves that might be seen as compromising ASEAN's non-
alignment and moving too far towards a formal alliance.

On several occasions in recent years, therefore, ASEAN members have
signalled that there are real limits to the US presence. In 1989, Singapore
encountered considerable resistance from fellow ASEAN members when it
suggested that the benefits of a US military presence should be openly
acknowledged.[7] In 1994, Thailand, with the support of Indonesia and
Malaysia, rejected a US request for prepositioning six military supply ships
in the Gulf of Thailand on the grounds that it would 'generate regional
tensions.' Shortly afterwards, the Philippines rejected an agreement to
facilitate US Navy port calls.[8]

ASEAN anxiety to keep any military relationship with the US at arms
length could change quickly in the event of a crisis, for example as a result

of Chinese aggression in Taiwan or the South China Sea. Until then, however, ASEAN states are likely to continue to emphasise the potential for co-operation with China over a wide range of issues, even when this may involve taking sides with China against the US. Both parties remain suspicious, for example, about the human rights agenda pursued by the major Western powers, seeing in it a neo-colonial attempt to dictate to Asian countries how they should conduct their internal affairs. Above all, there is the common interest of ASEAN states and China in the continuation of the Asian economic miracle, and their consequent common interest in avoiding any event - such as a major armed conflict - that could derail it.

ASEAN governments still have a clear preference for a policy of 'engagement' towards China, rather than one of 'containment'. But they are also uncomfortably aware of the possibility of a new Cold War in Asia. While seeking to engage China in a process of diplomacy and confidence-building, therefore, they are also seeking to make provision 'just in case' by modernising their own defences and urging the US to maintain a role as a regional balancer.

III   China: a rising power?

If the recent rapid rate of economic growth in China continues, the US's relative power is likely to erode and that of China to increase. The reversion of Hong Kong to Chinese rule in 1997 will further increase China's weight in the international economic system. By early in the twenty-first century, the Chinese economy could be larger than that of Japan.[9] Since the end of the Cold War, there has been widespread speculation that China's rapid economic growth will lead to growing regional tensions. As one pessimistic, but not entirely unrepresentative, Singaporean analyst has argued:

> 'a more economically-powerful China will face increasing pressures to behave more aggressively. ... China is a large (increasingly) powerful state in a region filled with smaller, weaker states. This circumstance often tempts large states to military aggression - as was the case with Nazi Germany, fascist Japan, and the Soviet Union.'[10]

Such an analysis is finding echoes in the US policy community, where China is increasingly seen as a potential superpower rival, and where calls for a policy of 'containment' of China - echoing the comparable policy in the Cold War itself - are gaining growing support. As an indication of its growing concern, the Pentagon, which had previously played war games in which China was the enemy behind closed doors, made it known that it had held such an exercise near the end of 1994 (and that China had been the winner). Another report suggested that, during 1994, Chinese ships and aircraft more than once deliberately challenged a US aircraft-carrier battle group in international waters.[11]

It is not always easy to disentangle self-serving threat inflation from genuine worry about the development of Chinese policy. In contrast to the short-lived attempts in the late 1980s to talk up possible Japanese and Indian military threats to ASEAN, however, concern with China appears deeper-rooted and likely to be more sustained. In addition to continuing tensions in the South China Sea, there is considerable apprehension about China's support for the military regime in Myanmar. China has supplied Myanmar with military equipment and technical assistance, and has provided considerable economic assistance in order to open up high quality transport links from China to the Indian Ocean. Chinese military personnel are helping to develop naval bases and radar stations along Myanmar's coast, fuelling fears of Chinese military expansionism.[12]

ASEAN states also view other developments in Chinese policy with apprehension. In 1995, its continuing programme of nuclear weapon tests, in violation of pledges made at the 1995 NPT conference to exercise utmost restraint, reinforced concern that China was reluctant to abide by international arms control norms. Sabre rattling over Taiwan - including missile tests conducted near Taiwanese territory in August 1995 - increased concern at the possibility of open conflict in the region.

Underlying these specific concerns, ASEAN governments fear that China is seeking to restore the broader regional hegemony it enjoyed before the colonial period. ASEAN governments have always feared that such an effort by China could exploit their own sizeable Chinese minorities (in Singapore's case, a majority). The Chinese practice of giving 'overseas Chinese' a different status from other ASEAN citizens has not been reassuring in this respect.[13]

IV   The South China Sea disputes

The main current focus of contention between China and ASEAN member states is the complex set of disputes over ownership of the Spratly Islands in the South China Sea. The conflict is key to an understanding of recent military developments in the region. Many fear it could provide a trigger for a major armed conflict.

The Spratlys are made up of 200 or so tiny islands, cays, atolls and reefs, spread over 388,000 square kilometres of the South China Sea. Geographically, they are much nearer to Vietnam, Malaysia and Philippines than to mainland China. But China claims sovereignty over all the Islands, using historical records, maps and cultural relics to support its claim.[14] Official Chinese maps show the boundary of the People's Republic passing within 75 km of Brunei, Malaysia, Vietnam and the Philippines, enclosing the entire area in a 'Chinese lake'.[15]

As part of its assertion of sovereignty over the South China Sea, and taking advantage of Vietnam's preoccupation with its war in the south, the Chinese Navy evicted Vietnamese forces from the more northerly Paracel Islands in 1974 and occupied some of the islands. Until the 1980s, however, China took little action in pursuing its claim to the more southerly Spratlys. The main foreign policy priority of the new Chinese leadership under Deng Xiao Ping which took power in 1978 was to oppose Soviet hegemony, and to this end it needed the support of ASEAN countries in seeking the withdrawal of Vietnam from Cambodia. Moreover, the need to protect the northern border with the Soviet Union meant that the Navy remained a primarily coastal force, unable to project power as far south as the Spratlys.[16]

As a result of the focus of the armed forces of both ASEAN and China on internal security and/or disputes over land borders, the South China Sea disputes tended to be marginalised during most of the Cold War. In some respects the area even acted as a 'confidence-building' buffer zone, minimising military contacts between ASEAN states and China, and reassuring both parties that they faced little direct military threat from the other.

This buffer zone function did not last. Since the 1980s, several new developments have ensured that competition over the Spratlys has intensified dramatically, turning it into a patchwork of competing claims and occupations that could yet plunge the whole region into war.

First, there is a widespread belief, not least in China, that the area contains massive mineral wealth. In 1989 the China Geology Newspaper reported a survey by the Ministry of Geology and Mineral Resources that found that oil and natural gas deposits in the Spratlys amounted to 17.7 billion tons: greater than the reserves of Kuwait and the fourth largest in the world.[17] In 1992, Chinese scholars claimed that more than one thousand oil and gas drills had been set up by other countries in the South China Sea, of which 120 were within China's traditional sea border.[18]

Second, the process of 'island snatch' has intensified, spreading the dispute beyond a bilateral China/ Vietnam affair. In the 1950s, the Democratic Republic of Vietnam - which became the government of all Vietnam in 1975 - had acknowledged Chinese sovereignty over the Spratlys. But it reversed this position after 1975, and subsequently occupied a number of islands in the area. The Philippines issued a Presidential claim to part of the Spratlys in 1978, landing 1000 marines to back up its claim. Malaysia followed by staking a claim to 12 of the islands in 1979, and has been actively developing one of the islands (Swallow Reef) as a tourist resort. In 1988, Brunei established an Exclusive Economic Zone that included Louisa Reef, though it has so far made no move to occupy it.

Indonesia has no territorial claims in the Spratlys themselves, and its ownership of Natuna Island itself - south of the Spratlys - is not under dispute. But it is developing the rich Natuna gas field 220 km north-east of Natuna Island: an area that is 120 km inside the sea area claimed by China. The Indonesian government recently signed a $35 billion agreement with Exxon for the development of the field.[19]

Third, after a long period of relative inactivity, China has begun to assert its claims to the Spratlys forcefully. Its longer range naval forces, although still modest by Great Power standards, increased considerably in capacity during the 1980s, in part as a result of technology transfer from Western countries. The Chinese Navy began to exercise more regularly in the South China Sea, and in 1987 it began to occupy islands in the Spratlys itself. In 1988, it sunk two Vietnamese naval boats and took six islands. In early 1995, it took control of Mischief Reef, a rock outcrop to the west of the Filipino island of Palawan: prompting vigorous protests from the Philippines government and a more general apprehension throughout ASEAN. As of late 1995, China had occupied seven islands and reefs and Taiwan (which sometimes acts in cooperation with China on this issue) had occupied one. Vietnam had occupied twenty-seven, the Philippines eight and Malaysia three.[20]

More such incidents seem a distinct possibility as military capabilities improve, economic stakes grow, and all the claimants seek to strengthen their position on the ground in preparation for eventual negotiations. Additional uncertainty is created by the succession struggle in Beijing. It is often suggested that the PLA Navy is keen to take more decisive action to assert Chinese sovereignty over the Spratlys, but has been blocked by the strong opposition of the Foreign Ministry. A post-Deng leadership, however, may be more beholden to the armed forces for power, and may be unable to resist pressure for further military action.

China's legal position may be as strong as those of its rival claimants. But all parties to the conflict realise that the conflict is not simply about legality, or about economic resources. It is also about security and political symbolism. The ASEAN countries involved are concerned that Chinese assertiveness in the region may be the first step in an attempt to restore military hegemony in the region, and that ceding it control of the South China Sea would bring all of their coastlines within range of Chinese forces, allowing China to 'play a role in the region similar to that of the US in Central America.'[21] Even Singapore - one of only two ASEAN members not involved in the dispute directly - is worried by China's claim that the South China Sea is a inland sea, through which it has the right to control traffic. ASEAN states remember previous disputes over Malaysian and Indonesian attempts to limit passage through the Malacca Straits in 1971, and the accompanying sabre rattling by Japan. With much of Japan's overseas trade still passing through the area, the possibility of Japanese involvement in the conflict in future cannot be excluded.

Yet China's leaders also have security concerns. They believe that China's legal claim is a strong one, and consider the ASEAN claims as unjustified and opportunistic. They believe China has exercised restraint in the past, allowing Vietnam and other countries to seize far more islands than it has done itself. And they also view the degree of condemnation of its actions as part of a broader attempt by the US to encircle China: creating a structure of anti-China alliances from Japan through Taiwan and ASEAN to India.

These Chinese fears are not necessarily a source of instability. Chinese leaders are much less convinced of their own strength than others often are, and they may thus be deterred from taking action that could drive ASEAN into an explicit alliance with the US. If this is right, ASEAN leaders may be right to take an ambivalent attitude towards US overtures, maintaining a US presence 'just in case' while also reassuring China of their neutrality.

It is even possible that the greatest period of danger in the Spratlys has already passed. Many Chinese military strategists believed that 1988 would have been the best opportunity to take all the islands occupied by the Vietnamese.[22] Moscow's response to the naval conflict between China and Vietnam had been lukewarm, and the US was still anxious not to push China into an alliance with the Soviet Union. ASEAN countries could have been reassured by taking military action only against those islands occupied by Vietnam. Thus, for example, one Chinese analyst contends:

> 'Beijing made a strategic mistake ... the PLA Navy lost the rare chance to recover the Spratlys Islands from the Vietnamese. The Tianmen incident (in June 1989) doomed this chance. The extremely unfavourable situation that followed the incident made any such action impractical.'[23]

Such favourable circumstances are unlikely to repeat themselves. The US no longer needs China as an ally against the Soviet Union, and increasingly fears it as a potential rival superpower. Vietnam is now a member of ASEAN, and would strongly resist any attempt to isolate it from its new colleagues. China would risk driving the rest of Asia into an alliance against it, to the detriment of both its economic development and its security.

Despite these considerations, some elements in the PLA Navy, as part of the continuing campaign to acquire an aircraft carrier, may still be arguing for a military solution. For example, what claims to be a leaked internal Chinese government document paints the following scenario:

> '... we must establish dominance over the Vietnamese air force as much as possible and prevent the Vietnamese from sending reinforcements to the Spratlys. The attack on the sea should focus on Indonesia's submarines and escort vessels .... If necessary, we could consider 'surgical' strikes against the mainland of (Southeast Asian) countries in order to subdue them by destroying their military bases.'[24]

Yet an attempt to seize the Spratlys by force would be fraught with risks for China. There is no obvious political window of opportunity emerging, in which - as perhaps in 1988 - other powers need China so much for other purposes that they are willing to defer to it on this issue. Nor would a military operation necessarily produce a clear-cut victory. A Chinese task force would almost certainly be able to expel the other claimants from the 38 islands and reefs they occupy. Even with some Taiwanese support, however, the Chinese Navy would then face considerable difficulty in retaining control in the face of attempts by ASEAN states to disrupt their lines of supply. China would be unlikely to strike at air bases on the mainland of ASEAN states since this would almost certainly trigger a wider conflict. But without such strikes, its forces in and around the islands would be the target of continuing air attack, as well as harassment by ASEAN submarines and surface ships.

China could defeat Vietnam and Philippines - both of whom currently occupy more islands than China itself - in short order, given the virtual obsolescence of their naval and air forces. But it would encounter more sophisticated opposition from Malaysia, whose forces are being bolstered by the acquisition of modern Mig-29 and F/A-18 aircraft, together with two new British-built frigates. China would have to reckon with the possibility that Indonesia and/or Singapore - the latter through the FPDA - might be drawn into a conflict on Malaysia's side, adding additional assets to those lined against China's vulnerable lines of supply. Although direct US or Australian involvement might be avoided, an ASEAN coalition would almost certainly benefit from - and be able to afford - substantial logistical support and arms supplies from the West.

Even if ASEAN were to back down from a prolonged war, a victory could soon prove disastrous for China. A forcible seizure of the Spratlys would trigger a massive arms build-up throughout the region, a probable imposition of sanctions against the Chinese economy, and the start of a prolonged period of Cold War between China and most of the rest of the region. The fact that ASEAN governments still feel they cannot exclude such a possibility in itself indicates the depth of the current concern about the direction of Chinese policy.

It seems unlikely that Chinese leaders would be willing to risk so much for such an uncertain prize. They may therefore, if a domestic political opportunity presents itself, be prepared to adopt a compromise solution. Virtually all the inhabitable islands - that is, those above the water at low tide - have now been occupied, so there are few remaining opportunities for seizing additional islands or reefs without coming directly into conflict with the forces of one or other ASEAN state. At some stage, therefore, China may decide that it can enhance its international standing - and its position on other issues - by acceding to pressure for a negotiated settlement.

Many possible compromises have been suggested, both in ASEAN and in China itself.[25] In what appears to be a significant development, Chinese Foreign Minister Qian Qichen told the 1995 ARF meeting that Beijing would be willing to recognise international laws, including the 1982 Law of the Sea, as a basis for negotiating differences. He also agreed that China would discuss differences over the South China Sea with all seven ASEAN members, and not only in bilateral meetings.[26] ASEAN states have applauded these statements as a 'positive step forward'.[27]

The form of any settlement, within broad limits, may be less important for regional stability than the fact that it is reached. Such a settlement would be unlikely to entirely assuage the security concerns of either China or ASEAN. But it would make possible a sharp increase in the level of investment in the disputed seas, to the benefit of all the states concerned. In parallel with moves designed to deter precipitate military action, therefore, ASEAN leaders couod provide China with considerable economic incentives for a peaceful resolution of current tensions.

V   The military balance and China

Closely related to the Spratlys dispute is uncertainty about what is happening to the regional military balance, and in particular the balance between China and its neighbours. Within Asia as a whole, as within ASEAN itself, an important element in regional stability has been provided by the fact that the potential hegemon (Indonesia in the case of ASEAN, China in the case of Asia) has been extremely underdeveloped economically and primarily defensive in military orientation. China maintained impressively large armed forces throughout the Cold War period, organised to conduct a Maoist 'people's war' against an invading army as well as playing a central role in crushing internal dissent. But these same forces were relatively ineffective in offensive operations outside national territory, as was most clearly demonstrated in the 1979 invasion of Vietnam. Moreover, at least until the late 1980s, the bulk of China's armed forces were tied down defending the long land frontier with the Soviet Union: a source of some relief to China's southern neighbours.

With the easing of Chinese/Russian tension, some commentators expected a reduction in the level of Chinese military activity. In the absence of such reductions, there has been increased concern within South-East Asia at what China is doing. This concern has been most evident in relation to military spending and trends in force modernisation. We consider each in turn.

Military spending

China's official 1994 defence budget was only 52.4 billion yuan ($6 billion at prevailing exchange rates): less than Taiwan's budget, and only a fraction of that of other major Asian powers.[28] But this estimate excludes most spending on R&D and defence procurement, spending on the 1 million strong People's Armed Police, and service pensions. It is widely regarded as underestimating the true level of resource allocation for military purposes.[29] David Shambaugh has estimated that, allowing for these additional items, net PLA spending in 1993 was around $35.6 billion.[30]

The extent of such differences could be reduced by greater openness on the part of the Chinese government as part of the process of economic reform. Some recent proposals for procurement reform, for example, would require the use of market prices for the sale of weapons to the armed forces: a reform which, if implemented, would transfer a significant amount from the 'hidden' defence budget to the official one.[31] But it will also require a greater recognition on the part of Chinese officials that excessive secrecy on this matter is not in their own interests. Some recent attempts to engage in a debate on this matter have been made.[32] Given the considerable concern expressed on this issue - most noticeably by the Japanese government - China will come under pressure to do more.

Increased Chinese transparency will not entirely solve the problems created by attempts to compare China's defence budget with those of other countries. It is widely recognised that official exchange rates are often not a satisfactory means of comparing the costs of non-traded products (such as national defence) between countries, particularly when the countries in question are at very different stages of economic development. In recent years, therefore, it has become increasingly common to compare the national income of countries using 'Purchasing Power Parity', a means of allowing for differences in price levels between countries. One of the most dramatic effects of the use of 'PPP' has been to suggest that the Chinese economy, rather than being the ninth largest in the world, would be vying with Japan for number-two slot behind the US.[33]

The use of PPP methodology leads to a much increased estimate of the level of Chinese military expenditure. Using official exchange rates, the Chinese defence budget was $7.3 billion in 1993, falling to $6 billion in 1994 because of the 35% devaluation of the yuan in January 1994. After adjusting for differences in purchasing power between the US and China, estimates for Chinese defence spending range from $27 billion (IISS) to $56 billion (Arms Control and Disarmament Agency) to $140 billion (RAND).[34]

The calculation of defence spending on a PPP basis, and its comparison with figures using official exchange rates, helps explain why China is able to maintain armed forces of some 3 million for an amount (in dollar terms) comparable to the defence budget of the Netherlands, which has only 71,000 in its armed forces. For China spends so little on defence in part because it pays its soldiers and other employees so little compared with Western countries, even allowing for the lower levels of individual effectiveness and productivity of average Chinese soldiers.

Yet PPP estimates, used without sufficient care, can create a misleading impression, particularly if they are used to make comparisons with other Asian countries. The problems involved in selective use of PPP can be seen by reference to the budget figures published by the US Arms Control and Disarmament Agency (ACDA). According to ACDA, Chinese military expenditure for 1993 was $56.2 billion, calculated on a PPP basis. This compares with a total ASEAN defence budget in that year of only $12.5 billion, calculated by ACDA using official exchange rates.[35] Yet, if ASEAN defence expenditure is also calculated using PPP, it comes to $33 billion: around 60% of China's own defence effort.[36]

Attempting to estimate the level of Chinese defence expenditure is, therefore, bedevilled with problems. So much depends on the methodology used that there is likely to be little relation between the figure produced and the level of military capability. International comparisons may be of some value between countries with similar economic and military structures (for example between France and Germany). They are much more problematic between countries such as the US and China.

Given these problems, it may be more productive to focus instead on analysing trends in China's defence budget. One can normally, though not always, assume that deficiencies in coverage or methodology in any particular series of budget numbers will be consistent over time. A budget trend may be of limited value in assessing trends in capability (which is the result of programmes of procurement and investment over many years). But it can provide a good indication of the priority currently being given to defence in resource allocation, and thus indirectly some insight into government strategic thinking.

Thus, as a direct result of the adoption of an economic reform programme in the late 1970s, and the publicly announced decision to give defence spending a low priority, Chinese defence spending (on the official definition) fell sharply in the early 1980s, and continued to fall in real terms through the mid 1980s.[37] From 1989 onwards, however, this trend was reversed. The defence budget rose from Y21.8 billion in 1988 to Y37.8 billion in 1992, Y42.5 billion in 1993, Y52 billion for 1994 and Y63 billion for 1995: an average annual rate of growth in money terms over the last seven years of 16%.

Yet China also experienced a high rate of inflation over this period. In 1994, David Shambaugh estimated that half of the increase in the defence budget between 1988 and 1994 had been in real terms, implying an average annual rise of around 8% per annum in real terms.[38] More recently, Gerald Segal has suggested that 'China is the only power whose defence spending is rising as a percentage of gross domestic product (GDP), and quite dramatically in absolute terms.'[39] By contrast, the 1995 survey of world military expenditure by the US Arms Control and Disarmament Agency suggests an average real increase of only 1.5% over the period 1988 to 1993, leading to a reduction in the share of national income devoted to defence from 3.8% in 1988 to 2.7% in 1993.[40] SIPRI calculates an average real increase of 3.6% over the period 1988-94.[41] Other authors suggest a rate of increase of around 2% per annum in real terms.[42]

The substantial divergence between these estimates illustrates clearly why greater transparency could contribute to an easing of regional tensions. Even if the higher estimates of budget growth are more convincing, however, they may be as much a result of trends which China shares with its ASEAN neighbours - such as rapid economic growth - as of a fundamental shift of national priorities towards the armed forces.

Force modernisation

Of more concern to ASEAN governments than the trends in the Chinese defence budget is the reorientation of that budget towards power projection. The number of Chinese military personnel has declined from 3.9 million in 1988 to 2.9 million in 1995, thus releasing resources for investment in forces capable of power projection. There has been a particular emphasis on forces capable of conducting air/sea offensives against Taiwan and the South China Sea.[43] The Navy has sought to transform itself into a true 'blue water' navy by the acquisition of logistic support vessels, global communications facilities, and amphibious landing capabilities. Its surface ships, while still outdated by Western standards, have acquired new missile defences and on-board helicopters, enhanced underway replenishment capabilities, and improved classes of destroyers and frigates. It is in the process of acquiring Kilo class submarines from Russia, with some analysts estimating a final buy of as many as twenty boats.[44] The Air Force's capability has been further boosted by the acquisition of 26 Su-27 fighter aircraft from Russia in 1992, with a further 22 on order. Agreement in principle has also been reached about future licensed production of the Su-27 in China, perhaps at an initial rate of 10 to 20 aircraft annually.[45]

Since the 1980s there have also been reports of the Chinese Navy's desire to acquire an aircraft carrier. In the early 1990s, China sought to buy the former Soviet carrier *Varyag*, only to fall foul of American pressure on Russia not to proceed with the deal.[46] In January 1996, China also held exploratory talks with the chairman of Bazan, the Spanish warship builder responsible for supplying an 11,500 tonne carrier for the Royal Thai Navy.[47] If such a deal were to become a serious possibility, however, it would undoubtedly provoke pressure on the Spanish government to prevent it going through.

If China is unable to purchase an aircraft carrier from abroad, it may seek to build its own, perhaps similar in capability to the one being purchased by Thailand. Such a vessel would probably have the capability to launch vertical take-off aircraft and helicopters. A full-fledged capability, of two or three carriers plus escorts, might be in place by 2010 or 2015.

Yet China is still many years away from attaining the capabilities of a military superpower. Its destroyers and frigates are vulnerable to the European-designed submarines being purchased by ASEAN nations and South Korea, and still lack many of the capabilities necessary to make them a real 'blue-water' force. China remains extremely reliant on procuring its weapons from the inefficient, and technologically backward, state industrial sector. In stark contrast to the defence industrial sector in the Soviet Union, but in a situation not dissimilar to that facing ASEAN armed forces, the Chinese arms industry in recent years has often been unable to attract the best young graduates, most of whom now prefer the greater attractions of the private sector. Progress is clearly being made, as the quality of new generations of equipment show. But, given that other countries in the region are also investing in military modernisation, it may be a long time before the quality of Chinese forces is able to match that of other Asian powers.

Moreover, it has become more difficult for China to gain access to foreign military technology since the Tianmen Square events of 1989. With only limited exceptions, it no longer has the degree of access to Western technology that it had during the 1980s, and this seems likely to remain the case for some time in the absence of a fundamental improvement in US/Chinese relations. In contrast, most of China's neighbours - including Taiwan, Japan, South Korea and most ASEAN countries - have relatively free access to advanced Western technology.

China has sought to offset the Western arms embargo with competitively-priced imports from Russia, itself anxious to stem the collapse of its own arms industry by selling abroad. As a result of both Western pressure and its own security concerns, however, Russia has been unwilling to give China full access to all its products. In addition to its refusal to sell an aircraft carrier, it is also reported to have turned down a request by China to buy Backfire bombers.[48] In part because of the lack of willing suppliers, and in part because China's own arms industry has blocked military pressure for larger-scale imports, most estimates suggest that Chinese arms imports have been relatively limited in volume over the last five years. SIPRI estimates that China's imports of major conventional arms were worth $2.9 billion (at 1990 prices) over the period 1990-94, compared with $8.3 billion for Japan, $3.9 billion for Taiwan, and $6.6 billion for ASEAN.[49]

China is stronger militarily than any individual ASEAN country, and the disparate nature of ASEAN forces might give it the edge even against an all-ASEAN alliance. But it is far from clear that the military balance is tilting in China's favour. China's mass army would be irrelevant in a war that required power projection, such as an air/sea conflict in the South China Sea. The most militarily advanced ASEAN states would also have the advantage of distance, allowing them easier resupply for their forces in a prolonged conflict.

Even if they could not count on direct military support from the US, Australia or the UK, (and such support cannot be ruled out) ASEAN would, unlike China, be able to gain access to substantial technical support and resupply of their military efforts. China may have much larger armed forces, but it still has good reasons to fear that it could suffer the fate of other states - such as Syria against Israel, or Iraq against the US - that seek to take on Western-equipped armed forces with Soviet-model weapons.

VI   Conclusion

ASEAN has legitimate security concerns regarding trends in Chinese military power, especially when these are viewed in the context of some of China's recent sabre-rattling gestures. So far, the Chinese military build-up appears to have been relatively modest in nature. But a worsening of the strategic situation (from the perspective of either China or other countries) could lead to an acceleration of current programmes, and in turn to a real 'arms race' across Asia. In order to avoid such a development, more will have to be done to strengthen processes of confidence-building in the region: reassuring both China and its neighbours that no one country is seeking 'hegemony'. The regional security dialogue, discussed in Chapter 6, will be crucial in this process.

Notes

1.   Douglas T. Stuart and William T. Tow, *A US Strategy for the Asia-Pacific*, Adelphi Paper Number 299, International Institute for Strategic Studies, Oxford University Press, 1995, p. 39.

2.   Tim Huxley, *Insecurity in the ASEAN Region*, Royal United Services Institute for Defence Studies, London, 1993, p. 26.

3.   J. N. Mak, *ASEAN Defence Reorientation 1975-1992*, Canberra Papers on Strategy and Defence Number 103, Strategic and Defence Studies Centre, Australian National University, 1993, p. 41.

4.   *Defense News*, September 11, 1995, p. 8.

5.   'US Navy eyes port in Vietnam', *Defense News*, September 11, 1995.

6.   Nigel Holloway, 'Jolt from the blue', *Far Eastern Economic Review*, August 3, 1995, p. 22.

Notes continued

7.   Philip Methven, *The Five Power Defence Arrangements and Military Co-operation among the ASEAN States*, Canberra Papers on Strategy and Defence Number 92, Strategic and Defence Studies Centre, Australian National University, 1992, pp. 69-91.

8.   International Institute for Strategic Studies, *Strategic Survey 1994/95*, Oxford University Press, 1995, p. 185.

9.   Audrey Kurth Cronin and Patrick M. Cronin, 'The Realistic Engagement of China', *The Washington Quarterly*, 19, 1, Winter 1996, p. 143.

10.   Denny Roy, 'Consequences of China's Economic Growth for Asia-Pacific Security', *Security Dialogue*, 24, 2, 1993, p. 182.

11.   International Institute for Strategic Studies, op cit, p. 165.

12.   J. Mohan Malik, 'Sino-Indian Rivalry in Myanmar: Implications for Regional Security', *Contemporary South-East Asia*, 16, 2, September 1994, pp. 137-156; Eric Hyer, *Sideshow: The Developing China-Myanmar Security Relationship*, paper presented to 35th annual conference of the International Studies Association, Washington D.C., April 1994.

13.   J. N. Mak, 'The Chinese Navy and the South China Sea: A Malaysian Assessment', *The Pacific Review*, 4, 2, 1991, p. 150.

14.   For some recent discussions of the competing claims, see Gerardo M. C. Valero, 'Spratly archipelago dispute: is the question of sovereignty still relevant?', *Marine Policy*, 18, 4, 1994, pp. 314-344; Michael Leifer, 'Chinese Economic Reform and Security Policy: The South China Sea Connection', *Survival*, 37, 2, Summer 1995, pp. 44-59; Mark Valencia, 'Troubled Waters: Disputes in the South China Sea', *Harvard International Review*, Spring 1994, pp. 12-15; Sheng Lijun, *China's Policy Towards the Spratly Islands*, Strategic and Defence Studies Centre Working Paper Number 287, Canberra, Australian National University, 1995; Brian Cloughley, 'No need for war in South China Sea', *International Defense Review*, 6, 1995, pp. 22-26.

15.   *Map of the People's Republic of China*, China Cartographic Publishing House, 1988.

16.   You Ji and You Xu, 'In Search of Blue Water Power: The PLA Navy's Maritime Strategy in the 1990s', *The Pacific Review*, 4, 2, 1991, pp. 138-139.

17.   Michael Leifer, op cit, p. 44.

Notes continued

18. Sheng Lijun, op cit, p. 7.

19. Ibid, p. 9; Nayan Chanda, Rigoberto Tiglao and John McBeth, 'Territorial Imperative', *Far Eastern Economic Review*, 23 February 1995, p. 16.

20. Nayan Chanda et al, ibid, p. 14; Sheng Lijun, ibid, p. 26.

21. You Ji and You Xu, op cit, p. 145.

22. You Ji, 'The PLA Navy in the Changing World Order: The South China Sea Theatre' in Dick Sherwood (ed), *Maritime Power in the China Seas*, Australian Defence Studies Centre, 1994, p. 103.

23. Sheng Lijun, op cit, p. 12.

24. Ross Munro, 'Eavesdropping on the Chinese Military: Where it Expects War - Where it Doesn't', *Orbis*, Summer 1994, p. 371.

25. For a useful discussion of compromise solutions proposed by Chinese experts, see Sheng Lijun, op cit, pp. 19-25.

26. Murray Hiebert, 'Comforting Noises', *Far Eastern Economic Review*, 10 August 1995, p. 16.

27. quoted in Douglas T. Stuart and William T. Tow, op cit, p. 43.

28. Stockholm International Peace Research Institute, *SIPRI Yearbook 1995*, Oxford University Press, 1995, p. 373.

29. Ibid, pp. 372-377.

30. David Shambaugh, 'Calculating Chinese military expenditure' in Nicole Ball et al, 'World Military Expenditure', *SIPRI Yearbook 1994*, Oxford University Press, 1994, p. 443.

31. Ibid, pp. 445-446.

32. For example, see Hu Ping, 'Refuting the Allegation of "China's Military Threat"', *International Strategic Studies (Beijing)*, 36, 2, June 1995, pp. 25-29.

33. 'China: a survey', *Economist*, 18 March, 1995, p. 9.

34. International Institute for Strategic Studies, *The Military Balance 1994/95*, Brassey's, 1994, p. 170; US Arms Control and Disarmament

Notes continued

Agency, *World Military Expenditures and Arms Transfers 1993-1994*, 1995, p. 58; Barbara Opall, 'Study Rings Alarm on PLA Budget', *Defense News*, June 1995. For a discussion of the uncertainties surrounding the Chinese defence budget, see Richard A. Bitzinger, 'China's defence budget: is the PLA cooking the books?', *International Defense Review*, 2, 1995, pp. 35-37.

35.   Does not include Vietnam.

36.   Calculated using PPP figures from World Bank, *World Development Report 1995*, Oxford University Press, 1995, pp. 220-221.

37.   Hadi Soesastro, 'Military Expenditure and the Arms Trade', *Asian-Pacific Economic Literature*, 8, 1, May 1994, p. 31.

38.   David Shambaugh, 'Growing Strong: China's Challenge to Asian Security', *Survival*, 36, 2, Summer 1994, p. 54.

39.   Gerald Segal, 'Tying China into the International System', *Survival*, 37, 2, Summer 1995, p. 69.

40.   US Arms Control and Disarmament Agency, op cit, p. 58.

41.   *SIPRI Yearbook 1995*, op cit, p. 442.

42.   Gary Klintworth and Desmond Ball, 'China's Arms Build-up and Regional Security', mimeo, 1994, p. 8.

43.   Derek da Cunha, 'Conventional Arms and Security in South-East Asia: China and the ASEAN', in Malcolm Chalmers, Owen Greene and Xie Zhiqiong (eds), *Asia Pacific Security and the UN*, Chinese People's Association for Peace and Disarmament/ University of Bradford, 1995, pp. 49-67.

44.   Jason Glashow, 'US says Chinese naval threat is years away', *Defense News*, October 1995.

45.   "Made in China' deal is forged for Su-27's', *Jane's Defence Weekly*, 6 May 1995, p. 3.

46.   You Ji, op cit, p. 94.

47.   David White, 'Spain may build carrier for China', *Financial Times*, 22 January 1996.

48.   Gary Klintworth and Desmond Ball, op cit, p. 25.

49.   *SIPRI Yearbook 1995*, op cit, p. 494.

CHAPTER 4

The ASEAN Arms Build-Up

I   Trends in ASEAN defence spending

South-East Asia has failed to enjoy a 'peace dividend' from the end of the Cold War. While defence budgets have fallen throughout Europe, spending in most ASEAN states has risen substantially over the last few years. According to the Stockholm International Peace Research Institute (SIPRI), Indonesia, Thailand and Malaysia have all experienced a marked increase in defence spending, with real increases of 32%, 33% and 50% respectively over the last four years. Singapore's defence budget has grown more steadily, with a real increase in spending of 60% since 1985. Only the Philippines, always marginal to ASEAN's balance of power, has seen no significant increase in real defence spending in recent years.[1]

The most important driving force for increased defence expenditure in the region has been the availability of resources. Spending has grown fastest in those countries - Singapore, Malaysia and Thailand - with the highest rates of economic growth. And spending increases have been concentrated in those periods - such as the first half of the 1990s - when growth has been highest. Figures on regional defence expenditure can vary considerably between different sources. Yet most sources agree that the long term trend in the proportion of national income devoted to defence has, until recently, remained downwards.[2] The proportion of government expenditure devoted to defence has also fallen in each of the ASEAN countries between 1980 and 1993 (except for Brunei, for which data were not available). Whereas four out of five ASEAN states spent more on defence than on education in 1980, only one (Singapore) did so in 1993.[3]

Decisions on the size of the peacetime defence budget in any country inevitably involve a trade-off at the margin between military requirements and alternative demands on limited resources. As total available resources increase, therefore, one would expect that (if the security risks facing the government remain unchanged) more will be spent on the armed forces, as on other government services. Rapid growth in military spending is still a matter of concern, not least for neighbouring states. But, in the absence of a rise in the share of military spending in national resources, it does not necessarily provide evidence of growing tension or insecurity.

Table 4.1: ASEAN Defence and Education Budgets

(as a percentage of total central government spending)

	Defence 1980	Defence 1993	Education 1980	Education 1993
Indonesia	13.5	6.2	8.3	10.0
Malaysia	14.8	11.8	18.3	20.3
Philippines	15.7	10.6	13.0	15.9
Singapore	25.2	24.5	14.6	22.3
Thailand	21.7	17.2	19.8	21.1

Source: World Bank, *World Development Report 1995*, Oxford University Press, 1995, pp. 180-181.

Most of the increases in ASEAN defence outlays in recent years have gone into capital investment and procurement. The end of the Cold War has meant that there are many bargains available in the international arms market, and some ASEAN states have become adept at obtaining good terms from suppliers. Armed forces have therefore sought to acquire new weapon systems, and replace ageing ones, for which they previously lacked sufficient resources. In particular, recent years have seen an effort to make up for the shortfall in modernisation programmes caused by the cutbacks in defence spending in the mid 1980s.

The ability of regional states to finance significant growth in arms budgets has been helped by the shift of resources away from personnel spending that has been made possible by changes in strategic circumstances. Vietnam, although still possessing the largest armed forces in the region, has made the sharpest reduction - from 1,052,000 in 1990 to 572,000 in 1995 - as a consequence of its withdrawal from Cambodia. Reductions in force levels have also been possible in Malaysia and Thailand, where resources have been shifted from the personnel-intensive armies needed for counter-insurgency operations to the more capital-intensive, and more 'modern', air forces and navies required for new roles. Insofar as there is a 'race' in the region, therefore, it is confined to arms rather than military forces more generally.

Table 4.2: ASEAN Armed Forces: Personnel Numbers

	Indonesia	Malaysia	Philippines	Singapore	Thailand	Vietnam
1990	283,000	129,500	108,500	55,500	282,900	1,052,000
1995	274,500	114,500	106,500	53,900	259,000	572,000

Sources: International Institute for Strategic Studies, *The Military Balance 1990/91*, Brassey's, 1990; International Institute for Strategic Studies, *The Military Balance 1995/96*, Oxford University Press, 1995.

The acceleration in procurement spending in recent years is linked to the process of societal modernisation. Modern 'high tech' armed forces are often seen as an important symbol of modernity and economic progress, part of the process of moving from predominantly agrarian societies to urban capitalist economies. The investment in modern armed forces is seen as every bit as natural a part of this transition as are investments in modern roads, ports and universities.

There are also more concrete reasons why development has tended to increase demands for military modernisation. Perhaps the most important is that the 1982 UN Convention on the Law of the Sea has led to the creation by ASEAN members of 200 nautical mile Exclusive Economic Zones (EEZ's) in South-East Asia. Policing these Zones is becoming increasingly important to ASEAN economies. Oil and gas revenues are important elements in the economies of Malaysia, Indonesia and Brunei, and new technologies continue to increase the attractiveness of offshore drilling. Access to the rich fish stocks of the region is an important part of many regional economies. Not least, continued freedom of navigation through the EEZ's is vital to a region that is increasingly dependent on trade.

ASEAN states argue that they require additional maritime forces in order to protect these resources, both against piracy (perceived to be a growing problem in the region) and against rival claimants to often disputed territorial claims. In order to obtain these new capabilities, a high proportion of ASEAN procurement over the last decade has been in areas such as surveillance aircraft, offshore patrol vessels, corvettes and frigates.[4]

The growth in arms spending in the region is also linked to the domestic politics of ASEAN states in various ways. The distribution of government resources is inevitably, at least to some extent, a result of a process of balancing the demands of competing interest groups. The groups most closely connected to military expenditure - the armed forces and military-related industries - have considerable political clout in this process. Defence procurement is often a lucrative source of pay-offs for influential individuals, who may be more concerned with opportunities for 'kickbacks' than with military effectiveness.[5] Governments are wary of giving their armed forces reasons to become disgruntled with civilian leaders, fearing that the lack of a clear military role may tempt them to acquire a political one. Even in Singapore, where there is a long tradition of civilian rule, Tim Huxley has pointed to the growing role of senior military officers in politics.[6]

It is thus significant, and apparently paradoxical, that ASEAN's lowest level of defence spending (as a proportion of national income) is in Indonesia, where the armed forces dominate the state, yet have been conscious of the national need for low defence spending. As J. N. Mak has observed:

> 'the military can become so much part and parcel of government that national interests often override service interests, as in the case of Indonesia.'[7]

There are, therefore, good reasons why there is not a simple relationship between military spending levels and recent changes in the international environment. But this does not mean that ASEAN defence policy is unaffected by broader trends in the strategic environment, and by changes in the balance between Asia's Great Powers in particular. The questionmark over future Chinese intentions, demonstrated most forcefully by recent events in the South China Sea, continues to exert upward pressure on ASEAN defence budgets.

Finally, any explanation of the recent ASEAN military build-up also needs to take into account the existence of rivalries and balancing behaviour within ASEAN itself. As discussed in Chapter 2, the armed forces of ASEAN have evolved a complex 'spiderweb' of joint exercises and consultation, and the 'ASEAN Way' has undoubtedly strengthened the commitment to peaceful resolution of conflicts within the organisation.

Yet tensions still remains in several bilateral relationships, with unresolved territorial disputes and minority problems continuing to generate suspicions. As a result, despite its progress over the last 25 years, ASEAN is not yet a 'security community' in the sense of having made war unthinkable between its member states. The military balance of power within ASEAN remains of keen interest to the armed forces of the region. And the desire to maintain or improve this balance may, at least for some countries, be as powerful a motivation for military investment as the potential threat from outside powers such as China.

Most analysts are anxious not to characterise what is occurring as an 'arms race:' a value-laden term which is increasingly reserved for very specific, and narrowly defined, circumstances.[8] Yet there are strong elements of competition and emulation in ASEAN procurement patterns. One example often cited in recent years was the Thai decision to buy the F-16A from the US in 1985, followed by F-16 orders from Singapore and Indonesia, and the Malaysian decision to sign a Memorandum of Understanding with the UK for the purchase of its own fighter aircraft. Other factors were clearly at play in this process, not least a common requirement to balance Vietnamese air power. But the maintenance of the balance of power within ASEAN also appears to have been a significant factor.

The process of 'emulation' is not necessarily an antagonistic one. With the end of most domestic insurgencies in the region, and the increasing importance of maritime resources, ASEAN armed forces have tended to evolve increasingly similar military requirements. The purchase of a new capability by a neighbour, even if viewed entirely as a potential ally, can be a powerful argument in favour of a similar purchase by one's own government.

Yet the armed forces of ASEAN also continue to watch the military developments in their neighbours with a view to maintaining or improving their own ability to prevail against them should conflict occur. The extent to which intra-ASEAN factors play a determining factor in procurement is a matter of judgement, and is in any case likely to vary between projects and between countries. There is little doubt, however, that it plays a significant role in ASEAN defence planning in several instances, or that there is scope for further, and potentially destabilising, competition in future.

In order to understand more fully the nature of regional defence programmes, and the extent to which they should be a cause for concern, we now discuss each ASEAN member state in turn, before returning to thematic issues in the last section of the Chapter.

II   Singapore

Singapore is the ASEAN member whose defence programme is most clearly driven by concern about other ASEAN states. Since its independence in 1965, its leaders have been acutely aware of just how small Singapore is in comparison with its two neighbours, Malaysia and Indonesia. As Prime Minister Goh Chok Tong commented in his August 1995 National Day speech:

> 'We have overcome great odds to stand at the threshold of a developed country. But our constraints and vulnerabilities are still there. ... Recently I met several groups of Singaporeans .. and shared with them my priorities and worries. I started with a geography lesson. I showed them a map of South-East Asia which marked out the boundaries of Malaysia, Indonesia and Singapore. Many had forgotten their geography. They never realised that Singapore was that small. They were awed by the size of Indonesia. Do you know that Indonesia from east to west is as far as from Singapore to Tokyo? Do you know that between last year's National Rally and now, one Singapore has been born in Indonesia?'

In military terms, Singaporean leaders do not anticipate an attack, but they do plan for the possibility that external events might lead without warning to a threat emerging. Although concern regarding Indonesia remains, the main focus of current defence policy appears to be to deter military attack, as well as other forms of intervention in its affairs, by Malaysia.

Because of this primary focus, the end of the Cold War has had no discernible effect on Singaporean defence plans. It has continued to maintain a policy of allocating 6% of its national income to defence: by far the highest proportion in the region. As a result of the rapid growth in its economy in recent years, the Singaporean armed forces have therefore

Table 4.3: Singapore

Vital statistics

Population	2.8 million
1993 GNP	$55.8 billion
Real GNP growth 1983-93	+ 99% (7.1% per annum)

Trends in military spending and arms imports

Year	Military spending constant 1993 $	Military spending as % of GNP	Arms imports constant 1993 $
1983	1176	4.2	271
1984	1607	5.2	232
1985	1839	5.9	224
1986	1722	5.5	397
1987	1756	5.2	223
1988	1994	5.3	442
1989	2062	5.0	194
1990	1926	4.3	241
1991	2356	4.9	306
1992	2599	5.1	215
1993	2700	4.8	60

Source: US Arms Control and Disarmament Agency, *World Military Expenditures and Arms Transfers 1993-94*, 1995.

benefited from ASEAN's fastest growth in defence spending. This trend appears to have continued over the last two years, with a 14% increase in spending in real terms in 1994, followed by a 16% real increase in the defence budget in 1995.[9]

In an achievement that can be seen as the counterpart of its impressive economic success, Singapore now also has the region's most modern and combat-capable armed forces. Its procurement policies appear rational, extremely cost-effective, and unburdened by the corruption or prestige considerations common in other ASEAN members. Its armed forces have proven as adept at learning how to operate high technology military equipment as its increasingly well-educated and adaptable civilian workers have proven in carving out a high-income niche in the regional and global economy.

Because of its lack of manpower, Singapore relies heavily on the training and mobilisation of reserves. Its active forces of 54,000 are smaller than Malaysia's 114,000, but on mobilisation it could have 312,000 military personnel compared with Malaysia's 172,000. Through an extensive training programme, including annual training camps lasting several weeks for most reservists and involving a range of overseas facilities (in Australia, US, Brunei, Indonesia, Taiwan and, some reports suggest, Myanmar[10]) its forces are the most operationally ready of all the forces of ASEAN.

Defence policy is based on the assumption that, in the event of conflict, Singapore needs to ensure that fighting does not take place on its own, very small, territory by launching an offensive campaign. Because of Singapore's vulnerability to a cut-off of its water supplies, the key task of such an offensive would be to capture and hold a zone in the south of Malaysia. This region has the additional advantage, from Singapore's point of view, of being disproportionately populated by ethnic Chinese.[11]

In order to ensure it a military advantage in any crisis, Singapore not only maintains a higher degree of operational readiness than its neighbours. It also seeks to maintain clear technological superiority, and is often the first to introduce new capabilities into the region. The clearest reflection of this policy is that Singapore's air force is now the largest and most technically sophisticated in the region. According to Tim Huxley, Singaporean planning is based on the precept that it should deploy more front line combat aircraft than Malaysia and Indonesia combined. Moreover, the effectiveness of Singaporean air power is further increased by its deployment of airborne early warning aircraft (delivered in 1987-88), in-flight refuelling tankers, and hardened air bases.[12] If a conflict were to occur between Singapore and its neighbours in the near future, there is little doubt that Singapore would be able to establish clear air superiority very quickly.

Singaporean ground forces have also gained growing capabilities for offensive operations, converting three infantry divisions into combined arms units, equipped with locally upgraded AMX-13 light tanks, the locally-developed FH-88 155mm artillery, and M-113 APCs. Equipment is constantly upgraded, with recent purchases including the Legaun vehicle-launched bridge, 105mm heli-portable GIAT guns, and the AMX-10 PAC 90 light tank.[13] According to one recent report, the US government is believed likely to approve a Singapore request to purchase Apache attack helicopters, which would be the first sale of this advanced system to South-East Asia.[14]

If war should come, these forces would be well-equipped to conduct a rapid advance into neighbouring territory in order to secure Singapore's water supplies and provide substantial strategic depth in preparation for an enemy counter-offensive. As Malaysian analyst J. N. Mak suggests:

> 'From a purely military point of view, it makes sense for Singapore to plan never to make the island a battlefield, but to defend the republic on the soil and waters of its neighbours. However, this doctrine has upset Indonesia, and more especially Malaysia, leading some defence analysts in Kuala Lumpur to argue that Singapore's armoured force is meant for only one purpose, a deep strike against Malaysia.'[15]

Until recently, the Singaporean navy was given a lower priority than air and ground forces. Since the mid 1980s, however, increased defence resources have permitted a rapid, but carefully planned, build-up of naval capabilities. Unlike other ASEAN countries, Singapore has no extensive Exclusive Economic Zone to police. Rather, the declared aim of the new naval policy is protection of freedom of navigation through the Sea Lines of Communication (SLOCs) vital for Singapore's economy: not least in the event of a conflict in the South China Sea.[16] In pursuance of this further extension of its military reach - described by one analyst as having 'a strategic intent which is very much defensive, even if some of the equipment and tactical methods rely very much upon the tactical offensive'[17] - Singapore introduced six missile corvettes into service in 1991, upgraded existing missile gunboats with Harpoon missiles, and is in the process of acquiring mine counter-measures vessels and maritime patrol aircraft. According to a one analyst:

> 'These improvements have resulted in the RSN (Republic of Singapore Navy) now having, among the navies of South-East Asia, an unmatched missile strike capability.'[18]

Despite some suggestions that premature development of such a capability might be viewed as aggressive by its neighbours[19], the next stage in the development of Singapore's naval capabilities seems likely to be the acquisition of a submarine force. In September 1995, Singapore announced that it was purchasing a second-hand diesel-electric submarine from Sweden in order, according to the Singapore Defence Minister, to 'learn more about submarine operations and how they add to the capabilities of our fleet'. Discussions are also continuing about the possible acquisition of further Type 206 submarines from Germany.[20]

With economic success spreading to its much more populous neighbours, however, Singapore may not always be able to maintain a military doctrine based on technological supremacy and pre-emption. Thailand and Malaysia, in particular, have joined the club of 'NIC's' (newly industrialising countries), and are gradually developing the technological and organisational skills necessary for modern warfare. Moreover, now undistracted by internal insurgency threats, their armed forces are pursuing ambitious procurement programmes that may already be starting to narrow the qualitative gap between Singapore and its neighbours.

If Singapore were to sustain annual growth rates of 7-10% into the 21st century, this process of catch-up could take a long time. Singapore could afford further rapid military modernisation without increasing the burden of military spending on the economy, and it could compensate for its falling number of conscripts (as a result of a declining birth rate) by vigorous investment in new technologies.

With Singapore likely to be enjoying an average level of national income comparable with that of the US before the end of the century, however, it may - like Japan in the 1980s - soon find that it cannot sustain a breakneck pace of growth when there is no more 'catching up' to do. Even allowing for the possibilities for a city-state to achieve a higher average level of development than a large country like the US, the stage seems set for a marked economic slowdown within the next decade or so. Once this occurs, Singapore may find that it cannot avoid both its relative economic position and its margin of military advantage beginning to erode quite rapidly. The latter could be threatened even sooner if its neighbours seek to match the 5-6% of national income which Singapore currently spends on its armed forces.

Aware of the potential of competitive programmes in neighbouring states for eroding its current edge, the Singapore government has tried to soften the impact of its own acquisitions in various (not always successful) ways. Its official policy states that its defences are not built on the premise of an existing external threat, even though many observers have suggested that it is the ASEAN member for whom specific external threats are most important. It prefers to retain its superiority 'in a very discrete, non-abrasive, and sometimes consultative manner.'[21] For example, in order not to be the first state to introduce such advanced aircraft into the region, it kept its first F-16's in the US for two years after they were purchased in 1988; and it opted to buy a second batch only after Thailand decided to buy a second squadron towards the end of 1991. It consulted both Indonesia and Malaysia before signing an agreement to locate its fighter training school near Perth in Western Australia.[22]

This diplomatic track in Singaporean security policy, however, is in uneasy coexistence with the strongly entrenched tradition of worst case defence planning, which encourages the armed forces to pursue a policy based entirely on military considerations. This tendency was illustrated most graphically by the espionage controversy with Malaysia in 1989, which was reportedly due, at least in part, to Singapore's efforts to collect information on Malaysia's arms deal with the UK.[23] This did nothing to reassure Malaysia that it need not fear Singapore's 'forward defence' policy.

Singapore may seek to maintain its current military edge, even at the risk of an intensified intra-ASEAN arms race. Faced with rapid military modernisation in Malaysia and Thailand, however, it may eventually have little choice but to progressively rely more for its security on factors other than its own military strength: including greater intra-ASEAN confidence-building and/or a strengthening of links with outside powers.

III   Malaysia

Until recently, the main focus of the armed forces of Malaysia was internal insurgency. Even as other concerns - notably maritime policing - began to take on more prominence, the onset of economic recession in the mid 1980s meant that for several years no significant procurement orders were placed. While Singapore has been engaged in an incremental, but continuous, improvement in its conventional forces almost since its independence in 1965, it is only in the 1990s that the Malaysian armed forces have been able to devote substantial resources to meeting potential external threats.

The last five years, however, have seen a major effort to improve Malaysian conventional defences. The development budget for defence (i.e. excluding operations costs) in the Sixth Malaysian Plan (1991-95) quadrupled compared with the previous Plan.[24] After remaining at under $100 million a year since 1985, imports of major conventional arms shot up to $350 million (at 1990 prices) in 1994.[25] In 1994, the manpower budget is reported to have been cut by 6% to accommodate a 27% increase in the procurement budget.[26]

There has been a particular emphasis on the upgrading of air and naval forces. 28 Hawk aircraft armed with Sea Eagle and ALARM missiles have been supplied as part of a 1988 deal with the UK. 18 Mig 29 fighter aircraft from Russia were delivered in 1995, in a contract reputedly worth $550 million.[27] 8 American F/A-18 fighter/ground attack aircraft should come into service in 1997, armed with a comprehensive range of US-built missiles (AIM-7M Sparrow, AIM-9S Sidewinder, AGM-56 Maverick and AGM-86 Harpoon).[28] For the Navy, two new British-built Exocet-armed frigates have been bought at a cost of $600 million, and should enter service in 1996. A second squadron of patrol vessels was formed in August 1995, and stationed on Labuan island in order to cover the South China Sea.[29] Two Italian corvettes, originally due to be sold to Iraq, now seem likely to be purchased by Malaysia, and may be joined by two more if terms can be agreed.[30] Not least, despite the considerable expense, options are being considered for the procurement of submarines. Personnel have already been sent to various European countries for training in submarine operations and maintenance.[31] Malaysia's programme is likely to be spurred on by the decisions to introduce submarines into the navies of both Singapore and Thailand.

One of the most important driving forces for the Malaysian naval expansion has been concern at the threat posed to its maritime resources. This is a particularly acute problem with relation to fish stocks, where sustained overfishing around Thailand itself has pushed Thailand's massive, and largely unregulated, fishing fleet to seek stocks elsewhere.

Table 4.4: Malaysia

Vital statistics

Population	18.8 million
1993 GNP	$61.3 billion
Real GNP growth 1983-93	+ 91% (6.7% per annum)

Trends in military spending and arms imports   (e = estimate)

Year	Military spending constant 1993 $	Military spending as % of GNP	Arms imports constant 1993 $
1983	1638e	5.1	399
1984	1314e	3.8	545
1985	1276e	3.8	618
1986	1456e	4.2	77
1987	1645	4.5	87
1988	1067	2.7	36
1989	1271	2.9	80
1990	1297	2.7	33
1991	1930	3.7	21
1992	2456	4.4	10
1993	2642e	4.3	80

Source: US Arms Control and Disarmament Agency, *World Military Expenditures and Arms Transfers 1993-94*, 1995.

Partly in response, Malaysia is investing $1.6 billion in replacing its fleet of offshore patrol vessels: the largest single fleet modernisation project in the country's history.[32] As B. A. Hamzah of the Malaysian Institute of Maritime Affairs has commented:

> 'Our sea area is four times as large as our land area. We need to prevent our resources from being taken away by other people. The navy takes this very seriously.'[33]

Although at first disoriented by the loss of its counter-insurgency mission as a result of the peace settlement with the Communist Party of Malaya in December 1989, the Army has also received a substantial share of new resources. Two new army bases are being built at Gemas and Mersing in the south of peninsular Malaysia, a national command and control network is being established, and in October 1994 a brigade-sized Rapid Deployment Force was launched.[34] This new formation, which it is hoped will expand to divisional size in due course, is intended to give the Army the capability for conducting pre-emptive strikes or counter-offensive action, deploying rapidly to Sabah and Sarawak to counter a possible secessionist movement. It is made up of elements of the parachute battalion, support and mechanised infantry, spearheaded by light tanks.[35] 114 infantry fighting vehicles have been bought from South Korea.[36] In order to support the new formation, the Navy is acquiring a 8450 ton landing ship tank and the Air Force is purchasing five new Hercules aircraft.[37] Funding permitting, it is also hoped to acquire transportable light artillery, utility and attack helicopters and possibly main battle tanks.

Malaysian procurement policy in recent years has been highly politicised and has therefore tended to attract more international attention than Singapore's quieter and more technocratic approach. For example, the 1988 Memorandum of Understanding with the UK, effectively the starting point for the recent military modernisation programme, was also the catalyst for a wider improvement in relations between the two countries: only to become the focus for a high-profile international row once it became clear that it involved a $234 million aid package for the Pergau Dam in northern Malaysia in return for the promise of defence sales.[38] More recently, the decision to buy Mig 29's from Russia - making a powerful point to the US, the dominant supplier of fighter aircraft in the region - was made by the Prime Minister himself, reportedly overruling scepticism in the armed forces.

The desire to use the armed forces for purposes of broader foreign policy has also been seen in the considerable contribution which Malaysia now makes to UN peacekeeping missions. Since 1988, it has contributed forces to 15 UN missions, of which the most substantial so far have been in Namibia, Cambodia, Somalia and Bosnia.[39] The 1995 Malaysian request to double its presence in Bosnia to a brigade level of 3,000, although rejected by the UN[40], further illustrated the willingness to use Malaysia's peacekeeping forces to promote the country on the world stage, as did the decision to set up a dedicated peacekeeping centre. Peacekeeping operations also have the welcome side-effect of providing the Malaysian armed forces with a practical opportunity to test their personnel and equipment.[41]

The provision of a substantial UN contribution, together with the politicisation of other aspects of defence policy-making, reflects the leadership's perception that Malaysia does not face any pressing immediate military threats and that, therefore, defence policy can be placed at the service of broader external and internal policy objectives. Yet one should not overstate the impact of such factors. The driving force for Malaysian military modernisation remains the perception that, in the long run, Malaysia faces an uncertain strategic environment in which the armed forces may have important roles to play in the protection of Malaysian interests.

The most important of these roles is defence of Malaysia's maritime claims. Malaysia is involved in maritime disputes with all its regional neighbours, with conflicts in the South China Sea being of particular concern. The current build-up of Malaysian air and naval forces in the area can thus be justified as necessary both in order to deter China from attempting military action against Malaysian-controlled territory in the area, and to provide effective military superiority in this theatre over fellow ASEAN members Brunei, Philippines and Vietnam.

In addition, the nature of the Malaysian build-up may also be influenced by the desire, over time, to overcome the country's vulnerability to attack by its smaller island neighbour. Recent combat aircraft purchases will help to erode, though will not end, Singaporean superiority in the air. Plans for new Army equipment, together with the development of major bases in the south of the country, may be in part motivated by a desire to be able to counter Singapore's combined arms divisions should they seek to establish a bridgehead on Malaysian territory.

There is no immediate prospect of conflict between Malaysia and any of its neighbours. But recent incidents suggest that such a possibility cannot be ruled out by regional leaders. The April 1988 arrest by the Malaysian navy of 49 Filipino fishermen operating in a disputed border area apparently provoked a military mobilisation by the Philippines.[42] The case of Singaporean espionage against Malaysia in 1989, which led to a marked chilling of relations between the two countries, only brought to a head the tensions surrounding Singapore's forward defence posture. In 1991, Singapore expressed its own concerns when it accused Malaysia and Indonesia of insensitivity for holding major joint manoeuvres in Johor, next to Singapore, without prior notification.[43] In 1992, after the Malaysian government breached an agreement to freeze development on disputed islands off the Sabah/Kalimantan border, a build-up of Indonesian military forces took place before the issue was resolved.[44] In 1994, both Singapore and Indonesia reportedly voiced their concern about the launch of the Rapid Deployment Force, complaining of a lack of prior consultation or explanation.[45]

Malaysia has some way to go before its armed forces are as technologically capable as those of Singapore. Although it was agreed to press ahead with new procurement programmes in the late 1980s, it was not until 1993 that the level of arms imports began to rise sharply. It will therefore require several more years of sustained investment to fill some of the more obvious gaps in conventional warfighting capabilities. Moreover, investment in new equipment is only one, and in some ways the more straightforward, part of enhancing military capability. If new weapons are to be of military value, they need to be supported by well-trained personnel, logistics, munitions, and maintenance, and all these require sustained investment and attention. The decision to buy a combination of American and Russian aircraft may further increase the burden of maintenance and training.

Malaysia may also find this element in its military modernisation programme to be hampered by the difficulty of recruiting skilled personnel into its armed forces at a time of economic boom and full employment. This difficulty is compounded by the fact that, for historical reasons, the military has always been predominantly a Malay organisation: thus limiting participation from what is a relatively well-educated, and large, section of the population. It may be possible to recruit Malay personnel of a high enough calibre only by offering more competitive salaries: thus putting further strain on the military budget.[46]

Yet Malaysia's military is no paper tiger. The Malaysian Army already has a reputation as highly successful in counter-insurgency warfare, and its recent experience in UN peacekeeping gives it operational experience. It has proven its ability to strike hard bargains with arms suppliers, taking advantage of the current buyers' market. The growing educational level of the population, together with the increasing sophistication of the civil economy, also help provide a favourable environment for military modernisation.

It is difficult to say at what point the modernisation of Malaysian armed forces may contribute to a regional arms race, or otherwise destabilise regional security. As in the rest of the region, much of the current increase in procurement spending can be justified by the requirements of force replacement. Moreover, recent rates of economic growth make this increase much more affordable than in the past. But, because resource availability is increasing, the armed forces are also seeking to go beyond replacement to the acquisition of new capabilities. Plans to buy attack helicopters, battle tanks, and submarines are perhaps the most obvious examples of this tendency; but acquisitions that entail significant qualitative enhancements - such as purchases of combat aircraft with enhanced range and armaments - can also be regarded as providing more than simply replacement capabilities.

As Malaysia acquires increasing offensive capabilities, it is beginning to provoke some unease amongst neighbouring states. Concern has not reached a level at which it is a serious threat to intra-ASEAN relations, and it is often tempered by support for a process that may strengthen ASEAN resilience against China. But concern might grow if there were to be a significant further increase in the proportion of GNP devoted to defence, as some reports suggest may be a possibility in the next five year plan. If the late 1990s do see a further shift in Malaysian priorities towards defence, this may influence other countries - including Singapore, Thailand, Indonesia and the Philippines - to do likewise. Indeed there are growing indications that such an interactive dynamic is already under way.

IV   Thailand

Over the last decade, Thailand has spent more than any other ASEAN member on defence, even before allowing for substantial off-budget expenditures. Its position as a 'front line' state against Vietnam, in the wake of the invasion of Cambodia in 1978, drove a marked increase in defence spending, especially in the early 1980s. In contrast to Malaysia, there was no significant procurement 'pause' in the late 1980s. Instead, Thailand consolidated its position as ASEAN's biggest military spender.

With the end of the Cold War, many observers expected a slowdown in the rate of growth of Thai military spending. The internal threat from the Communist Party disintegrated in the late 1980s, and the threat of conventional attack from Vietnam disappeared not long thereafter. In addition, the long-standing policy of seeking to weaken neighbouring regimes through support of rebel armies (for example in Myanmar and Cambodia) now appears to have been abandoned in favour of a policy of seeking a dominant position through economic means, using aid and investment to further the interests of Thai business in regional markets and resources.[47]

Despite this apparent shift towards a less military-focused security policy, however, the period since 1990 has seen an acceleration in the rate of growth of military spending. Between 1990 and 1993, defence spending in real terms rose by 47%. Recent estimates suggest a further 11% increase between 1993 and 1995.[48]

Many analysts see this continuing growth as inexplicable. As one recent study concluded:

> 'The developing force structure seems out of proportion to probable threats to Thailand. Bangkok remains somewhat preoccupied with land-based threats from Cambodia and Burma; it is also concerned about activities in the eastern Indian Ocean. Still, these do not seem to warrant either the scale or the direction of Thailand's arms acquisition program.'[49]

The Thai procurement programme involves all three services. The Cabinet has recently approved Army plans for the purchase of 101 decommissioned M60A3 main battle tanks from the US at a cost of $71 million.[50] 30 L-39 combat capable training aircraft from the Czech republic were delivered in 1993. A second squadron of F-16A/B aircraft is being delivered in 1995/96,

Table 4.5: Thailand

Vital statistics

Population	58.7 million
1993 GNP	$122.0 billion
Real GNP growth 1983-93	+ 127% (8.5% per annum)

Trends in military spending and arms imports

Year	Military spending constant 1993 $	Military spending as % of GNP	Arms imports constant 1993 $
1983	2058	3.8	470
1984	2194	3.9	382
1985	2482	4.2	250
1986	2344	3.8	166
1987	2256	3.3	496
1988	2208	2.9	627
1989	2243	2.6	320
1990	2396	2.5	263
1991	2777	2.6	554
1992	2971	2.6	318
1993	3511	2.9	90

Source: US Arms Control and Disarmament Agency, *World Military Expenditures and Arms Transfers 1993-94*, 1995.

and the Thai air force is actively seeking a further squadron of combat aircraft, with the F-16C/D, the F-18C/D and the Su-27 Flanker apparently the leading contenders.[51] There are also plans to buy three E-2C Hawkeye early warning aircraft.[52]

The most dramatic shift in Thai defence policy in recent years has been the increased priority being given to the Navy, transforming it from a coastal defence force into a fleet with the most ambitious plans for power projection of any country in ASEAN. Already, the number of personnel in the Navy has increased from 32,000 in 1985 to 63,000 in 1994.[53] China supplied four new frigates in 1991 and 1992, and two Knox-class frigates have been bought from the US Navy. A further two missile frigates, built in China but armed with Harpoon missiles and Western sensors, are due to be commissioned shortly. With the purchase of 18 A-7 fighters from the US in 1995-96, the Navy has acquired a land-based strike capability.[54] Navy plans reportedly envisage the building of three new bases (two facing westwards on the Andaman Sea, one eastwards in the Gulf of Thailand), as well as a force of 16 to 20 frigates.[55] Preparations are also being made for a $800 million programme to introduce a submarine capability, probably with an initial order for three boats.[56]

By far the most controversial programme is the plan to bring a 11,485 tonne light carrier, currently under construction in Spain, into service in 1997. The carrier will be equipped with Harrier V/STOL aircraft and helicopters, and it is planned to order a second carrier in due course. It will make Thailand only the second Asian power (after India) to possess such a capability. Although it is not comparable to the full-scale aircraft carriers deployed by the US, Russia and France, it will provide Thailand with a highly visible, and potentially provocative, instrument of power projection.

During the Cold War, there was relatively limited strategic interaction between the arms programmes of Thailand and its fellow ASEAN members because the region was, in large measure, divided into two security complexes: a continental complex centred on the relationship between Indochina, Thailand and, to some extent, Burma; and an archipelagan complex centred on the Singapore / Indonesia / Malaysia triangle, with a more marginal role for the Philippines. The shift of Thailand towards a more maritime defence posture, however, threatens to undermine this division, thereby increasing the potential for intensified ASEAN-wide competition in procurement.

Certainly, statements from Thai military leaders suggest that one of the important factors explaining the current naval build-up is the desire to balance the power of its neighbours. Thai navy chief Admiral Vichet Karunyavanji has argued that:

> '(although) Thailand has friendly relations with all its neighbours, especially ASEAN countries, we cannot afford to be complacent. We need to maintain our military preparedness.'[57]

The Thai decision to increase its capability for maritime power projection is sometimes welcomed by other ASEAN governments as a useful contribution to 'regional resilience' against external threats (e.g. from China and India). But the Thai carrier decision has led to increasingly public concern being expressed about the direction of Thai policy by leading Malaysian commentators. In March 1994, J. N. Mak and B. A. Hamzah of the Malaysian Institute of Maritime Affairs suggested that:

> 'Thailand's naval expansion is the most dramatic within ASEAN. Naturally these moves have made some in ASEAN nervous ... though the Thai navy's current chief, Adm. Prachet Siridej, has completed a regionwide visit to reassure his counterparts that Thailand's purchases are for purely defensive purposes, the question remains: defence against whom - and what?
>
> (Thailand's) neighbours harbour strong suspicions about Bangkok's aspirations for blue-water status, not least because Thailand over the last 300 years has had expansionist tendencies whenever it was militarily strong.'[58]

Thailand's recent economic success has already made it South-East Asia's largest NIC, (its GDP is as large as those of Singapore and Malaysia combined), and has helped finance the region's largest defence budget. Given the economic backwardness of its immediate neighbours in Indo-China and Burma, it is already seen by some to be well on the way to achieving its ambition of being the dominant power in continental South-East Asia. With Indonesia continuing to face severe internal problems, it may also be tempted to see itself in a leadership role in the wider ASEAN region.

Such an ambition, if it exists, would be unwelcome to many of Thailand's ASEAN partners. To assuage their concerns, Thai officials have undertaken a number of visits to neighbouring states, including Malaysia, to explain the rationale for their maritime build-up. Yet such reassurance, by itself, is unlikely to prevent others from considering whether they may need to respond to Thailand's programme with measures to improve their own forces. In January 1996, managers of Bazan, the Spanish shipbuilding firm supplying the Thai carrier, were reported to be

> 'counting on the Thai deal to generate more contracts in the region since the new carrier, due for delivery next year, would create an imbalance in naval forces.'[59]

Despite these commercial hopes, the Thai carrier acquisition is unlikely to be matched directly by other ASEAN countries, not least because of the enormous expense involved. But it will become more difficult for ASEAN countries to contest China's plans to build a light carrier of its own once one of their own members has acquired a similar capability.

Despite the possible effects on Chinese decision-making, the carrier decision is unlikely to stimulate a rapid process of emulative purchasing. More worrying in this respect are Thai acquisitions of submarines and aircraft, although in neither case is Thailand the clear 'leader' in the process as it is with carriers.

Intra-ASEAN comparisons are not the only ones made, with Chinese procurement plans in particular a subject of intense interest. But it is hard to argue the case that the recent rapid pace of Thai procurement is driven primarily by concern over China. Thailand is concerned by long term changes in the regional balance of power, and in the shorter term has particular concerns over Chinese military involvement in Burma. But much of recent Thai procurement, not least in the naval field, has been from China, and there remains a historical legacy from the close cooperation against the Vietnamese-backed government in Cambodia. Not least, Thailand is one of only two ASEAN members (along with Singapore) which has no direct involvement in territorial disputes in the Spratlys.

Yet an explanation of recent Thai procurement that focuses only on military requirements and potential threats would be seriously lacking. Much more than in Singapore or Malaysia, observers of Thai politics agree that other factors play a critical role. Since the creation of a constitutional monarchy in 1932, the armed forces have been active participants in politics. As David Van Praagh argues:

> 'The Thai military has not been primarily a fighting force. It has been a self-serving hierarchy devoted to controlling politics and extracting profits from the productive Thai economy. Even more important, it has been the self-appointed custodian of the core Thai values of Chart-Sassana-Phra Mahakasaat - nation, religion (Theravada Buddhism) and monarchy.'[60]

In the aftermath of the Thai military's involvement in the brutal suppression of pro-democracy demonstrations in Bangkok in May 1992, the King intervened to restore civilian rule and the new Prime Minister acted to sideline some of the most discredited military leaders, removing generals from the boards of Thailand's biggest state enterprises and authorities.[61] At the same time, the military's role in procurement policy came under an unprecedented level of scrutiny. Arms sellers anonymously admitted that commissions to senior military decision-makers were essential to secure contracts:

> 'These kickbacks vary widely according to the type of contracts and countries involved, but average 15-20% of any deal. Commissions for spare parts and other after-sales services - where companies reap most of their profits - are much higher.

> Analysts say the highest commissions are given to the armed forces' top generals, including the supreme commander and chiefs of the armed services. Arms dealers estimate these senior officers can makes as much as $50-100 million in commissions and income from other business dealings during a normal three-to-four-year tenure.'[62]

> '(according to) an arms-sale specialist, the important thing to remember when you sell to the Thai military is not what a weapon can do, it's how much it can produce in under-the-counter payments.'[63]

One of the consequences of widespread corruption is that the Thai military has had a long-standing predilection for high-tech and expensive weaponry, often at the expense of the necessary, but more mundane, efforts necessary to make front-line equipment effective. During the 1970s, when the main threat facing the government was domestic insurgency, the armed forces went ahead with purchases that were largely inappropriate for this threat.[64] Despite a massive infusion of arms and military support from both China and the US during the 1980s, the lack of investment in appropriate logistical capabilities for the army contributed to the Army's humiliation in clashes along the Laos border in 1987-89, in which it lost an estimated 400 troops.[65] According to one Bangkok source:

> 'Rather than repair something, it's easier and more lucrative to buy another something from outside. Preferably that something is not compatible with anything you've got so that you can also buy a new support system.'[66]

Given this climate, it is not surprising that the weapons that are bought often do not work effectively. For example, the 106 Stingray tanks bought from Cadillac Gage in the US in 1987 for $160 million were bought while still at a prototype stage, and have since been bought by no one else in the world. They have suffered from hull cracks on 44 of the vehicles, probably because, as one observer put it, it is 'a cross between a tank and a self-propelled howitzer chassis'.[67]

The related problems of corruption and ineffectiveness have been especially severe in relation to weapon systems ordered from China in the late 1980s, and often supplied at 'friendship prices'. The antiquated T-69 tanks bought during this period are already out of commission and 'in store'. The four Chinese-built frigates turned out to be riddled with problems, and of questionable value even in very limited roles.[68] And the armed forces nearly succeeded in buying two squadrons of Chinese F-7 aircraft (a development of the Soviet Mig 21) in 1990 before being forced to accept that their engines would last only 150-200 flying hours before overhaul or replacement (only available in China), compared with 1000-5000 hours for the Western alternatives.[69]

It is possible that these Chinese systems were never intended to fulfil an operational role and that - aside from the opportunities for kickbacks provided - their main purpose was to send a political signal to Vietnam and the Soviet Union of the determination of the Sino-Thai alliance to resist their presence in Cambodia.[70] Certainly, for a combination of political and military reasons, the last 3-4 years have seen few new orders for Chinese weapons, together with a move back to buying proven US systems (such as the M-60 tank, Knox-class frigate and F-16 aircraft). After the Stingray affair, the government issued new contract rules that preclude the procurement of prototypes and specify that imported systems must be in use in the home military and must be involved in ongoing production to ensure the availability of spare parts. In August 1995, a $12 million sale of Shadow unmanned aerial vehicles from the US was delayed pending an enquiry into whether these conditions had been met.[71]

Despite these improvements in procurement practice, however, the Royal Thai Navy will face a formidable challenge in seeking to make its carrier (due to come into service in 1997) fully operational. The logistical challenges involved in supporting the carrier and its on-board airpower alone are considerable, and the Thai record in this regard is not encouraging. Moreover, if it is to operate in the South China Sea, it will need to be able to defend itself not only against the surface fleets of other states but also against the land-based air forces of neighbouring states and against the growing number of states that are now planning to acquire submarines. Such a defence will in turn require a massive investment in missile defences, escorts and sensors in the anti-air, anti-surface and anti-submarine roles. The extreme vulnerability of the UK's VSTOL carriers in the 1982 Falklands War, despite the presence of a large protective screen of escort ships, provides a warning about the difficulties involved even for a Navy with considerable experience of managing such a capability.

These potential difficulties help explain why other countries in the region appear to be in no hurry to follow the Thai carrier initiative, and may also reduce the destabilising effect which it may have. Neighbouring states can hope that, however valuable it may be in prestige terms (special quarters are provided for the Royal Family on board)[72], the carrier may turn out to be of only limited military value. It may even serve the useful function, from their point of view, of diverting scarce military resources from other, potentially more worrisome, projects.

After the events of May 1992, some analysts predicted a levelling off in the trend in Thai defence procurement.[73] So far, however, there is little indication of such a trend. The Navy - which was as powerful as the Army before the failed 1951 coup led to a drastic reduction in its status - may now be reaping its reward for its unwillingness to take part in the Army's suppression of democracy protesters in 1992. More generally, it is far from clear that the armed forces have given up their political role for ever, despite the peaceful handover of power to a new civilian government after the 1995 elections. The threat of a future coup continues to make civilian politicians nervous about interfering with military privileges. Even on optimistic assumptions, it will be some time before Thai politics are as 'civilianised' as those of Singapore or Malaysia.

Moreover, if the regional security environment were to worsen and neighbouring states were to continue with ambitious modernisation programmes, it is far from clear that a civilian government in Bangkok would want to challenge their own armed forces' assessments of their requirements. It is more likely that political modernisation will lead to a professionalisation of the armed forces than that it will lead to a substantial reduction in their access to national resources.

If the regional security environment appears more benign, a consolidation of civilian leadership may allow a reduction in the military's share of national resources in order to meet the many pressing gaps - not least in education and infrastructure - that Thailand will need to address if it is to continue its recent economic success. But such an environment is unlikely to appear of its own accord without reassuring those of Thailand's neighbours who remain perplexed and concerned at the recent Thai military build-up.

V   Indonesia

Although the largest ASEAN state in terms of population, Indonesia is the region's sleeping giant in military terms. Its government remains preoccupied with holding together a multi-ethnic empire in which many minority groups are profoundly unhappy with Javanese dominance. Not least, after twenty years of repression, the Army has yet to finally defeat the rebellion in East Timor, a former Portuguese colony illegally invaded in 1975. The Indonesian Army, with 214,000 personnel, is the largest in ASEAN after Vietnam. But two-thirds of these, together with a large proportion of the defence budget, are committed to the internal security role. As Bob Lowry has commented:

> 'Internal security is a very personnel-intensive activity. For example, at least 12 battalions are deployed in East Timor and Irian Jaya from elsewhere in the archipelago and a minimum of another 12 battalions are required to replace them periodically. Moreover, even in quiet areas a presence is required to dissuade dissidents from resorting to force to achieve their goals.'[74]

Table 4.6: Indonesia

Vital statistics

Population	197.2 million
1993 GNP	$135.9 billion
Real GNP growth 1983-93	+ 82% (6.2% per annum)

Trends in military spending and arms imports

Year	Military spending constant 1993 $	Military spending as % of GNP	Arms imports constant 1993 $
1983	1934	2.6	228
1984	2019	2.5	150
1985	1933	2.4	197
1986	2038	2.4	205
1987	1716	1.9	335
1988	1703	1.8	299
1989	1751	1.7	240
1990	1807	1.6	296
1991	1873	1.6	21
1992	1872	1.5	41
1993	2031	1.5	160

Source: US Arms Control and Disarmament Agency, *World Military Expenditures and Arms Transfers 1993-94, 1995.*

The resources available to the Indonesian armed forces for external defence have been further reduced by the deliberate decision of President Suharto to make sharp cuts in the defence budget inherited from Sukarno in the mid 1960s. While Indonesia was by far the most powerful ASEAN state in military terms in the mid 1970s, its defence budget failed to grow at all in real terms over the next 15 years or so, and declined sharply as a proportion of GNP. As a result, the official Indonesian defence budget is now no greater than those of Singapore or Malaysia.[75]

The official defence budget does not fully reflect the allocation of resources to defence, with pension spending excluded, and with presidential discretionary funds and contributions from government and military-owned enterprises providing off-budget sources of revenue.[76] A 1994 report by the US-based Project on Demilitarization and Democracy has estimated that the official budget was from 25 to 50 per cent below actual military spending.[77]

Even allowing for some under-reporting, however, it is clear from Indonesia's order of battle that its level of spending, as a proportion of GDP, is modest by regional standards. Its capability for conventional warfare is hampered by the difficulties that result from the low levels of education and technical expertise amongst service personnel, by the fact that many service personnel are obliged to seek additional sources of income to supplement their low levels of pay, and by the low levels of resources devoted to maintaining equipment.[78] Even as it prepares to buy a further squadron, it has been estimated that only about 10% of Indonesia's existing F-16's are in service at any one time, compared with an estimated 70% in Singapore.[79]

Since the recession of the mid-1980s, which had led to a sharp decline in procurement spending, defence spending has been rising. There has been a 12% real increase between 1990 and 1993 (see above), and IISS figures estimate real growth in defence spending accelerating to around 7% per annum between 1993 and 1995.[80] Although this still leaves Indonesian spending well behind that of its three neighbours (Malaysia, Singapore and Thailand), it does appear to have brought to an end the trend towards a decline in the proportion of GNP devoted to defence.

As a country made up of over 13,000 islands, separated by some of the world's busiest shipping routes and with offshore mineral resources (not least around Natuna Island) of critical economic importance, there is an increasingly pressing requirement to be able to police the waters within and around the Indonesian archipelago. As a detailed discussion of Indonesian naval policy in 1991 suggested:

> 'As the largest maritime country in sea, Indonesia is beginning to see itself at a disadvantage as its ASEAN neighbours begin to re-equip. The likely acquisition of submarines by Malaysia, Singapore and Thailand also gives the (Indonesian Navy) a feeling of insecurity, as it realizes that passage through or into its archipelagic territory is all through a very small number of straits which it does not have the capability to either control or monitor totally.'[81]

The main focus of increased procurement activity in the last decade has therefore - as in most other ASEAN countries - been on air and naval forces. 12 F-16 aircraft entered service in 1989-90, and Indonesia is considering the purchase of a further squadron. In addition to 14 British Aerospace Hawks already in service in the training and counter-insurgency roles, a further 24 are on order. Despite considerable international controversy over their alleged use in East Timor, these 24 are due to be delivered in 1995 or 1996.[82]

Yet the biggest increase in capability in recent years has been in the Indonesian Navy, which is now probably the most formidable naval force in ASEAN. Three ex-Tribal class UK frigates were brought into service in 1985-6, and six Van Speijk class frigates were bought from the Netherlands in 1989-90 and fitted with Harpoon missiles.[83] Two German Type-209 submarines came into service in 1981, and underwent major refits in 1986-89; and orders for two or three more remain under discussion.

The most dramatic acquisition of recent years is the purchase of half of the former East German Navy. 39 ships, including 16 corvettes, 12 amphibious landing ships, nine coastal minesweepers and two support ships, were delivered during 1993 and 1994 to Indonesia (see Appendix 1), where they will be refurbished for service in the Navy. The purchase cost is reported to be only $12.3 million, but initial estimates for the cost of refurbishment in Indonesia range from $640 million upwards[84]: tying up most of the Navy's procurement budget until the end of the century.

This contract, while it may eventually lead to a substantial addition to naval power, is also a graphic illustration of the way in which, in an apparently military-dominated state, the armed forces can be overruled even on issues of military requirements. The purchase was opposed both by the armed forces and by the Ministry of Finance. In a rare display of opposition to government policy, it also led to open criticism of the costs of the project in news magazines, three of which were banned for their pains. But it still went ahead because of the influential support of B. J. Habibie, the Minister of Science and Technology, who sees the refurbishment of the ships as an important part of his ambition to build high technology industry, with the state-owned aerospace and shipbuilding industries at the centre of these efforts.[85] For Habibie and other 'economic nationalists'[86], greater self-sufficiency in arms production is desirable because it can contribute to the development of Indonesia as an industrial power. The cost to the armed forces of this approach - a diversion of resources from more cost-effective foreign procurement - is one that, it is argued, the armed forces will have to accept.

It remains to be seen whether the Habibie strategy will survive the opposition of the armed forces who, at least on this issue, are joined by those - both amongst economic technocrats and in the donor community - who are concerned at the escalating subsidies required. Indonesia already has foreign debt of over $100 billion, and critics are concerned that $2 billion plan to build an Indonesian jet airliner will further drain resources from more competitive sectors of the economy.[87] Habibie's recent proposal for a Pacific Rim consortium for combat aircraft development suggests the extent of his ambitions.[88]

The fact that Indonesia is able to prioritise its industrial ambitions over its immediate military requirements reflects the commonly held view amongst the governing elite that Indonesia will not face major external military threats in the near to medium term. It thus casts doubt on the common argument that the arms build-up in South-East Asia is being driven primarily by concern over China. Indonesia's New Order regime has a long history of antipathy to China dating back to its support for Sukarno in the early 1960s. As a result of this antipathy, Indonesia was the ASEAN power most sympathetic to Vietnam during the 1980s, and it was not until August 1990 that Indonesia and China restored full diplomatic relations. If China were a serious threat, one would therefore expect Indonesia to be one of the first to respond. The fact that it has not responded in a dramatic fashion suggests that other factors - such as intra-ASEAN rivalries - may be more important. Indonesia's own reluctance to be drawn into an intense arms competition with its neighbours may reflect a perception that it has little to fear. It may also demonstrate Jakarta's continuing sensitivity to its

ASEAN neighbours' fears of a return to the expansionist policies of the Sukarno years.

Such a possibility at present seems remote. But those who fear an Indonesian attempt to overcome its relative military weakness through some dramatic gesture cannot have been reassured by the Chief of the Air Staff's comment in August 1992 that the air force was considering the purchase of Scud missiles.[89] Such an acquisition would be highly controversial in the region. Ballistic missiles would be a highly dubious investment in military terms unless armed with weapons of mass destruction, and the latter have been disowned by all South-East Asian countries. And attempts to acquire such missiles could encounter strong opposition from the Missile Technology Control Regime (MTCR), adding to Indonesia's vulnerability to arms embargo as a result of its occupation of East Timor. Fortunately, this proposal seems to have been squashed. The fact that it was discussed at such a high level, however, must provide some grounds for concern.

Another cause for concern is the possibility that the arms build-up elsewhere in the region - both in China and in other ASEAN countries - may be starting to strengthen the hands of those in the armed forces who are arguing for Indonesia to counter with a more ambitious modernisation programme of its own. In December 1994, the Commission for Politics and Security of Indonesia's House of Representatives urged the government to increase defence spending from its present level of 1.7% of GNP to at least 3%.[90]

If Indonesia did begin to increase its defence budget more sharply, it would take some time for it to remedy the many gaps in its capabilities. Even before it acquired a significant capability for large-scale offensive action, however, its sheer size, together with memories of the 1960s, would ensure that such a build-up would have much more serious consequences for regional stability than comparable buildups by other ASEAN countries.

In part, this is because Indonesia is already using up much of its international credit through its continuing inability to find a solution to the problem of East Timor. The inability of the government to consider alternatives to repression (either in East Timor or Irian Jaya or Aceh) contributes to an underlying feeling of wariness amongst neighbouring states (both in ASEAN and in Australasia). As long as Indonesia remains a model of self-restraint in international affairs, others are likely to give it the benefit of the doubt on these matters, in line with ASEAN's norm of non-interference. If Indonesia were to become more assertive internationally, however, it might find itself losing its friends rather quickly.

Indonesia's internal political weakness is also a central factor in what is still - admittedly by ASEAN's exceptional standards - a poorly performing economy. Indonesia has been unable to match the stunning rates of economic growth seen in China, Thailand, Malaysia and Vietnam in recent years. Since the liberalising reforms of 1988, there has been greater success in promoting deregulation and the growth of export-oriented manufacturing. But corruption remains pervasive, income inequality is greater than in most neighbouring states, and a massive external debt burden could yet threaten a major financial crisis.

To overcome these weaknesses will require radical change. Events elsewhere in the region provide some hope that, over time, economic prosperity brings in its wake political liberalisation. Yet while the next years may see such an opportunity developing in Indonesia, they may also be a period of danger. The Suharto years have done little to promote voluntary participation in the process of nation-building, and there is no way of knowing how strong the centrifugal forces within the country will be if greater opportunities for self-expression are allowed. Nor can it be assumed that a new post-Suharto regime will necessarily be more successful economically. By the standards of anywhere in the developing world outside East Asia, the last 30 years of Indonesian economic history have been a period of considerable, if uneven, success. The continuation of this success cannot be taken for granted.

There is little doubt that governments in the rest of the region would prefer a strong and stable Indonesia, even if it was as a result better armed, to an Indonesia immersed in a prolonged internal crisis, with all the unpredictable consequences for its external policy that such a crisis might bring. Whether Indonesia succeeds in avoiding this latter fate may not become clear for some time. Until it does, uncertainty about the future direction of Indonesian politics is likely to remain a largely unspoken factor in the readiness of neighbouring states to pay growing military 'insurance premiums' against the possibility of a turbulent future.

VI The Philippines

Despite being a founding member of the Association, the Philippines' experience during the Cold War years was very different from the ASEAN 'model' of increasing self-confidence on the international stage backed up by growing economic prosperity. Its place in the regional security structure remained defined largely in terms of its position as the host for the largest US bases in the region. Its economic performance was more akin to those of the Latin American states than to those of East Asia, with per capita income falling at an average rate of 0.6% per annum between 1980 and 1993.[91]

These defining characteristics of uniqueness during the Cold War, however, no longer exist to the same extent. The closure of US bases in 1992 has left the Philippines, like the rest of ASEAN, looking more to its own resources to ensure its security. With GDP growing at 5.7% in 1995, there are also clear signs of economic recovery under way.[92]

Yet the Philippines faces some of the most serious security challenges of any country in the region. Serious insurgencies persist, fuelled by poverty and the rise of Islamic resistance. As of 1993, the communist New People's Army was reported to be still about 10,000 strong.[93] And 1995 reports suggest that one of the Islamic resistance movements on the island of Mindanao (the MILF) now has somewhere between 6,000 and 60,000 men under arms.[94]

The need to concentrate on counter-insurgency operations, together with the US presence, contributed to a long-standing neglect of external defence needs. Many of the navy's major combatants are of World War Two vintage, and the air force has only three F5-A combat aircraft operational, together with 13 OV-10B counter-insurgency aircraft.[95] It is unable to police adequately the 650,000 square nautical miles of maritime territory within the country's EEZ,[96] and loses an estimated $2 billion worth of fish annually to poachers annually, as well as a lesser amount to pirates.[97] In October 1994, the insurgents in Mindanao were able to use the opportunity of the 50th anniversary celebrations of the American landings in World War Two, when nearly all the government's coastal patrol boats were in Leyte, to bring in fresh supplies of weapons by sea.[98] In February 1995, China took advantage of Filipino military weakness to seize Mischief Reef, a disputed territory only 200 kilometres from Palawan Island.

Table 4.7: The Philippines

Vital statistics

Population	70.0 million
1993 GNP	$55.3 billion
Real GNP growth 1983-93	+ 14% (1.3% per annum)

Trends in military spending and arms imports

Year	Military spending constant 1993 $	Military spending as % of GNP	Arms imports constant 1993 $
1983	814	1.7	43
1984	551	1.2	55
1985	562	1.4	53
1986	832	1.9	51
1987	838	1.9	74
1988	1022	2.1	72
1989	1149	2.3	80
1990	1153	2.2	99
1991	1103	2.1	116
1992	1034	1.9	103
1993	1200	2.2	40

Source: US Arms Control and Disarmament Agency, *World Military Expenditures and Arms Transfers 1993-94, 1995.*

Partly in response to these pressures, and partly because of the signs of economic recovery, the armed forces have begun to have some success on obtaining more resources for modernisation. In 1995, Congress approved a government programme calling for an estimated $13 billion dollars to be spent on defence modernisation over the next 15 years, of which the navy is to receive around 40%. Over this period, the navy will replace its obsolete ships (with an average age of 41 years) with 12 offshore patrol vessels, 6 corvettes, 3 frigates and 40 patrol vessels. The air force is due to receive 36 multirole fighters, 6 air defence radars, 24 attack aircraft and 6 long range patrol aircraft. The Army plans to acquire howitzers, light armoured vehicles and communications equipment. New bases are to be established to thwart possible 'external threats from the west, north and south in that priority'.[99]

Such a programme would go a long way to remedying the Philippine armed forces' current deficiencies. At present, however, only a small part of it - $2 billion of the $13 billion - is budgeted to be spent in the first five years. This would still allow the Navy to acquire 2 guided missile corvettes, 3 offshore patrol vessels with medium range SSM, and 6 patrol craft with short range SSM. It has even been suggested that the air force may acquire 28 F-16 aircraft ordered from the US by Pakistan, but never delivered, at a reduced price: a step that could dramatically improve the Philippines' air defence capability.

It remains to be seen how far these plans are fulfilled in the light of many other competing pressures on government resources. They do indicate the growing pressure in the Philippines, as in the rest of ASEAN, for increased levels of spending on maritime defences in the light of the increasing economic and strategic importance of the sea. Even a limited level of investment may have a marked impact on the ability of the Philippines' armed forces to raise the stakes for others seeking to challenge its maritime claims. Yet it will take a sustained period of growing defence spending before the Philippines will be able to match the capabilities of its ASEAN partners.

VII Brunei

After avoiding absorption by either Malaysia or Indonesia in the 1960s, Brunei became an independent state, and a member of ASEAN, in 1984.

Table 4.8: Brunei

Vital statistics

Population	0.3 million
1991 GNP	$4.1 billion
Real GNP growth 1983-91	+ 4% (0.5% per annum)

Trends in military spending and arms imports

Year	Military spending constant 1993 $	Military spending as % of GNP	Arms imports constant 1993 $
1983	pre-independence		
1984	260	6.6	0
1985	308	8.0	0
1986	513	13.6	6
1987	376	9.8	6
1988	486	12.5	6
1989	401	10.5	6
1990	330	8.4	11
1991	not available	not available	0
1992	not available	not available	0
1993	not available	not available	0

Source: US Arms Control and Disarmament Agency, *World Military Expenditures and Arms Transfers 1993-94*, 1995.

ASEAN membership has afforded the oil-rich Sultanate a degree of reassurance that it will not suffer the fate of East Timor in 1975, but its continuing security concern is indicated by the fact that, expressed as a proportion of GDP, it has the highest level of defence spending in ASEAN (funding is so lavish that the Ministry of Defence has difficulty in spending more than 60% of its allocated budget).[100] The Sultanate's defence commitments have been increased by the perceived need to protect its declared Exclusive Economic Zone in the South China Sea, together with its 1988 claim to one of the Spratlys reefs, against competing, and well-armed, claimants.

Because of the limited recruiting pool, the Bruneian armed forces consist of only 4,400 active personnel (it is not clear what role the 900 British Gurkhas and 500 Singaporean personnel in Brunei would play in the event of a conflict). Its main naval capability consists of three Exocet-armed fast attack craft bought from Singapore in the 1970s. An ambitious 'Defence Protocol' was signed with the UK in 1989, but so far with few actual deliveries as a result. A recent report suggests, however, that Brunei has decided to order three corvette-sized offshore patrol vessels from Yarrow Shipbuilders, armed with anti-ship (Exocet or Harpoon) and anti-air (Seawolf) missiles.[101] The air force is reported to want to order 16 Hawk aircraft from the UK. Given the limited size of the Bruneian armed forces, however, it remains a moot point whether Brunei will have the capability to operate these complex systems. Like the procurement of some of the Gulf states in recent years, Bruneian purchases may be as much about preserving links with potential external protectors - in this case the UK - as about building an effective domestic defence capability.

VIII Vietnam

Vietnam was until recently widely regarded as the single most capable military power in the region. In the 1970s, it had defeated the US and gone on to establish military hegemony over Cambodia and Laos. The quality of its military leaders had been proven over decades of almost constant warfare against technologically superior powers. And, faced with a civil war in Cambodia, it was the region's largest importer of arms throughout the 1980s. Between 1979 and 1987, Soviet military aid to Vietnam averaged nearly $1.7 billion a year. Soviet economic and military aid together accounted for about 20% of Vietnamese GNP.[102] This Vietnamese military

Table 4.9: Vietnam

Vital statistics

Population	71.8 million
1993 GNP	$18.5 billion
Real GNP growth 1986-93	+ 17% (2.3% per annum)

Trends in military spending and arms imports

Year	Military spending constant 1993 $	Military spending as % of GNP	Arms imports constant 1993 $
1983	not available	not available	2136
1984	not available	not available	2181
1985	not available	not available	1973
1986	2406	19.4	2689
1987	not available	not available	2358
1988	not available	not available	1793
1989	not available	not available	1487
1990	723	5.2	1206
1991	720	4.8	211
1992	not available	not available	21
1993	not available	not available	10

Source: US Arms Control and Disarmament Agency, *World Military Expenditures and Arms Transfers 1993-94*, 1995.

buildup was in turn a key factor in explaining the buildup of ASEAN military power in the late 1970s and early 1980s, helped by American military aid. The ASEAN-Vietnam confrontation during this period was the concrete manifestation of the Cold War in South-East Asia, and of the sometimes uncomfortable US/China/ASEAN alliance against the Soviet Union and Vietnam. Yet Vietnam had overstretched itself. As famine threatened and the economy faltered, there was an increasing realisation that the invasion of Cambodia in 1978 had been a profound and costly error, born of the excessive self-confidence of the post-1975 years. In a region where the 'economic miracle' was now spreading to involve even communist China, Vietnam appeared increasingly impoverished by comparison.

What brought matters to a head was the decision of the Soviet Union to withdraw its financial support from the Hanoi government. In a region where it had many enemies, Vietnam was now faced with losing its only friend. To its impoverishment was added isolation. As we discussed earlier, China was quick to take advantage of Vietnam's weakness to press its claims in the Spratlys in the clashes with the Vietnamese Navy in 1988. If China had not itself had to face international outcry, brought about by the Tianmen Square incident of 1989, Vietnam's claim to the Spratlys might have suffered much more than it did.

Since the nadir of the late 1980s, however, Vietnam's recovery has been impressive. Starting with the announcement of doi moi (renovation) in December 1986, and the decollectivisation of agriculture in 1988, Vietnam moved to implement a vigorous programme of economic reform. Agricultural production rapidly increased, making the country the world's third largest exporter of rice.[103] From 1992 to 1995, it recorded rates of GDP growth of between 8 and 10%:[104] equal to the best perfomers in ASEAN. With better levels of education and health than in most other low income countries, and a relatively high degree of nation-state cohesion, it seems poised to join the region's economic success stories. On a purchasing power parity basis, Vietnam's GDP per head is only $1200, compared with China's $2400 and Thailand's $5500.[105] But, if recent growth rates continue, Vietnam could begin to catch up with some of its poorer fellow ASEAN members within the next 10-15 years.

In parallel with economic reform, Vietnam made radical changes in its defence posture from 1987 onwards. By withdrawing its armed forces from

Laos and Cambodia, it effectively abandoned the 'forward defence' doctrine of the previous decade. In addition, troops along the border with China were ordered to take a non-provocative stance, and were reduced in number. By the end of 1990, 600,000 regular soldiers had been released from service.[106]

It soon became clear how dependent Vietnam's military position had been on Soviet aid. From being the Prussia of South-East Asia in the 1980s, Vietnam had become one of ASEAN's weakest military powers by the mid 1990s. Its armed forces were increasingly obliged to resort to commercial activities to supplement their meagre state income.[107] Much of its equipment became non-operational as a result of a shortage of spare parts and fuel. While other ASEAN states increased their spending on modernisation in the early 1990s, Vietnam was unable to afford any significant new acquisitions.

Vietnam still has the largest armed forces in ASEAN, with more than twice as many personnel as Indonesia (572,000 compared to 274,500).[108] The government is wary about the dangers of social unrest as a result of hasty demobilisation, preferring instead to allow the armed forces to seek new means of generating their own income. Even so, it seems probable that further reductions in force structure and personnel numbers will take place in future.

At the same time, some investment in new capabilities is taking place. According to official statistics, the defence budget increased by 49% in 1994.[109] Not least, the government is aware of the need to defend Vietnam's claims to the mineral and fishing wealth of the South China Sea. Economic development is leading to increasing requirements for policing the long Vietnamese coast against smuggling, piracy, and illegal fisheries, as well as against threats from rival claimants.

The first sign of a more active procurement policy was the order placed in late 1994 for six Sukhoi Su-27 fighter aircraft from Russia, which is expected to be followed by an order for a further six in the near future. This marks a significant advance in Vietnam's ability to police the air space over the South China Sea, since existing aircraft (such as the Mig 21) lack the endurance required for spending more than a very limited time over the Spratlys.[110] Given current weaknesses in training and maintenance, it remains to be seen whether Vietnam will be able to translate these purchases into operational capability. But it seems likely that, as available resources increase, Vietnam will be able to make further incremental improvements in its maritime warfare capabilities.

If and when such a process of improvement takes place, Vietnamese air and naval forces will add a further dimension to the already complex strategic interaction in the South China Sea. Initially, the main focus of interest is likely to be on the military balance between Vietnam and China. With Vietnam's claims also a matter of dispute with Malaysia, the Philippines and Brunei, however, the possibility for discord with fellow ASEAN members cannot be ruled out.

In addition, even a modest revival of Vietnamese defence capability has the potential for reviving traditional rivalry with Thailand. Economic success has led Thailand to see itself as the leader of continental South-East Asia, a position that has been considerably enhanced by Vietnam's isolation. As Vietnam becomes more of an economic force, this position may become more difficult to sustain, and old fears may re-emerge. According to Lt-Gen Poonsak Nakphat, Chairman of the Thai National Defence Committee drafting Thai defence strategies for 1995-1999, Vietnam is still regarded as a threat by Thailand.[111] If such fears persist, some element of competitive arming between Thailand and Vietnam may be a possibility. Indeed recent Thai acquisitions of M-60 tanks from the US might be explained, in some part, by continuing concerns of this sort.

The Vietnamese military faces formidable problems in maintaining the operational effectiveness of its Soviet-made weapons systems. It has sought to tackle these problems in part through developing its contacts with both Russia and Ukraine. Over time, however, it is likely that Vietnam will move increasingly to diversify its sources for defence equipment by also buying from Western suppliers. It has already laid the foundations for such a policy through its success in overcoming its diplomatic isolation. It has announced plans to place defence attaches with each present and proposed ASEAN partner, except Brunei.[112] In the next years, it is likely to move further towards being a 'normal' participant in ASEAN's (usually friendly) arms rivalry.

IX   Dangers and opportunities

The marked shift of government priorities away from defence spending that took place in the 1980s, both in ASEAN and in China, has now come to a halt. In some cases, defence spending is even taking a growing proportion of national budgets that are themselves going rapidly.

Many factors play a part in explaining these trends. It is clear that the rapid economic growth of recent years has played a key role in making the arms build-up possible by easing the financial constraints on all components of government budgets. To some extent, increases in defence budgets in the 1990s have also been seen as necessary in order to make up for spending cuts imposed during the economic recession experienced by some states in the mid 1980s: requirements that were in large measure independent of what others were doing.

But, as the regional arms build-up continues and the replacement backlog diminishes, procurement is starting to shift increasingly towards the purchase of systems that either provide completely new capabilities or are such an improvement on the systems they 'replace' that they must be considered new capabilities. In explaining both the persistence and the composition of the arms build-up, moreover, a central role is being played by changes that have taken place in regional security concerns since the end of the Cold War.

New security concerns

The 1990s have seen significant changes in the type of challenges which the region's armed forces are being designed to meet. In the past, Singapore was the only ASEAN country without a domestic insurgency, and whose armed forces could therefore give undivided attention to external defence. As a result of the intensity of its external security concerns, Singapore became the region's leader in terms of military innovation and modernisation, introducing the most modern new capabilities before others, experiencing the fastest rate of growth in defence spending, and, by the late 1980s, spending a higher proportion of its GDP on defence than any other ASEAN country. Moreover, as its margin of superiority over its neighbours grew, Singapore increasingly moved towards a doctrine of forward defence: first in air forces, then in ground and naval forces.

Given Singapore's geography, such a defence posture seemed to make sense in narrow military terms. But it could only be sustained in circumstances where Singapore's larger neighbours were more concerned with tackling the problems of insurgency and low economic growth, and in any case lacked the technical and economic resources needed to march Singapore's capabilities. As these circumstances have changed in the last few years, so too has the military balance of the region began to shift.

Firstly, and paradoxically, the recent ASEAN defence build-up appears to have been encouraged by a marked reduction in the threats that dominated defence planning in the Cold War. Peace agreements with communist insurgents in Malaysia and Thailand in 1990 ensured that the armed forces of ASEAN's two leading industrialising powers (after Singapore) were no longer tied down in internal security operations. The withdrawal of Vietnamese troops from Cambodia removed the main threat of external aggression facing Thailand, and to some extent ASEAN as a whole. And the security situation of China itself was dramatically improved by the sharp reduction in Soviet military capabilities, both on its northern land border and in the Pacific Ocean.

In some countries, notably in Indonesia and Philippines, internal security concerns remain considerable and little progress has been made in their resolution. These countries have tended to see the slowest increases in procurement. But in most of the countries where there has been a clear improvement in strategic circumstances (with the exception, so far, of Vietnam), there has also been a marked process of reorientation of security concerns, and with it an increase in spending. In part, this appears to reflect the continuing political weight of the armed forces who, deprived of a previous role, are now seeking to build a new case for a share of national resources. In part, it also reflects the fact that countries are now able to address concerns that always existed, but which until recently had been forced to take second place.

Second, the diminishing of old concerns has been accompanied by a marked increase in interest in the protection of maritime resources. The 1982 Law of the Sea resulted in the creation of vast Exclusive Economic Zones, containing considerable mineral and fishing resources. The governments of the region, preoccupied as they were with defence on land, possessed few of the capabilities necessary to effectively police these new acquisitions. As the considerable value of the EEZ resources became known, therefore, and as land-based security concerns faded in significance, governments moved to increase investment in maritime military capabilities.

To a significant extent, the new maritime security roles were, like traditional counter-insurgency roles, concerned with controlling non-state actors, such as illegal fishermen, pirates, smugglers. In contrast to traditional roles, however, maritime security also involved a significant element of interstate competition. A multiplicity of conflicts over sovereignty, especially in the South China Sea, led to armed forces being used as a means of asserting control over territory at the expense of other claimants. Concern over the Chinese military build-up in the region played a particularly important role in encouraging defence modernisation, given the growing concern that it might have long-term aspirations towards regional hegemony.

Finally, the recent arms build-up has reflected continuing concerns between ASEAN states. These concerns have not become more serious in recent years, but the spread of economic success in the region has meant that more countries now have the resources to act on those concerns. Increasingly the region's armed forces have been able to finance modernisation plans based on what might go wrong in future.

The regional balance of power depends to some degree on a complex set of bilateral and multilateral (the FPDA) arrangements which, although not formal alliances, do provide for the possibility of joint action. Given the uncertainty involved in these arrangements, however, national 'contingency planning' seeks to minimise dependence on others' support and achieve a greater degree of defence 'self-reliance'.

Yet when four or more, roughly equivalent, military powers in a region seek self-reliance - that is, the ability to defend themselves without help - they cannot all attain it simultaneously. If one country seeks to maximise its own security in technical military terms, it will generate increased concerns amongst its neighbours, and will tend to provoke countervailing action. Even when, as is the case at present, ASEAN political leaders have no reason to fear their existing counterparts, they still harbour concerns about future political trends. Signs of arms builds in neighbouring states will, therefore, tend to encourage precautionary build-ups in response.

A non-offensive arms build-up?

It is still common to play down the significance of the arms build-up in South-East Asia. For example, IISS's *Military Balance 1995-1996* comments that:

> 'It would be incorrect ... to see in these increasing levels of defence expenditure an arms race threatening regional stability. In several cases, strong and sustained economic performance has allowed for increased investment in non-offensive defence and security.'[113]

The regional arms build-up is certainly non-offensive in the sense that no individual country intends to use its forces for offence against others. Viewed purely in terms of the capabilities for offence that the build-up provides, however, the picture is much less clear. During the Cold War period, defence postures were so clearly non-provocative that, even if offensive intent had been present, offensive action would have been very difficult. Current trends are creating capabilities which are more versatile and, potentially, offensive in nature.

Singapore is only the most obvious example of a country whose defence posture is increasingly hard to characterise as non offensive in terms of capabilities. In most regional armed forces, new capabilities are often characterised by greater range and lethality, providing increased capabilities for projecting power beyond national borders. Much more than in the past, the new weapons systems of regional states can be used - and are designed to be used - in attacks on the territory (at sea or on land) of neighbouring states.

This can perhaps be seen most clearly in the case of air forces, precisely because of the inherent versatility of air power. In addition to the procurement of shorter range Hawk aircraft, regional air forces are acquiring the longer range F-16, F-18 and Mig 29, supplemented by investments in refuelling, airborne command and control capabilities, and maritime patrol aircraft. As a result, increasing attention is being given to possible future vulnerabilities to surprise attack, and thus also to possible incentives for pre-emption in a crisis. In order to minimise vulnerability, some countries - most notably Singapore - are investing in defensive measures - such as hardened airfields, higher alert statuses, and overseas basing. If the acquisition of strike capabilities by regional states continues, pressures for further expensive defensive investments are likely to intensify.

At sea, competition for control of the air is complemented by investment in surface ships and longer range missile systems. Regional states are increasingly graduating from coastal patrol boats to corvettes and frigates. Investment in both submarines and other anti-submarine warfare is gaining an increased priority. The combined effect of the increasing importance of maritime resources to regional economies and serious territorial disputes has led most states in the region to give a high priority to strengthening their ability to assert power at sea.

Finally, as internal threats subside, regional armies have sought to protect access to resources by developing plans for rapid deployment and assault forces. Capabilities for combined arms warfare are being improved, and armies that had previously focused on counter-insurgency are being reoriented. Increased mobility should allow regional armies to defend national territory with fewer soldiers than before. But it may also have the effect of increasing offensive capabilities and, in some cases (most obviously the Singapore/ Malaysia relationship), adding to action-reaction dynamics.

As the reach of regional armed forces increases, and as overlap between areas of concern increases - especially in the South China Sea - procurement in ASEAN is becoming more competitive than in the past. It would be wrong to suggest that competition with neighbours - both within ASEAN and with non-ASEAN powers - is now the primary driving force for procurement. But its importance is probably increasing as a result of both technological and strategic developments. Part of the explanation for near-simultaneous procurement may lie in the fact that ASEAN countries are responding to similar military requirements and similar market opportunities. But the need to preserve the balance of military power between ASEAN countries undoubtedly also plays an important role.

Thus, for example, Thailand is one of three ASEAN countries - along with Singapore and Malaysia - that now seem likely to obtain their first submarines within the next decade. It is generally recognised that submarines are a necessary element in the creation of a balanced anti-submarine warfare (ASW) capability, not least in order to be able to train surface ships and maritime aircraft in ASW roles. Yet the perceived need for ASW capability is itself being driven by the fact that more states in the region are acquiring submarines: making ASW an indispensable component in an increasing number of possible scenarios.

There is also evidence of interaction between plans for acquiring modern combat aircraft, with each state seeking to maximise its ability to defend against the air forces of its neighbours. Thus it is generally believed that Thailand's initial decision to buy F-16s in the later 1980s was prompted in part by Singapore's decision to do the same. When, in response to the Thai and Singaporean decisions, Malaysia began to consider the possible purchase of the Tornado strike attack aircraft, Thailand immediately began to make enquiries of its own about Tornado. Thailand's decision to seek the US AMRAAM missile is reported to have been spurred by Malaysia's purchase of the similarly capable R-77 Vympel (AA-12 Adder) missiles from Russia as part of its Mig 29 package.[114] The prospective AMRAAM sale to Thailand, stalled until December 1995 by US officials 'for fear of triggering an arms race in Southeast Asia', is in turn expected to pave the way for AMRAAM sales to Singapore, Malaysia and, eventually, Indonesia and the Philippines. [115]

In these circumstances, fuelled by the increased financial resources available to governments, there is a danger that the defence budgets of the region may be shifting in tandem onto a higher, and self-justifying, level. What appeared in the early 1990s to be an overdue adjustment in response to previous underinvestment is now in danger of becoming an arms build-up with its own dynamic. New procurement will continue to be justified by legitimate defence needs. Yet the calculation of these needs cannot be made without reference to neighbours that are themselves rearming. And the approximate balance of power between regional states means that no single state can be fully secure in military-technical terms.

The arms dynamic in South-East Asia is not confined to ASEAN members. One of the consequences of both the purchase of longer range weapons and the increasingly maritime orientation of defence policies is that ASEAN states' security policies increasingly interact with those of extra-regional powers. China's capability for maritime power projection is an increasing factor in ASEAN force planning. More broadly, other powers - such as Japan - are concerned that conflict in the region might impact directly upon them through disruption of the sea lines of communication on which they depend.

The arms build-up in South-East Asia has been under way for several years now, but concern was until recently tempered by the perception that, even if defence budgets are rising, the proportion of national income devoted to defence is still falling. As recently as 1993, Desmond Ball could comment that:

> '..in South-East Asia ... the high growth rates of the late 1980s (have) given way to little real growth in most defence budgets (apart from Singapore and Burma).'[116]

By late 1995, however, defence budgets still seemed to be growing in real terms in virtually all countries in the region, and in several cases are either stable or rising as a proportion of GDP. Defence budget growth rates of between 5% and 10% per year, combined with relatively stable personnel budgets, are in turn leading to procurement spending growing at rates of 10-30% per annum in real terms. Even where growth in total defence spending has slowed - as may be happening to some extent in Thailand - past budget increases have allowed procurement spending to be maintained at historically high levels.

The connection between arms purchases and capability is always problematic, not least when large numbers of new systems are being introduced into service at once. Modern weapon systems require sophisticated logistical support and highly qualified personnel, and these are often not present. As general educational levels improve in the region, one can expect the armed forces' ability to absorb new technologies to improve also. But this will take time. The same growth in national economies that has allowed increased defence budgets is also making it difficult for the armed forces to recruit and retain skilled and educated personnel when more lucrative opportunities are available in the civil economy. If the new equipment now coming into service in the region is to work well, much more needs to be done, and much more needs to be spent, to improve the ability to operate it.

A risk of war?

The recent intensification of the arms build-up in the region does contribute to concern that, at some point, this will lead to an increased risk of open conflict. The long experience of ASEAN conflict management has helped regional states to evolve a modus vivendi between themselves in which the possibility of the use of force has been sharply reduced. Yet the region's peace remains vulnerable to political changes in ASEAN member states that could upset the fragile balances that currently underlie the regional peace. Not only might political change - such as a resurgence of Muslim/Chinese strife in Indonesia or Malaysia - lead to increased tension between ASEAN states. Intra-ASEAN conflict could also encourage China to miscalculate the extent of ASEAN responses to a more assertive policy in the South China Sea.

Moreover, while the high rate of economic growth in the region contributes to peace in many ways, it also brings with it rapid political and social change, as well as the possibility of sharp changes in the balance of power between states. The combination of rapid economic growth and the domestic requirements for further nationbuilding is encouraging some governments to pursue more assertive national foreign policy goals that are not always welcome to their immediate neighbours. ASEAN can play an invaluable role in containing and directing these tendencies in policy, providing a mechanism through which changes in the regional balance of power can be managed peacefully. But its ability to do so may be undermined if member states are increasingly concerned at the arms build-ups of their fellow members.

An increase in the level of sophistication of the weapons deployed in the region does not in itself increase the chances of war. But the process of rapid change in the military technologies and capabilities deployed in the region is a source of potential instability. It increases uncertainty about others' warfighting capability and may appear to create short-lived 'windows of opportunity': both in terms of the possibility of victory now but not in the future, and in terms of the tactical advantages of pre-emption. The combination of small forces deployed at low states of readiness without adequate self-defence, alongside increased capabilities for longer-range offensive operations, could well increase the incentives for resolving crises by force.

The costs of the arms build-up

In assessing the costs of the regional arms build-up, strategic analysts have tended to focus above all on whether it may increase the chances of war through increasing distrust or misunderstanding between states. Arguably as important, however, are the direct economic costs of financing ambitious, and highly import-intensive, procurement programmes. Most of the countries of the region are not so rich, or so assured of an effortless transition to developed country status, that they can afford to ignore the considerable opportunity costs of high defence budgets. Even in Singapore - the richest country in the region - the allocation of 25% of government spending to the armed forces severely restricts government flexibility to use resources for other purposes. In less well-off states, where future development often depends on the government's ability to finance increased investment in infrastructure, education, and poverty alleviation, the trade-off between defence and civil needs may be even more stark.

It has been suggested in the past that, because the proportion of GDP devoted to defence spending (often called the 'defence burden') in the region is stable or falling, the economic cost of arms spending is not a matter of great concern. This argument needs to be treated with some caution. It is true that over a longer time frame - of ten years or more - the defence burden has fallen in most ASEAN states, as well as in China and most of the rest of the world. But, in contrast to most of the rest of the world, there are now some indications that this trend may have reversed in ASEAN. Evidence remains somewhat fragmentary, and not too much should be read into the defence budgets of one or two years. But, as we have already argued, the defence burden has increased in Singapore, Myanmar, Malaysia and, less clearly, in Thailand. Defence spending as a proportion of national income has stabilised in Indonesia and Philippines after a period of decline, and a future increase in the defence burden seems a distinct possibility. In Vietnam, recent procurement decisions - as well as published defence budget figures - may suggest that the process of defence spending cuts that began in the late 1980s has now run its course. Last, but not least, the 'real' Chinese defence budget may now be growing as rapidly as China's economy.

Even if the proportion of regional product that is devoted to the military is stable rather than rising, the opportunity cost is still noteworthy. With regional growth rates of between 5% and 10% per annum, a stabilisation of defence spending as a proportion of GDP implies a real increase in defence budgets of between 60% and 160% over a decade. If, on the other hand, the growth in defence spending can be brought down to a level well below that of GDP, savings of between 1% and 2% of national GDP could be made within a decade: amounting to a substantial regional 'peace dividend.' Even if there were no concern at the strategic implications of the current arms build-up, therefore, it would still be worth examining whether it is possible to find means of reducing the burden of military spending in the region in ways that are compatible with necessary defence requirements.

X   Towards new ASEAN norms?

The increasingly important - albeit not yet dominant - role of interactive factors in determining procurement programmes in the region calls into question some of the basic premises of the 'ASEAN Way' of conflict resolution outlined in the last Chapter. During the first twenty years of ASEAN's existence, the primary security concerns were internal insurgencies and the possibilities of internal conflicts becoming internationalised, and the primary response was a rigid adherence to the principle of non-interference. The governments of ASEAN would set aside considerations of short term advantage, and resist domestic political pressures to intervene in each others' affairs.

The norm of non-interference worked well. The fragile new states established in the aftermath of European colonial rule consolidated themselves internally, and began to make progress - remarkable in some cases, less so in others - along the road of economic development. Even in Singapore - the only ASEAN member with no internal insurgency problem - the 'ASEAN Way' worked because the internal security problems of Indonesia and Malaysia helped to reduce the possibility of an external threat to its own existence developing.

Since the end of the Cold War, however, the norm of non-interference has become less relevant to the security concerns of some ASEAN members. The end of insurgency in Malaysia and Thailand means that the security policies of the Association's three most economically advanced members - Malaysia, Singapore and Thailand - are now primarily externally-oriented. Internal security is still a major, at times predominant, concern in the Philippines and Indonesia. But the norm of non-interference, in itself, is not enough if ASEAN is to prove relevant to the post Cold War security concerns of its members. Increasingly - as both the recent focus of ASEAN discussion on the Spratlys dispute and the ARF's decision to highlight its support for the UN Arms Register at its first meeting in 1994 illustrate - external security concerns are paramount in regional security discussions.

The existence of ASEAN, and the culture of consultation and mutual accommodation which it has engendered, means that the region already has a firm basis upon which to build measures and processes that can manage, and if possible scale back, the regional arms build-up. Moreover, there is some cause for optimism that the same interdependence and economic growth that is fuelling the arms build-up can also contribute to tension reduction. Regional leaders are aware of their profound common interest in a continuation of the region's remarkable economic success of the last two decades. They are well aware of the fragility of that success, and of the political costs to those who might destroy it.

Yet, in contrast to the Cold War period, no clear 'norm' has yet emerged around which the countries of ASEAN, or the broader region, can unite in addressing the problems created by the conventional arms build-up. Indeed, the very norm that contributed to regional stability during the previous period may in a certain sense be undermining the prospects for ASEAN developing new norms appropriate to its new situation. For the norm of non-interference can be used to suggest that governments should determine their own defence requirements without outside 'interference', and without reference to how others might view them. The very philosophy of 'national resilience' and strong national government that proved such an important part of securing regional stability in the past, therefore, may now be making it more difficult for governments to fashion security policies that take adequate account of their neighbours' concerns.

Notes

1.   Stockholm International Peace Research Institute, *SIPRI Yearbook 1995*, Oxford University Press, 1995, p. 442.

2.   For useful discussions, see Amitav Acharya, *A New Regional Order in South-East Asia: ASEAN in the post Cold War Era*, Adelphi Paper Number 279, Brasseys, International Institute for Strategic Studies, August 1993, pp. 64-68; Bates Gill, 'Arms Acquisitions in East Asia', *SIPRI Yearbook 1994*, Oxford University Press, 1994, pp. 551-562; Desmond Ball, 'Arms and Affluence: Military Acquisitions in the Asia Pacific Region', *International Security*, 18, 3, Winter 1993/94, pp. 79-95.

3.   World Bank, *World Development Report 1995*, Oxford University Press, 1995, pp. 180-181.

4.   J. N. Mak, *ASEAN Defence Reorientation 1975-1992*, Strategic and Defence Studies Centre, Australian National University, Canberra Papers on Strategy and Defence Number 103, 1993, pp. 29-35.

5.   For an exposure of corruption in procurement in Thailand, see Kenneth Stier and Bao Anyou, 'The Bitter Truth Behind Thailand's Khaki Commerce', *Asia Inc*, October 1992, pp. 28-37.

6.   Tim Huxley, *The Political Role of the Singapore Armed Forces' Officer Corps: Towards A Military-Administrative State?*, Strategic and Defence Studies Centre, Australian National University, Working Paper Number 279, December 1993.

7.   J. N. Mak, op cit, p. 20.

8.   According to one recent study, there have only been four true arms races between 1840 and 1991. Colin Gray, reviewing Grant Hammond, *Plowshares into Swords: Arms Races in International Politics, 1840-1991*, University of South Carolina Press, 1993, in *Survival*, 37, 1, Spring 1995,

Notes continued

pp. 177-179. For discussion of the 'arms race' hypothesis in relation to South-East Asia, see J. N. Mak, op cit, pp. 141-148; Desmond Ball, *Arms and Affluence*, op cit, pp. 94-95.

9. Expressed in local currency terms. International Institute for Strategic Studies, *The Military Balance 1995-1996*, Oxford University Press, 1995, p. 193.

10. Tim Huxley, 'Singapore forces shape up', *Jane's Defence Weekly*, 19 November 1994, p. 26.

11. Tim Huxley, 'Singapore and Malaysia' , *The Pacific Review*, 4, 3, 1991, p. 208.

12. Tim Huxley, *Insecurity in the ASEAN Region*, Royal United Services Institute for Defence Studies, London, 1993, p. 59.

13. Ministry of Defence, *Defence of Singapore 1994-95*, p. 40.

14. *Kyodo News Service*, August 13, 1995.

15. J. N. Mak, op cit, p. 97.

16. Ibid, p. 101.

17. James Goldrick, quoted in Shannon Selin, *Asia Pacific Arms Buildups Part One: Scope, Causes and Problems*, University of British Columbia, Working Paper Number 6, November 1994, p. 50.

18. Derek da Cunha, 'Conventional Arms and Security in South-East Asia: China and the ASEAN', in Malcolm Chalmers, Owen Greene and Xie Zhiqiong (eds), *Asia Pacific Security and the UN*, University of Bradford, 1995, p. 59.

19. J. N. Mak, op cit, p. 103; Shannon Selin, op cit, p. 58.

20. Joris Janssen Lok, 'Singapore to buy Swedish submarine', *Jane's Defence Weekly*, 30 September 1995, p. 5.

21. J. N. Mak, op cit, p. 142.

22. Shannon Selin, op cit, p. 28; J. N. Mak, ibid, p. 144.

23. Shannon Selin, ibid, p 56.

24. Tim Huxley, 'Insecurity in the ASEAN Region', op cit, p. 25.

Notes continued

25.   US Arms Control and Disarmament Agency, *World Military Expenditures and Arms Transfers 1993-94*, 1995, p. 121; personal communication, Ian Anthony, SIPRI.

26.   International Institute for Strategic Studies, *The Military Balance 1995-1996*, Oxford University Press, 1995, p. 173.

27.   *SIPRI Yearbook 1995*, op cit, p. 431. Some reports suggest, however, that one of the greatest attractions of this deal, from a Malaysian point of view, was that only limited new amounts of hard currency were involved, and that payment was made primarily through a combination of debt cancellation and the supply of palm oil.

28.   'Malaysian Modernisation', *Armed Forces Journal International*, October 1994, p. 65.

29.   'Country Briefing: Malaysia', *Jane's Defence Weekly*, 25 November 1995, p. 28.

30.   'Malaysia poised to buy corvettes', *Jane's Defence Weekly*, 23 September 1995, p. 16.

31.   Shannon Selin, op cit, p. 21.

32.   *SIPRI Yearbook 1995*, op cit, p. 430; 'Malaysian Military Shifts its Emphasis Outwards', *Defense News*, September 11-17, 1995, p. 12.

33.   Ted Bardacke, 'Fish war crisis brings Thai and Malaysian PMs to the table', *Financial Times*, 14 December 1995.

34.   'Malaysian Army Raids Budget', *Defense News*, October 10-16 1994, p. 1.

35.   Major-General Dato Nordin Yusof and Abdul Razak Abdullah Baginda, *Honour and Sacrifice: the Malaysian Armed Forces*, Malaysian Ministry of Defence, 1994, p. 53.

36.   'Malaysian MoD orders further 47 KIFV's', *Jane's Defence Weekly*, 8 July 1995, p. 14.

37.   'Country Briefing: Malaysia', op cit, p. 25.

38.   'Malaysians bemused about UK aid row', *Financial Times*, 19 January 1994.

39.   Major-General Dato Nordin Yusof and Abdul Razak Abdullah Baginda, op cit, p. 191.

Notes continued

40.   'Malaysia seeks to increase its involvement in Bosnia', *Jane's Defence Weekly*, 19 August 1995, p. 12.

41.   Chandran Jeshurun, 'Malaysian Defence Policy Revisited: Modernization and Rationalization in the Post-Cold War Era', *Southeast Asian Affairs 1994*, pp. 194-206.

42.   Shannon Selin, op cit, p. 56.

43.   J. N. Mak, 'ASEAN maritime insecurity: contingency planning in an uncertain world', *International Defense Review: Defense 1995*, p. 63.

44.   Bob Lowry, *Indonesian Defence Policy and the Indonesian Armed Forces*, Canberra Papers of Strategy and Defence Number 99, Strategic and Defence Studies Centre, 1993, pp. 45-46.

45.   Interviews.

46.   J. N. Mak, 'Armed But Ready? ASEAN Conventional Warfare Capabilities', *Harvard International Review*, Spring 1994, p. 24.

47.   Surin Maisrikrod, 'The Peace Dividend in South-East Asia: The Political Economy of New Thai-Vietnamese Relations', *Contemporary Southeast Asia*, 16, 1, June 1994, pp. 46-66; Bertil Lintner, 'Building new bridges with a former foe', *Jane's Defence Weekly*, 9 September 1995, p. 46.

48.   In local currency terms. International Institute for Strategic Studies, *The Military Balance 1995-1996*, Oxford University Press, 1995, p. 195.

49.   Shannon Selin, op cit, p. 52.

50.   'Thai Army gets green light for US tank buy', *Jane's Defence Weekly*, 23 September 1995.

51.   'US to clear AIM-120 for Air Force', *Flight International*, August 3, 1995; 'Thailand gets 18 F-16A/B's', *Jane's Defence Weekly*, 23 September 1995.

52.   Mark G. Rolls, 'Thailand's Post-Cold War Security Policy and Defence Programme' in Colin McInnes and Mark G. Rolls (eds), *Post-Cold War Security Issues in the Asia-Pacific Region*, Frank Cass, 1994, p. 107.

53.   International Institute for Strategic Studies, *Military Balance, 1985-1986* and International Institute for Strategic Studies, *Military Balance 1994-1995*.

Notes continued

54.   'First A-7 fighters delivered to Navy', *Jane's Defence Weekly*, August 12, 1995.

55.   J. N. Mak, *ASEAN Defence Reorientation*, op cit, p. 88.

56.   'Royal Thai Navy Submarine Program: Dossier', *International Defense Review*, June 1995, pp. 90-93.

57.   J. N. Mak, *ASEAN Defence Reorientation*, op cit, p. 89.

58.   J. N. Mak and B. A. Hamzah, 'Navy Blues', *Far East Economic Review*, March 17, 1994, p. 30.

59.   David White, 'Spain may build carrier for China', *Financial Times*, January 22 1996.

60.   David Van Praagh, 'Democracy and Asian Security', *Global Affairs*, Winter 1993, p. 74.

61.   Mark Baker, 'Is Thailand's new democratic face just a mask?' *The Age*, August 18, 1992, p. 13.

62.   Tai Ming Cheung, 'Officers' commission: arms procurement driven by profit rather than need', *Far Eastern Economic Review*, 2 July 1992, p. 13.

63.   Kenneth Stier and Bao Anyou, 'Khaki Commerce', *Asia Inc.*, October 1992, p. 36.

64.   J. N. Mak, *ASEAN Defence Reorientation*, op cit, p. 82.

65.   J. N. Mak, *Armed But Ready?*, op cit, p. 21.

66.   Kenneth Stier and Bao Anyou, op cit, p. 36.

67.   Kenneth Stier and Bao Anyou, op cit, p. 37.

68.   Shannon Selin, op cit, p. 51.

69.   Kenneth Stier and Bao Anyou, op cit, p. 28.

70.   J. N. Mak, *ASEAN Defence Reorientation*, op cit, p. 84.

71.   '$12 million Shadow 600 UAV deal On Ice', *Defense News*, August 7, 1995.

72.   'Royal Thai Navy Submarine Program: Dossier', op cit, p. 92.

Notes continued

73.   Arujunan Narayanan, 'Thailand's Strategic and Defence Policy', *Military Technology*, 9, 1993, p. 45.

74.   Bob Lowry, op cit, p. 78.

75.   Ibid, p. 24.

76.   Ibid, p. 23. Lowry also notes, however, that some items not normally included in defence spending - such police and coast guard functions - are included in the Indonesian defence budget. According to SIPRI, 20% of the defence budget is for spending on the national police. *SIPRI Yearbook 1995*, op cit, p. 429.

77.   'Indonesia under-reporting arms spending', *Reuters News Service*, 19 April 1994; *SIPRI Yearbook 1995*, ibid, p. 429.

78.   Bob Lowry, op cit, pp. 91-92.

79.   Shannon Selin, op cit, p. 51.

80.   International Institute for Strategic Studies, *The Military Balance 1995-1996*, op cit, p. 179.

81.   R. Supartha, 'Indonesia's navy: balancing strategy and introspection', *International Defense Review*, 3, 1991, p. 195.

82.   European Campaign Against Arms Trade, *Stop Arming Indonesia*, 1994, p. 67.

83.   Richard Sharpe, *Jane's Fighting Ships 1993-1994*, Jane's, 1993, pp. 294-295.

84.   *SIPRI Yearbook 1995*, op cit, p. 429.

85.   J. N. Mak, *ASEAN Defence Reorientation*, op cit, p. 159.

86.   Andrew McIntyre, 'Ideas and experts: Indonesian approaches to economic and security cooperation in the Asia-Pacific region', *The Pacific Review*, 8, 1, 1995, pp. 105-107.

87.   'The flying puppet', *Economist*, 19 August 1995, p. 58.

88.   Gregor Ferguson, 'Indonesia Proposes Pacific Rim Consortium', *Defense News*, 11-15 June, 1995, p. 3.

89.   Bob Lowry, op cit, p. 110.

Notes continued

90.   *Xinhua News Agency*, 7 December 1994, cited in *Military and Arms Transfer News*, 94, 15, 16 December 1994.

91.   World Bank, *World Development Report 1995*, p. 162.

92.   'Emerging Market Indicators', *Economist*, 13 January 1996.

93.   Tim Huxley, *Insecurity in the ASEAN Region*, op cit, p. 63.

94.   Rigoberto Tiglao, 'Crescent Moon Rising', *Far Eastern Economic Review*, 23 February 1995, p. 26.

95.   'Philippine military joins regional arms race', *Kyodo News Service*, 13 August 1995.

96.   Robert Karniol, 'Philippine Navy lines up for 1996 changes', *Jane's Defence Weekly*, 9 September 1995, p. 58.

97.   Shannon Selin, op cit, p. 25.

98.   Rigoberto Tiglao, op cit, p. 24.

99.   Kyodo News Service, op cit.

100.   Tim Huxley, *Insecurity in the ASEAN Region*, op cit, p. 61.

101.   Joris Janssen Lok, 'Brunei picks Yarrow for offshore patrol vessels', *Jane's Defence Weekly*, 9 December 1995, p. 5.

102.   quoted in Richard K. Betts, 'Vietnam's Strategic Predicament', *Survival*, 37, 3, Autumn 1995, p. 79.

103.   Carlyle A. Thayer, *Beyond Indochina*, Adelphi Paper Number 297, International Institute for Strategic Studies, Oxford University Press, 1995, p. 10.

104.   Edmund Fawcett, 'A Survey of Vietnam', *Economist*, 8 July 1995.

105.   Ibid, p. 12.

106.   Carlyle A. Thayer, op cit, p. 23.

107.   Murray Hiebert, 'Corps business: Vietnam's military is learning to turn profits', *Far Eastern Economic Review*, 23 December 1993.

108.   International Institute for Strategic Studies, *The Military Balance 1995-1996*, Oxford University Press, 1995.

Notes continued

109. Ibid; Carlyle A. Thayer, 'Vietnam's National Budget', *BBC World Service*, 27 January 1994.

110. 'Vietnam modernizes aircraft', *Jane's Defence Weekly*, 19 August 1995; Clive Schofield, 'An Arms Race in the South China Sea?' *IBRU Boundary and Security Bulletin*, July 1994, p. 43.

111. Carlyle A. Thayer, *Beyond Indochina*, op cit, p. 47.

112. Robert Karniol, 'New channels of Asian diplomacy unfold', *Jane's Defence Weekly*, 24 June 1995, p. 28.

113. International Institute for Strategic Studies, *The Military Balance 1995-1996*, Oxford University Press, 1995, p. 172.

114. *Reuters*, August 4, 1995.

115. Jason Glashow and Theresa Hitchens, 'Thailand to Get AMRAAMs in F/A-18 Fighter Package', *Defense News*, January 8-14 1996.

116. Desmond Ball, *Arms and Affluence*, op cit, p. 80.

CHAPTER 5

The ASEANization of Australia

I   Self-reliance in defence

For much of the period since it gained its independence from the UK in 1901, Australia has not been seen as an independent actor in Asian security, but as a junior member of the Western security club. The new state remained so closely linked to the 'mother country' that it was willing to send hundreds of thousands of its young men to fight in Europe in two world wars. During most of the Cold War, the Australian government tended to see its armed forces as essentially an adjunct to a much bigger US effort: the necessary price to pay for the American security guarantee, but not performing a distinct and independent role of their own.

In recent years, however, the orientation of Australian foreign and security policy has undergone a quite fundamental change. Asian economic dynamism has made Australia more aware of the economic opportunities presented by its relative closeness to the region, as well as the potential risks that this closeness might entail. As Gareth Evans, Australia's Foreign Minister, argued in 1991:

> '... the region from which we sought in the past to protect ourselves - whether by esoteric dictation tests for would-be immigrants, or tariffs, or alliances with the distant great and powerful - is now the region that offers Australia the most. Our future lies, inevitably, in the Asia-Pacific region. ... it is no longer an option for Australia to see itself first and foremost as a transplanted European nation.'[1]

In one of the earliest indications of this shift, the Labour government that came to power in 1983 set in place a major review of defence policy, the central result of which was the decision to adopt a policy of defence 'self-reliance'. Starting with Paul Dibb's Review of Defence Policy, published in 1986, together with the 1987 Defence White Paper, force planning increasingly assumed that the defence of Australia would be a national responsibility. Help from Australia's allies would continue to be welcome, and Australia would continue to host US defence facilities. But it would no

Table 5.1: Australian Trends

Vital statistics

Population	17.8 million
1993 GNP	$281.9 billion
Real GNP growth 1993-1993	+ 35.4% (3.1% per annum)

Trends in military spending and arms imports

Year	Military spending constant 1993 $	Military spending as % of GNP	Arms imports constant 1993 $
1983	5425	2.6	313
1984	5736	2.6	818
1985	6037	2.7	1184
1986	5959	2.6	1281
1987	6354	2.6	900
1988	5743	2.3	1434
1989	5674	2.2	686
1990	5986	2.3	438
1991	6609	2.5	253
1992	6760	2.5	185
1993	7441	2.6	300

Source: US Arms Control and Disarmament Agency, *World Military Expenditures and Arms Transfers 1993-94*, 1995.

longer assume that Australia could always count on the US providing military help in a crisis, far less that this help would be timely and appropriate. Australia took the US seriously, but sought to define its own distinct position and to take its own initiatives. The US was still seen as playing a vital role in enhancing the security of the Asia-Pacific region, not least in its relationships with Asia's biggest powers. But, as in ASEAN, the demise of the Soviet Union and the increased importance - at least in relative terms - of other threats meant that, as the 1994 White Paper argued:

> 'Australia's security is not so vital to other nations that we can assume others would commit substantial forces to our defence. This will become increasingly so as our strategic environment becomes more complex. Our alliance with the US does not mean that we can expect it to provide for our defence.'[2]

The shift towards self-reliance has been made easier by the end of the Cold War. As a result, Australia is arguably more secure from attack than at any time in its history as an independent nation:

> 'No country in Asia has developed the forces required to mount a major conventional attack on Australia sufficient to seize and hold significant amounts of territory on our continent.'[3]

Rather than preparing to meet the possibility of an imminent attack, therefore, Australian defence planning since the end of the Cold War has concentrated on preparing for the longer term. First, defence planning and defence infrastructure has been reoriented geographically. In the past, Australian armed forces were based almost entirely in the heavily populated parts of the country: appropriate for forces designed primarily to fight as part of an allied coalition in foreign wars, but questionable in the context of the new focus on defence in depth. Now land forces are increasingly being relocated to northern Australia, and naval forces relocated to the west of the country.

Second, Australia is investing heavily in modern technology in an attempt to maintain the qualitative edge of its armed forces for as long as possible. In contrast to fellow 'Western' countries in Europe and North America, its defence budget has continued to rise in real terms since 1990. A recent US government report suggests that Australia will spend $7 billion (in 1991 prices) on arms imports over the period from 1994 to 2000, including major planned purchases of maritime patrol aircraft, frigates and submarines. Its projected purchases over this period are greater than those of any individual South-East Asian country, and about twice as great as those of China.[4]

As part of this ambitious programme, the surveillance capabilities critical to the defence of the approaches to Australia are being improved, for example by the purchase of over-the-horizon radar and an upgrading of the two squadrons of P3C maritime patrol aircraft. The purchase of 75 F/A-18 multi-role aircraft was completed in 1990, and 15 F-111 bombers have been bought from the US to supplement the 22 previously in service. As well as extending the life of Australia's six existing frigates, eight Meko ANZAC-class frigates are due to be commissioned over the next decade. Six new Swedish-designed Collins-class submarines will be introduced into service by the end of the decade, replacing existing Oberon-class boats. Recent reports suggest the government is considering arming the new submarines with Tomahawk sea-launched cruise missiles.[5]

Australia's economy remains significantly larger than those of any of the ASEAN countries (measured at official exchange rates), and this relative economic strength is reflected in a defence budget which is still greater, in absolute terms, than any of those of its northern neighbours. As Gareth Evans has pointed out in regard to recent ASEAN equipment acquisitions:

> 'Certainly there is no basis for being overawed by them, given that - quite apart from the benign political relationships we employ - the pattern of Australian defence expenditures, until very recently, has been roughly equivalent to that of all the ASEAN countries combined.'[6]

Yet this relatively comfortable balance is almost certain to change over the next two decades. Australia cannot hope to match the growth rates of the economies of ASEAN. Nor can it hope to match the rate of growth in their military capabilities. Extrapolating recent trends, the defence budgets of individual ASEAN countries could approach the Australian level within the next 15 years without further increases in the proportion of GDP they devote to defence. As their economies become more sophisticated, their armed forces' ability to maintain and operate advanced weapon systems will increase. And major arms suppliers are likely, with few exceptions, to be eager to supply ASEAN countries with whatever systems they can afford.

It will be many years before any Asian power possesses the 'extensive amphibious and air capabilities to land and support a substantial land force' in Australia.[7] Yet, as Chapter 4 illustrates, force modernisation in Asian countries is now leading to an increase in capabilities - such as advanced maritime aircraft, Harpoon-armed surface ships and modern submarines - that will soon have the ability to pose real problems for Australia's sophisticated, but still relatively small, naval and air forces. As in Australia, ASEAN armed forces argue that it is essential that defence planning 'focuses on capabilities rather than threats.'[8] As in Australia, ASEAN armed forces argue that the best way to counter potential aggressors is to construct a layered defence stretching well beyond the territory of the country itself. The argument for forward defence is particularly cogent in countries like Singapore, which - unlike Australia - have no scope for conducting a 'defence in depth' on their own territory.

The adoption of a 'capabilities approach' to defence planning by ASEAN states includes efforts to counter the very capabilities on which Australia relies for its own defence. For example, ASEAN force modernisation may include a combination of defensive and retaliatory forces that can blunt Australia's current ability to launch strikes (for example with its F-111 aircraft) against air bases and other targets on ASEAN territory. ASEAN states may also increasingly seek surveillance capabilities that allow it to monitor Australian military activity and communications as closely as Australia already watches their own.

As the capabilities of regional armed forces develop further, an over-reliance on 'capabilities-based' force planning could mean that Australia is also drawn into this process: increasing the expense of defence in both Australia and ASEAN, reducing the prospects for military cooperation, and contributing to mutual mistrust more generally.

Australia should be able to maintain the most technically sophisticated armed forces in the immediate region for some time to come. In the long term, however, it cannot escape the logic of demographics. As the process of Asian economic development continues, Australia's strategic advantage in purely military terms is bound to diminish. A country of less than 20 million people cannot hope to maintain its military superiority indefinitely over the much more heavily populated states to its north. The erosion of Australia's advantage may be slowed if there is now a pause in the regional arms build-up. It could occur more rapidly than anticipated if the regional security situation deteriorates. But the long term trend is clear.

II   Regional engagement

It is because of this long term trend, rather than because of any immediate dangers, that Australia has complemented its more self-reliant defence policy with an increased emphasis on the need for dialogue and consultation on defence matters with its immediate neighbours.[9] Indeed, so extensive have Australia's defence contacts with the region become that - in every respect except actual ASEAN membership - Australia is now an additional member of ASEAN's 'spiderweb' of defence cooperation. For many years, Australia has been the major external power in the Five Power Defence Arrangements, and the associated Integrated Air Defence System, thus helping to cement its close ties with fellow Commonwealth members Singapore and Malaysia. An extensive programme of exercises takes place every year, in which the armed forces of the three countries (together with the UK and New Zealand) have an opportunity for sharing perceptions, addressing misunderstandings, and learning from each other.

In addition, Australia has close bilateral defence relations with Malaysia and Singapore. Its air force continues to deploy P3C maritime patrol aircraft to the Royal Malaysian Air Force base at Butterworth in order to conduct surveillance missions in South-East Asian waters, and Army rifle companies rotate through Butterworth on three-month deployments. Malaysia is also co-operating with Australian firms in the development of a possible collaborative programme to purchase and support a new class of offshore patrol vessels (12 for Australia, as many as 20 for Malaysia). For its part, Singapore has reached agreement with Australia in 1992 to deploy its aircraft and personnel to Australian air bases for up to ten months a year. In 1993 it was agreed that the Singapore Air Force would establish a permanent training school at Pearce, near Perth in Western Australia.[10] In December 1995, agreement was reached on a further intensification of the military relationship between the two countries.

Australia has also made extensive efforts to expand its programme of bilateral exercises and training with other ASEAN countries, especially Indonesia (discussed further in the next section). Desmond Ball has estimated that, even in the late 1980s, the schedule of joint exercises with ASEAN countries included an average of one exercise a month.[11] Of particular importance, Australia has sought (in addition to its FPDA involvement) to provide a structure for multilateral exercises involving several ASEAN countries: a structure that ASEAN has so far found it difficult to provide for itself. Thus, in the exercise 'Fleet Concentration Period - Kakadu', Australia brought together naval forces from Malaysia, Singapore. Thailand and Australia, as well as Singaporean fighter aircraft and Indonesian observers.[12]

Observers and participants have been invited from ASEAN members for Australia's own wargames. The latest example is from the 'Kangaroo' exercise in July and August 1995, held over two months over an area of 4 million square kilometres, involving over 17,000 Australian Defence Force (ADF) personnel, and described as 'perhaps the longest and most complex exercise ever undertaken by the ADF'. In addition to contingents from the UK and US, foreign participants included: a parachute company and 2 C-130 aircraft from Indonesia (160 people); a mechanised battalion HQ staff from Malaysia (60 people); an armoured battalion staff HQ from Singapore (60 people); and a patrol craft from Papua New Guinea.

K95 was also notable in another respect. In a further example of the ADF's efforts to promote transparency on its operations, a series of special Web page were prepared on the K95 exercise: making this what is believed to be the first military exercise ever reported directly via the Internet. The K95 Web pages had an average of 715 "hits" per day during the period of the exercise. Digital photos were also down loaded and used by the press, as well as being viewed directly on-screen.[13]

ASEAN and Australian military personnel are engaged in many smaller modes of personnel exchange. Military personnel from Indonesia alone attended training courses in Australia in 1994/95, while 32 Australian officers attended Indonesia's Staff and Command School.[14] The extent of Australian commitment to advanced officer training for the region will be further increased by the recent establishment of the Australian College of Defence and Strategic Studies. The College will provide postgraduate level education to both senior military officers and civilian officials, and will focus on strategic and defence issues in the Asia-Pacific region. Around a quarter of the intake will come from the region.[15]

The Australian policy of regional engagement is not without its risks, and could be seen as increasing the possibility that Australia might be drawn into military support for its friends in the region if they were faced with armed conflict (for example in the Spratlys). If Australia's policy were truly one of national self defence, critics have argued, it may be unwise to give the impression that Australian forces were committed, for example, to the defence of Singapore in the event of attack. As Graeme Cheeseman has argued:

> 'The increasing emphasis on CSBM's and other forms of defence cooperation could ... serve to divert the attention and resources of Australia's defence establishment away from its primary task of defending Australia and its immediate surrounds. ... Australia's formal involvement in any future regional security arrangements increases the chances of being embroiled in some future conflict between ASEAN and an outsider or between the ASEAN states themselves.'[16]

Notwithstanding these risks, Australia has decided that it cannot afford to isolate itself from the region to its north. There would be considerable opposition to a NATO-style Australian commitment to the defence of ASEAN states if this were proposed. But it is in Australia's interests to develop its cooperation with ASEAN governments and armed forces. Not only can dialogue and cooperation help to reduce misunderstanding, and thus the potential for conflict, between ASEAN and Australia. Perhaps of even greater importance, Australia has a clear interest in maintaining a resilient and independent ASEAN as a strategic buffer against great power intervention in the region. As the Australian government has argued:

> 'Australia's security is enhanced as Indonesia develops its capacity to defend its own territory, because this makes it less likely that in the future any hostile third power could mount attacks from or through the archipelago across our sea or air approaches.'[17]

While the central feature of Australian defence policy remains the search for self-reliance, therefore, its security policy also recognises that this aspiration - as in ASEAN - needs to be complemented by policies designed to enhance cooperation and common security. Nowhere is this more important than for the medium powers of South-East Asia and Australasia, whose independence from outside domination depends in large measure on their ability to avoid conflict between themselves.

The shift in Australian security policy since the late 1980s has also led to convergence with ASEAN thinking in another important respect: the determination to emphasise the multi-dimensional nature of the security problematic. As part of this new orientation of 'Comprehensive Engagement with South-East Asia', Australia has devoted considerable effort to a wide-ranging process of dialogue and networking with its northern neighbours, both in ASEAN and more broadly, that is not unlike the trust-building activity that has characterised ASEAN itself. It is an incremental process that cannot be expected to produce a transformation of national attitudes - either in Australia or in Asia - overnight. But Australia's commitment to sustaining and developing the dialogue now seems irreversible, whichever party is in power. As evidence of the new Asian orientation, Australian leaders can already point to the fact that between a third and a half of annual immigration has been from Asia since the late 1970s, as well as to the plan to ensure that all Australian school pupils are taught at least one of six Asian languages.[18]

Australian initiatives, not least in the area of arms control and transparency measures, are not always welcome in the region, where they are still often regarded as too 'Western' and too obsessed with content rather than process. But Australia's diplomatic efforts - which are out of proportion to those characteristic of most powers of its size - continue to have a substantial impact on the regional agenda. After an initiative from Prime Minister Hawke gained widespread support, the Asia-Pacific Economic Cooperation (APEC) process - now in its sixth year - held its first meeting in Canberra in November 1989. Similarly, the idea of a Conference on Security Cooperation in Asia, floated by Gareth Evans at ASEAN's 1990 Post-Ministerial Conference in Jakarta in July 1990, was widely criticised by both ASEAN members and by the US. Yet it helped to provoke a debate that led, four years later, to the establishment of the ASEAN Regional Forum. Australia is sometimes seen as over-enthusiastic in its promotion of transparency and confidence-building measures, and of being unaware of the differences in political systems between itself and most Asian countries. But it continues to play an important role in promoting these ideas in the region.

III   Australia and Indonesia

Australia's relationship with Jakarta is the key to its policy of regional engagement. But it is also fraught with continuing problems resulting from the massive political, economic and cultural gaps that separate the two countries. By the late 1980s, the Australian public came to regard Indonesia as the most likely possible threat to Australia's security. In 1993, a national survey reported that 57% of Australians believed that Indonesia would pose a security threat to Australia within 10 to 15 years.[19]

On the Indonesian side, concerns have been expressed at the implications of the northwards shift of Australian defence policy adopted in the 1987 White Paper. Most of these concerns, which were not necessarily held by all members of the Indonesian elite, were expressed in private. But in May 1989, former Ambassador Lieutenant-General Hasnan Habib told the Fifth Australian-Indonesian Conference in Canberra of his concern that Australian policy appeared to be based on an assumption that Indonesia was the most likely source of a threat to its territory, and that Australia had defined Indonesia as part of Australia's area of 'direct military interest'. Australian defence policy, he argued, 'gives the impression of an aggressive military doctrine'.

A second public critique emerged in two articles in the Jakarta Post by a resident senior analyst in the Indonesian Institute of Sciences, Hilman Adil, who argued that Australian defence planners might be seen to be attempting:

> 'to gain regional influence by establishing Australia as the dominant Western-aligned nation of sea and the Southwest Pacific through the projection of military, especially naval, power ... The availability of superior naval power might encourage greater risk-taking as it places Australia in a position to intervene militarily in another country in the region as it deemed necessary.[20]

Perhaps in part as a response to these difficulties, both the Australian and Indonesian governments began to give new impetus to mutual dialogue. The appointment of two new Foreign Ministers in 1988 - Ali Alatas and Gareth Evans - marked a turning point in this process, with their close personal relationship often seen as being a critical factor in the improvement of relations since that time. Thirty ministerial level meetings took place in the three years since mid-1988,[21] and a parallel process of regular contacts between leading military officers was also set in motion. Regular Bilateral Defence Discussions were institutionalised, as well as regular meetings and exchanges between the intelligence services of the two sides. The number of Indonesian officers involved in visits to Australia for exercises, training and intelligence exchanges increased from just 17 in 1991 to more than 300 in 1994.[22] The level of joint Australia Indonesia military exercises has increased sharply in the early 1990s. And the level of

Indonesian participation in Australia's annual Kangaroo exercises has been upgraded from a full briefing during the preparations for the 1989 exercise to observers at the 1992 exercise to the participation of an Indonesian parachute battalion in 1995.

The culmination of this process came on 19 December 1995 with the signature of a bilateral security accord between the two countries. Negotiated in eighteen months of secret talks, the 'Australian-Indonesian Agreement on Maintaining Security' commits the two states to consult one another in the event of a threat to either country or to regional security, and to considering measures which might be taken by them in response. It includes a commitment to regular consultation on mutual security issues at ministerial level, and was accompanied by an agreement to develop commonality and interoperability between the two countries' armed forces, and increase the level of combined training and exchanges of personnel and intelligence.[23]

The Australian government sees the Agreement as an important 'building block' in its efforts to develop closer military ties with the region, complementing its formal ties with Singapore and Malaysia through the FPDA, and increasing Australia's role as a key player in South-East Asia's defence architecture. As Prime Minister Paul Keating suggested:

> 'The agreement is, essentially, about building a structure for the future of Australia, to reduce uncertainties over the next 10 to 20 years. With it, Indonesia is offering us the opportunity to shape the region. The agreement will reinforce the security of the region as a whole by demonstrating to our friends and neighbours that Australia and Indonesia will continue to build a close and cooperative relationship.'[24]

It is also of historic significance for Indonesia, which for the first time has entered into a formal security arrangement with another country. In justifying the accord, Foreign Minister Ali Alatas explained that Australia and Indonesia now had 'common perceptions' of what can constitute a possible threat to the whole region, including 'an uncontrolled escalation in the South China Sea'.[25] Unnamed Indonesian government officials also suggested that the agreement represented an indirect strengthening of security ties with the US, which remains closely allied with Australia.[26]

Australia's relationship with Indonesia will, however, never be an easy one. Its character has been most starkly tested by the continuing controversy over Indonesia's 20-year occupation of East Timor. The Australian government recognised Indonesian sovereignty over the territory in 1978, but it remains unrecognised by the UN or by any other Western state. Yet in 1989, despite this controversy, Australia and Indonesia signed the Timor Gap Treaty, which provided for a 'joint development' regime, intended to exploit the substantial mineral resources in the area of the Timor Sea between Timor and Australia. The detailed arrangements for joint surveillance and security in the region may themselves be confidence-building measures, and have already included jointly-manned surveillance flights.[27]

The Australian government has been willing to court considerable controversy, both at home and internationally, in pursuit of its 'friendly neighbour' policy towards Indonesia. It has made clear its readiness to supply small arms to Indonesia to replace any gap left by the recent US embargo. It has contested, and won, a case brought to the International Court of Justice by Portugal over the Timor Gap treaty. In October 1995, Prime Minister Keating announced that Australia would refuse asylum to refugees from East Timor, dismissing their appeals as a 'phoney campaign,' and stating that Australia would not allow the issue to jeopardise its relationship with Indonesia. Keating went on to argue that, 'had it gone to a free vote, it's often argued that the people there would have voted for incorporation of Timor into Indonesia.'[28]

Australia's policy towards Indonesia is determined by the political elite rather than by public opinion. Yet this does not mean that Australia will always grant Indonesia a blank cheque for internal repression. Rather it reflects the view that, despite the continuing abuses in East Timor, Irian Jaya and Aceh, the current Indonesian regime also has, from an Australian perspective, important redeeming features. At least for now, Australia believes that a policy of ostracism towards the military regime in Jakarta could only be counterproductive, and that it is better to help the process of change in Indonesia through constructive engagement.

Australia's rejection of a more critical approach to Indonesia also reflects an awareness of its own vulnerability to Indonesian counter-measures, both in the economic field (Indonesia is now a major market for Australian exports) and in the field of security (Indonesia is central to Australian hopes for regional security cooperation). The growing degree of mutual interdependence between Australia and Indonesia has therefore made

Australia more, not less, reluctant to criticise the way that the latter conducts its internal affairs. In this respect - as in many others - Australia is adopting a norm of behaviour that has been central to ASEAN thinking since its formation.

IV   Conclusions

Australia may never be seen as an 'Asian' country. But, over time, a process of convergence in approaches to international politics and conflict management is readily apparent. The richer ASEAN countries, increasingly urbanised and market-oriented, appear more open to Western political ideas and culture than in the past. Australia, after two centuries of being isolated from the region to which it belongs, is coming to terms with its geography. The last decade has seen Australia adjusting in many ways to its new home, and in the process absorbing some of the norms of behaviour of its ASEAN neighbours. It remains to be seen where this process will lead. But it seems clear that Australia will continue to be an important part of the security jigsaw in South-East Asia.

Notes

1.   Gareth Evans and Bruce Grant, *Australia's Foreign Relations in the World of the 1990s*, Melbourne University Press, 1991, pp. 326-327.

2.   *Defending Australia: Defence White Paper 1994*, Australian Government Printing Office, 1994, p. 13.

3.   Ibid, p. 23.

4.   Department of Defense, *World-Wide Conventional Arms Trade (1994-2000): A Forecast and Analysis*, December 1994, pp. 23-24.

5.   'Australia studies Tomahawk as F-111 replacement', *Defense News*, 31 July 1995.

6.   Gareth Evans, 'Security in the Asia-Pacific region', *International Defense Review - Defense 95*, p. 54.

7.   *Defending Australia*, op cit, p. 23.

Notes continued

8.   Ibid, underlined in original.

9.   For a useful discussion, see Thomas-Durell Young, 'Assessing Australia's South-East Asian Strategy', *Contemporary South-East Asia*, 15, 4, March 1994, pp. 367-384.

10.   *Defence of Singapore 1994-95*, Singapore Ministry of Defence, 1994.

11.   Desmond Ball, *Building Blocks for Regional Security*, Canberra Papers on Strategy and Defence Number 83, Strategic and Defence Studies Centre, Australian National University, 1991, p. 40.

12.   J. N. Mak, 'ASEAN maritime insecurity: contingency planning in an uncertain world', *International Defense Review - Defense '95*, p. 65.

13.   Hts//www/adfa.oz.au/DOD/k95r12.html, Directorate of Public Relations, Department of Defence, Canberra, August - September 1995.

14.   'ADF-Indonesian training', *Jane's Defence Weekly*, 9 September 1995, p. 20.

15.   Desmond Ball, *The Political-Security Dimension of Australia and the Asia/Pacific Region*, paper prepared for conference on 'Australia and Indonesia: Diverse Culture, Converging Interests', Jakarta, July 1994, p. 31.

16.   Graeme Cheeseman, *The Search for Self-reliance: Australian Defence since Vietnam*, Longman Cheshire, 1993, p. 160. For another critical discussion of Australian defence policy, see Gary Brown, *Australia's Security: Issues for the New Century*, Australian Defence Studies Centre, 1994.

17.   *Defending Australia*, op cit, p. 87.

18.   Gareth Evans and Bruce Grant, op cit, p. 328.

19.   quoted in Desmond Ball, *The Political-Security Dimension of Australia and the Asia/Pacific Region*, op cit, p. 2.

20.   Philip Methven, *The Five Power Defence Arrangements and Military Cooperation Among the ASEAN States*, Canberra Papers on Strategy and Defence Number 92, Strategic and Defence Studies Centre, Australian National University, 1992, pp. 128-129. Methven reports on a series of interviews in Jakarta in mid-1990 in which a number of respondents expressed similar concerns. See also Graeme Cheeseman, op cit, pp. 150-151.

Notes continued

21. Gareth Evans and Bruce Grant, op cit, p. 188.

22. Desmond Ball, *The Political-Security Dimension of Australia and the Asia/Pacific Region*, op cit, pp. 21-22.

23. 'Keating justifies defence pact with Jakarta', *Straits Times*, 16 December 1995; Michael Richardson, 'Putting a 'Building Block' of Asian Security in Place', *International Herald Tribune*, 18 December 1995; 'Hands Across the Timor Sea', *The Economist*, 23 December 1995/ 5 January 1996, p. 87.

24. Gregor Ferguson, 'Indonesia's Australia Accord May Boost US Link', *Defense News*, 18/24 December 1995, p. 21.

25. Michael Richardson, op cit, p. 1.

26. Gregor Ferguson, op cit, p. 3.

27. Desmond Ball, *The Political-Security Dimension of Australia and the Asia/Pacific Region*, op cit, p. 31.

28. 'Keating spurns Timor refugees', *Guardian*, 11 October 1995; 'Australia and Indonesia', *The Economist*, 4 November 1995.

CHAPTER 6

The Regional Security Dialogue

'International relations in Asia today, to a large extent, consist of a set of mirrors reflecting the Association of South-East Asian Nations. As more countries and organisations find they must take ASEAN into account in their foreign policy planning, the result is the 'ASEANization' of Asian regional cooperation.'[1]

I   New Roles for ASEAN

In response to the new challenges facing the region, the period since 1992 has seen a process of rapid change in the security institutions of the region: a process that has not yet run its course. As in Europe, the end of the Cold War has meant that old certainties have been removed and the clear dividing lines of the past - between communist and non-communist in particular - no longer have the same significance. In Asia as in Europe, debates on the role and membership of institutions provide both an insight into, and a reflection of, processes of realignment that are far from over.

The end of the Cold War has seen both of ASEAN's previous main security roles called into question. The end of internal insurgency in Malaysia and Thailand has made ASEAN cooperation against this threat much less important. Vietnamese withdrawal from Cambodia, culminating in UN-supervised elections in May 1993, has also removed the Vietnamese threat as a unifying factor.

ASEAN's response to its new circumstances began at its fourth summit meeting, held in Singapore in January 1992, within a few months of the signing of the Paris peace agreements on Cambodia. At this meeting, ASEAN finally removed the taboo on open discussions of security matters which it had operated during the Cold War. As a consequence, the subsequent meeting of ASEAN Foreign Ministers in Manila in July 1992 was able to issue an ASEAN 'Declaration on the South China Sea', which urged the 'necessity to resolve all sovereignty and jurisdictional issues pertaining to the South China Sea by peaceful means, without resort to force'.[2] This was the first time that a security issue had been placed formally on ASEAN's agenda.

In addition, the Singapore summit adopted a proposal for the establishment of an ASEAN Free Trade Area (AFTA) within fifteen years. Subsequently overshadowed by the agreements to set up the World Trade Organisation (WTO) and the Asia Pacific Economic Cooperation (APEC) process, the AFTA agreement was nevertheless a significant indication of the increasing willingness of ASEAN members to deepen their economic integration.

Thirdly, a number of steps were taken to strengthen ASEAN institutionally. The position of the Secretary-General was upgraded to the same status as a Minister, allowing attendance at high-level political meetings for the first time. The Secretariat budget and personnel were increased. In addition, it was decided to institutionalise the ASEAN Summit of heads of government to regular meetings every three years.

Finally, it was decided to intensify 'external' security dialogues on political and security matters through the ASEAN-PMC mechanism: a decision that led directly to the decision of the ASEAN Post Ministerial Conference in July 1993 to establish the ASEAN Regional Forum.

On the military side, progress towards greater cooperation was more gradual. In the early 1990s, some commentators - anxious that ASEAN might lose its way in the wake of the Cold War - floated ideas for an ASEAN 'Defence Community' or military pact. In each case, however, these proposals failed to gain widespread support from ASEAN governments and were soon dropped.[3] In part, the failure to make progress on such ideas reflected the serious differences in security perceptions, and the continuing mistrust, between ASEAN members. But the determination that ASEAN's new emphasis on security should not be seen as the first step towards the creation of an alliance was also a result of an anxiety not to be seen as contributing to a new polarisation of the region: this time between China and ASEAN rather than between Vietnam and ASEAN. ASEAN political cohesion meant that the possibility of joint military action could not be ruled out in future. But there was widespread agreement that the formation of an ASEAN military block, even if it could overcome intra ASEAN suspicions, would reduce rather than increase the chances of a peaceful management of disputes with China.

Human rights and the future of ASEAN

Even as ASEAN moved to place security on its agenda, its leaders were anxious to emphasise their continuing belief that security could not be defined purely in military terms. The 'resilience' and security of the states and peoples of South-East Asia depended on mutual understanding and dialogue over a broad range of issues: social, economic, cultural, ideological. ASEAN's success in its first twenty years had been possible, it was argued, by its institutionalisation of a multi-layered dialogue involving a wide variety of actors and issue areas. In particular, advocates of the concept of 'comprehensive security' emphasised that regional security depended above all on individual states achieving political stability, economic development and national unity. Only if states were secure could the region be secure.[4]

While accepting the intimate connection between internal political stability and regional security, however, ASEAN members have always been anxious to reject any direct connection between democracy and peace. They argue that it takes time for new states to develop politically, and often emphasise the particular problems of nation-building in multicultural societies. When pressed by Western countries, they complain of Western arrogance and evoke the principle of non-interference in internal affairs.

ASEAN leaders' rejection of Western interference in their internal affairs stems in part from a determination to avoid dominance by any outside power. Yet it is accompanied by an awareness - not least in the 'comprehensive security' concept - that national political development and regional security are inextricably linked. Moreover, there are increasing signs that ASEAN itself may be placing greater emphasis on human rights in its agenda. The process of democratisation in most ASEAN members has advanced over the last decade, with multi-party elections now the norm in the Philippines, Thailand, Singapore, and Malaysia. The extent of press freedom varies, and only the Philippines and Thailand have seen a peaceful transition of power between parties. Moreover, the armed forces continue to play a major role in politics in Thailand and, to a lesser extent, some of the other countries. But no large-scale repression now takes place in these four countries, and the prospects for further political liberalisation appear good.

As the 'ASEAN Way' has increasingly become one of semi-democracy or soft authoritarianism, ASEAN itself may have become less tolerant of regimes that are more oppressive. The support given by ASEAN leaders to Philippines President Aquino in 1987, when faced with the possibility of a military coup, illustrated not only support for a sitting leader but support for a civilian democratic leader. Even more clearly, ASEAN was united in opposing the military regime in Myanmar for its gross violations of human rights, and in urging it to release the winner of the 1988 elections, Aung San Suu Kyi. Their methods tended to be more those of 'constructive engagement' than of ostracism. But their objective was, nevertheless, clear.

ASEAN leaders remain more reluctant to take action on human rights issues within their own ranks, not least because ASEAN's biggest member state is also its worst human rights offender. But human rights in Indonesia is a continuing topic of concern and discussion, both in the mass media and within the political classes of the region. And the balance of ASEAN opinion seems attracted by the idea of taking a 'middle way' or compromise between Western advocates of universal democratisation and those who argue that abuses of human rights, no matter how serious, are not a matter of international concern. For example, Jusuf Wanandi, a highly influential Indonesian academic, has argued for ASEAN to take a more pro-active role in fostering this 'Third Way' concept of human rights in the region:

> 'All ASEAN countries face the same major challenge: they are searching for a political system that will most appropriately maintain their values amidst global developments .... The ASEAN countries will succeed in meeting these challenges only if they develop forms of government that meet the demands of openness while maintaining a sufficient degree of stability.
>
> Human rights is one field in which the ASEAN countries can consult each other. ASEAN-ISIS has also proposed the establishment of an ASEAN Human Rights Committee .... Such consultation and cooperation aims to improve human rights policies and the development of democracy in ASEAN.'[5]

If the process of democratisation continues in the majority of ASEAN countries, the debate may evolve further. Even as the norm of non-interference remains in place, the pressures of competitive party politics and free mass media may make the more democratic countries of the region less tolerant of human rights abuses in neighbouring states.

Whether such debates will provide a source for rejuvenation or disintegration within ASEAN remains to be seen. It is clear, however, that the 'comprehensive security' of the region will depend as much on the political evolution of the region's states - not least Indonesia - as it will on dialogues limited to weapons and territorial disputes. The latter will remain important, but a full understanding of regional security requires that military security is viewed in a wider political context.

II ASEAN's expansion

With the end of the Cold War, the division of South-East Asia into two antagonistic blocs ended. The cessation of Soviet economic aid, together with the launch of its own economic reform programme, led Vietnam to make a radical reassessment of its international alignment. In 1992, it signed ASEAN's Treaty of Amity and Cooperation, and launched a campaign to end the country's diplomatic isolation. The campaign came to fruition in 1995, when the Vietnamese government was finally recognised by the US and accepted as a full member of ASEAN.

There is some concern that Vietnamese membership may provide a challenge to ASEAN cohesiveness, bringing an avowedly communist state into an organisation whose existing governments are still instinctively anti-Communist. Some fear that Vietnam could swing ASEAN to a more overtly anti-China stance, both as a result of historical antipathies and because of current disputes between the two states in the South China Sea. Finally, there is some doubt as to whether Vietnam will have sufficient resources to play its full part in ASEAN's numerous meetings and dialogues.

Yet, despite these concerns, the ASEAN consensus appears to be that Vietnam's membership is also an opportunity to influence the direction of its development in ways that encourage it to play a constructive role as a member of the regional community. The recent experience of a Vietnamese threat reinforces the importance of a future Vietnam having a stake in regional security and stability. By welcoming Vietnam, and in particular helping it in its drive for economic development, the rest of ASEAN can help prevent the (now remote) possibility of its reversion to North Korea-style isolation.

Beyond Vietnam, it has been agreed that ASEAN should expand to include Cambodia, Laos and Myanmar. Laos signed the Treaty of Amity in 1992, and was a founding member of the ASEAN Regional Forum in 1994. Cambodia only became an ASEAN observer in 1995, in part because King Sihanouk had discouraged Cambodian membership of ASEAN. With the King's ill-health increasingly taking him out of decision-making, however, the Cambodian attitude has now become more positive.[6] Speaking at the December 1995 ASEAN summit in Bangkok, officials said that both Laos and Cambodia could become full ASEAN members as early as 1997.[7]

Myanmar remains the most problematic possible ASEAN member. In recognition of the release of Aung San Suu Kyi from detention, it was allowed to accede to the Treaty of Amity and Cooperation in July 1995: an essential prelude to full ASEAN membership. Moreover, ASEAN businesses are prominent in the increasing flow of foreign investment into the country. Without further moves towards a reconciliation between the junta and the democratic opposition, however, there may not be a consensus within ASEAN to grant Myanmar full membership.

As in the case of the formative years of ASEAN in the late 1960s, the process of ASEAN expansion in the 1990s is being driven above all by considerations of security in a broad sense. ASEAN is anxious to extend the process of economic modernisation to its neighbours in the belief that the replication of ASEAN's own economic success will strengthen the resilience of the whole region.

Moreover, increased resilience within South-East Asia states helps reduce the opportunities for larger outside powers - such as China, Japan and the US - to dominate the region as they have done in the past. ASEAN membership is already helping to provide Vietnam with a means of avoiding a close alignment with any single major power, and it may in future help to provide Myanmar with an alternative to its current close alignment with China. In this way, the expansion of ASEAN to the whole of South-East Asia is in the security interests of both existing ASEAN members and of new members that wish to retain freedom from outside dominance.

III   The ASEANization of East Asia

ASEAN's continuing importance has perhaps been seen most clearly in the institutionalisation of a security dialogue for the Asia Pacific region as a whole, under the auspices of the ASEAN Regional Forum (ARF). The idea of a regional security forum was first suggested by Soviet leader Mikhail Gorbachov in a speech in Vladivostock in 1986, where he argued for a 'Pacific conference along the lines of the Helsinki conference.'[8] But the initiative was quickly denounced by the US, which feared that it would allow the Soviet Union a forum in which to press for arms control in the Pacific, where the US had unchallenged naval superiority. In reality, as long as the Cold War continued, any security dialogue in Asia was bound to be subordinate to the overarching superpower confrontation. It was not until the end of the Cold War that real possibilities opened up for a more multilateral approach to regional security dialogue.

The initial, and indirect, move towards an institutionalised regional security dialogue was the November 1989 founding, at a meeting in Canberra, of the Asia-Pacific Economic Cooperation (APEC) process. APEC's agenda was limited to trade and other economic issues. Nevertheless, as well as preparing the ground for other multilateral initiatives by its very existence, it also established two of the key principles on which the subsequent security dialogue would be based.

First, it institutionalised the tendency to privilege the concept of the 'Asia-Pacific' as a region, compared with rival possibilities (such as 'Asia' or 'East Asia' or (the recent Australian favourite) 'East Asian Hemisphere'). Initially, APEC included only Western-oriented countries (the six ASEAN countries, Australia, Canada, Japan, New Zealand, South Korea, and the US). But, in keeping with the logic of the 'Asia-Pacific' concept, it was expanded in 1991 to include China, together with the separate 'economies' of Taiwan and Hong Kong. It thus signalled an acceptance of a concept of region that saw both South-East Asia and North-East Asia as forming part of a single security complex, joined together by the common importance of China to both. By the addition of the word 'Pacific' to the more restrictive 'Asia', it also allowed four 'Western' countries - Australia, New Zealand, Canada and the US - to be included.[9]

Second, in a precedent that would prove of considerable importance for ARF, ASEAN succeeded in obtaining key organisational concessions in order to allay its fears of being swamped by the region's major powers. For example, it was agreed that APEC's secretariat (established in 1993) would be based in Singapore, and that ASEAN would provide the Chair for APEC Senior Officials and Ministerial Meetings every second year.[10]

Moreover, as in the case of ASEAN, APEC has been used to demonstrate the success of an evolutionary and non-confrontational 'Asian' approach to multilateral dialogue. It has spawned a growing number of technical working groups, covering issues such as standardising customs procedures. It has proven to be key forum for co-ordinating trade liberalisation, both on a regional and global level. It has established an annual summit of APEC leaders, which is already being favourably compared with the G7 summit of the world's most developed economies, and which inevitably - especially in bilateral discussions - provides an opportunity for bilateral discussion of both security and economic issues.

APEC is not a security forum. Yet many of the governments involved see it as playing an important role in regional security in a broad sense, most notably by cementing China's engagement with the outside world. At the November 1995 Tokyo summit, there were even suggestions (for example from US Defense Secretary William Perry) that APEC should take on a more explicit security role: signalling a continuing debate on the wisdom of having two separate Asia-Pacific organisations for security and economics when most of the countries involved accept that the two are so closely intertwined.[11]

For the foreseeable future, it seems unlikely that APEC will take on security issues, not least because its membership includes Taiwan (represented as an 'economy'), whose competence to speak on security matters would not be accepted by China. Moreover, with its already formidable agenda of trade liberalisation and its diverse membership of 18, APEC is not short of agenda items. Simply in terms of avoiding organisational overload, it may make sense to have some division of labour.

Instead of leading to an expansion of APEC's remit, therefore, its initial success helped pave the way for the establishment of a parallel security mechanism. Following the success of APEC, Australian Foreign Minister Gareth Evans, in remarks made at the ASEAN Post Ministerial Conference in Jakarta in July 1990, suggested the idea of a Conference on Security and Cooperation in Asia (CSCA), drawing explicitly on a parallel with the CSCE process in Europe. After vigorous criticism from both the US and Asian countries, Evans was careful to qualify his remarks, arguing that:

> 'if the idea of a 'CSCA' is to have any application, it is not so
> much as an institutional prescription, but as a metaphor for a
> process of dialogue and mutual confidence-building - leading
> to the gradual development of a sense of regional community,
> based in turn on a sense of shared security interests.'[12]

The criticism of Evan's proposal was more a reaction against importing a model for regional security dialogue than against the idea itself. Over the year that followed, a group of ASEAN strategic studies institutes began to develop their own proposal, but one based on the ASEAN, not the European, experience. The result was a memorandum, agreed in June

1991, that recommended that ASEAN take the initiative in establishing an Asia-Pacific Political Dialogue.[13]

Partly as a consequence of this work, ASEAN's 1991 Post-Ministerial Meeting agreed the first step towards a broader regional dialogue by inviting Russia, Vietnam and China to attend as observers. Both the Philippines and Thailand held informal seminars in 1991 involving participants from ASEAN, the Dialogue Partners, Laos, Vietnam, Myanmar, the then Soviet Union and China.[14] The Singapore summit of ASEAN in 1992 moved the process further forward by accepting that security fell explicitly within ASEAN's remit.

One of the most public indications that proposals for Asia-Pacific security dialogue now had high-level support in ASEAN governments came in a widely-discussed initiative launched by Malaysian Defence Minister Datuk Seri Najib Tun Razak at a defence conference in Australia in April 1992. Najib suggested that Malaysia was willing to host the first of a proposed series of Asia-Pacific Security Dialogue meetings, to which each of the countries of the region could send a delegation comprising representatives of their security agencies, from both the military and civilian organisations. Drawing on models of 'cooperative security' and 'common security' as well as 'comprehensive security', he proposed that such dialogues would perform the function of CBM's for the region, reducing suspicions and misperceptions. The initial reception to Najib's initiative was rather cool, apparently in part because it was taken without prior consultation with other ASEAN members.[15] But the 'Najib talks' went ahead, being held in Kuala Lumpur in June 1993. The initiative undoubtedly contributed to the momentum already developing within ASEAN in support of a wider regional dialogue.

As ASEAN began to move towards support of an Asia-Pacific security dialogue, supported by Australia and Japan, the attitudes of the region's two biggest powers - the US and China - also began to change. ASEAN support for multilateral dialogue led to a softening of the previously hard-line bilateralist approach of the Bush administration in the US; and the trend towards an acceptance of multilateralism accelerated with President Clinton's assumption of office. In May 1993, Winston Lord told the ASEAN Senior Officials' Meeting in Singapore of the US's support for a more multilateral approach to regional security.[16]

Because of its sheer size (two thirds of the total population of East Asia), China has traditionally been sceptical of regional multilateralism. From its point of view, it is more straightforward to conduct separate bilateral negotiations with neighbours that are invariably much smaller than itself than to risk being in a minority of one in a larger forum. Given its knowledge of regional attitudes, moreover, Chinese leaders feared that the proposed forum might easily become a means of restraining its own freedom of manoeuvre, without offering anything of substance in return.

Given these reservations, China might have been tempted to try to delay the establishment of a new regional organisation more or less indefinitely. By building on its existing Post-Ministerial Meetings framework, however, ASEAN made sure China did not have this option. If China had refused to take part, the process of regional dialogue could have gone ahead without it (as APEC did in its first two years), risking the very polarisation of the region that China wanted to avoid. Consequently, albeit reluctantly, China added its support for ASEAN's proposals.

With both the US and China on board, the stage was set for the announcement at the 1993 ASEAN Ministerial Meeting that an ASEAN Regional Forum would be established the next year. It would bring together ASEAN's 6 members with its 7 dialogue partners, 2 consultative partners (Russia and China), and 3 observers (Vietnam, Laos and Papua New Guinea). It would cover every aspect of regional security, not only those of direct concern to ASEAN members themselves.

The first ASEAN Regional Forum was held in Bangkok, Thailand on 25 July 1994. As the first of its kind, the meeting served in large measure as an 'icebreaker.' Nevertheless, the Chairman's statement did include some specific commitments. Moreover, as Chapter 7 will discuss, the meeting's endorsement of the United Nations Register of Conventional Arms does seem to have helped encourage ARF participants to take part in this global transparency measure.

True to the precedent established by both ASEAN and APEC, the second Forum, held in Bandar Seri Begawan, Brunei on 1 August 1995, proved more substantive. The number of participants increased to 19, with the addition of Cambodia. Participants agreed to a Chairman's statement urging all South China Sea claimants to abide by the principles in ASEAN's 1992 declaration; urged a renewed North-South dialogue in Korea; and agreed that 'those countries who plan to conduct further nuclear tests were called upon by all other ARF member states to bring an immediate end to such testing.'[17]

The ARF process is still in the early stages of the development of confidence-building measures, and it is therefore far from clear how far it will be able to proceed on the basis of consensual decision-making. Already, however, there are some signs of progress on the items specifically identified. Of ARF's 19 members, only 3 (Brunei, Cambodia and Laos) have not submitted replies to the Register in 1995.[18] Moreover, the recent publication of statements on defence policy by Thailand, Indonesia and China, suggests that on this issue progress is also being made. As in the case of ASEAN itself, it is not always easy to identify whether quiet diplomacy is producing results or not. What is clear is that much more remains to be done.

IV   ASEAN and ARF

One of the most significant aspects of ARF is the way in which it has given ASEAN a role in a regionwide security dialogue that is disproportionate to the relatively modest economic and military weight of its members. First, ARF has followed ASEAN in adopting the principle of equal representation of all member states, large or small. Any form of special representation (or 'Security Council') for major powers has been ruled out. Small and medium powers such as Singapore, Australia and Malaysia have as much right to be heard as the US, China or Japan. Second, because it has developed as an offshoot of ASEAN's own meetings, ASEAN's leading role has been recognised. Thus the 1995 ARF agreed that:

> 'A successful ARF requires the active, full and equal participation and cooperation of all participants. However, ASEAN undertakes the obligation to be the primary driving force.'[19]

Thus, the annual ARF meetings are to be held in an ASEAN capital, and will be attended by ASEAN's own Secretary-General. The ASEAN country that acts as the chair and host for the annual ARF meeting will also provide the secretariat for the previous year. (Indonesia fulfils this role for 1995-96). All ARF working groups will be jointly chaired by one ASEAN state and one non ASEAN state. Not least, the very name of the Forum emphasises the central role which ASEAN continues to play.

Finally, even without such institutional privileges, ASEAN's own coherence, as well as its experience and competence in its own dialogue process, provides it with advantages which the rest of the region - with the possible exception of Australia - simply does not possess. There is no North-East Asian sub-regional security dialogue to balance ASEAN's influence, with military to military relations even between South Korea and Japan (both long-standing US allies) still underdeveloped.

ASEAN's leading role, if not handled with sensitivity, could be counterproductive. Some North-East Asian participants in the ARF process have already raised concerns on this point; and there must be a worry that ARF may lose its appeal to Asia's major powers if it is seen to be too dominated by ASEAN's own agenda. On the other hand, if the result of this dissatisfaction was simply to spur efforts to institutionalise a North-East Asian security dialogue, perhaps initially involving ARF participants China, Japan, Russia, South Korea, and the US, it could complement and strengthen a region-wide process in much the same way as already occurs with ASEAN.[20]

A different, and to some extent contradictory, concern has been expressed by some ASEAN commentators, who have suggested that the emergence of an Asia-Pacific identity, through both APEC and ARF, could undermine ASEAN's claim to being the primary focus of collective identity for its members.[21] Yet this may underestimate the extent to which some ASEAN members already have closer relations to external powers than others. Moreover, even ASEAN's largest members know that individually they are dwarfed in power resources by Asia's major powers. Far from undermining ASEAN, therefore, the experience of ARF may reinforce the message that ASEAN members are more likely to be able to protect their interests in the region by acting together rather than by acting separately.

ASEAN's influence on ARF has been demonstrated very clearly in ARF's adoption of a style of working similar to that of ASEAN itself. It works to prevent conflict through constructive engagement and informal consensus building rather than through the more formal, and goal-oriented, methods seen as being characteristic of Western-style negotiations. The governments taking part are 'participants' rather than members, its name does not mention its purpose (security), and it calls itself a 'Forum' rather than the more formal 'Conference' or 'Organisation' titles used in other regions of the world.

Moreover, as in ASEAN itself, the annual meetings of foreign ministers, although important, are seen as the culmination of a less public process, rather than as a setting for headline-grabbing negotiations. The key to the success or failure of ARF lies instead in its ability to sustain a growing number and variety of institutionalised dialogues below the Ministerial level. These dialogues, it is hoped, will allow ARF participants new opportunities to air their concerns to each other out of the glare of publicity and before they develop into open disagreements. By binding participants into a network of mutual commitments and reassurances, they help to establish norms of acceptable behaviour.

V   ARF membership

One of the indicators of ARF's success is that others want to join, including India, France and the UK (the latter two want to join in their own right, rather than being represented by the EU). The 1995 ARF meeting deferred consideration of the issue of membership by asking the next Chairman, Indonesia, to develop criteria for membership in time for consideration at the 1996 ARF.

The most obvious candidates for ARF membership in the near future are Myanmar and North Korea: the former because it has already taken the first steps towards becoming a member of ASEAN, the latter because its participation is a vital part of any North-East Asian security dialogue. Beyond these two, the future size and shape of ARF is still unclear. A comparison of APEC and ARF, both of which are ostensibly designed to cover the 'Asia-Pacific Region', reveals significant differences in the composition of their memberships. The explanation for the exclusion of Taiwan and Hong Kong from ARF - Chinese opposition - is clear, and will in the case of Hong Kong be largely irrelevant after 1997. A case can also be made for the exclusion of APEC members Chile and Mexico (and potential member Peru) from ARF on the grounds that they have no significant security interests in the (Western) Asia-Pacific. But the exclusion of Vietnam from APEC membership (it was even refused observer status at the 1994 Jakarta summit) is likely to be increasingly hard to sustain given its membership of ASEAN. Indeed by 1995 many APEC members were already said to have expressed their support for eventual Vietnamese membership of APEC.[22]

Nor is it clear why, other than as a result of historical accident, the EU is a member of the main forum for security dialogue (ARF) but not the forum for economic cooperation (APEC). The main competence of the EU is economics and trade, rather than military security (thus helping to explain the applications for ARF membership from the UK and France); and Europe's main interest in East Asia is also economic rather than military. If the EU can be considered part of the Asia-Pacific for the purposes of a security dialogue, therefore, it is not clear why the same cannot be said for economics. Fears of a further dilution of the Asia-Pacific concept may lead to this anomaly being resolved by the EU's progressive marginalisation from the security dialogue rather than by its inclusion in APEC. While such anomalies exist, however, they point to the fact that the Asia-Pacific concept remains a fluid and evolving one.

Perhaps the hardest case may be India, Asia's second power in terms of population. Its economic isolation from East Asia is declining as it carries out an economic reform programme of its own. Its relationship with China (which has improved in the 1990s) is widely acknowledged as being of critical importance to regional security. Not least, the direction of Indian security policy is of direct interest to several ASEAN members, and is likely to become more so with the accession of Myanmar.

As a significant step towards bringing India into an ARF-style regional security dialogue, Australia hosted a meeting of seven Indian Ocean states (including Australia, India, Singapore and South Africa) in Perth in June 1995. South Africa insisted that membership of the International Forum of the Indian Ocean Rim (Ifior) would have to be expanded if it were to continue; and there was some sensitivity towards Australia's insistence that discussions should include security matters. India itself is sensitive to taking part in any Indian Ocean process which it has not iself initiated. But the countries present did agree to establish a series of working groups on trade-related matters, as well as a series of 'second track' discussions on security and social issues.[23]

Until recently, direct Indian involvement in ARF has been stalled by existing participants' reluctance to be drawn into the intricacies of conflicts between and within South Asian countries. It might be difficult, it was argued, to admit India into ARF without also accepting the case for membership for Bangladesh and Pakistan as well. Even if this did not occur, ARF might find itself drawn into discussions on further issues - such as Kashmir - at a time when its agenda is already an ambitious one.

Despite these objections, however, India is reported to have become a full ASEAN 'dialogue partner' in late 1995:[24] apparently entitling it to become ARF's 20th participating state. It remains to be seen how this decision will influence the direction and priorities of the Forum as a whole.

Since the concrete obligations of membership are few (in contrast to the trade liberalisation commitments made by APEC members), it might be argued that the exact membership of ARF does not matter much, except insofar it leads to ever larger meetings of officials. Yet this would be to understate two crucial aspects of the symbolism of regional self-definition in international politics. First, those countries that are accepted into the regional community, in this case the 'Asia-Pacific', are more likely to be seen by others (and even by themselves) as sharing the characteristics of the region as a whole and as being part of a regional system or model. Potential aspirants to Asia-Pacific status may therefore hope to gain from the reflected glory of the rest of the region, especially in the field of economic development.

Second, it is in the nature of a regional community of states that some states are defined as outsiders. Relations with non-members need not be antagonistic. Yet the more that states develop special relationships of consultation and common security with their regional partners, the more likely it is that they will also seek to develop common policies for their relations with states outside the region. As ASEAN developed in internal cohesion, its members were able to use this to more effectively bargain with Japan, the US and others. APEC has proven to be an important instrument for orchestrating its members' views for global trade negotiations, not least in relations with the EU. If ARF gains in strength and cohesion, it too may find in time a need to complement its efforts at community-building within its membership with means of relating those efforts with the rest of the world.

Such a question is not of immediate concern for a process still at its initial stages. Moreover, it is in the nature of the style of working adopted by ARF that its role and boundaries are more likely to evolve slowly than as a result of a single definitive decision. The resolution of current uncertainty over its membership will, however, provide important clues not only to how ARF sees its own future role, but also to how the concept of Asia-Pacific itself is developing in a world where the familiar divisions of the past have disappeared.

VI   The Second Track

It is increasingly recognised that transnational 'epistemic' communities of experts can, in some circumstances, have a significant impact on government policies, contributing to the development and acceptance of new concepts and proposals.[25] Much of the work on such communities has focused on the rich industrial democracies, where governments are seen as being relatively open to non-governmental inputs. But a recent study by Matthew Evangelista suggests that 'policy entrepreneurs' can also, in certain conditions, influence policy in less open societies. He shows how, at a critical juncture in the evolution of Soviet arms control policy in the late 1980s, a transnational community of Soviet and Western experts played an important role in shaping new directions in Soviet policy through their access to Mikhail Gorbachov.[26] The Soviet bureaucracy's failure to provide a wide enough range of policy options meant that, once the top leadership had accepted that 'something had to be done,' it looked to outside experts (from both inside and outside the Soviet Union) to contribute ideas for new directions in policy.

The experience of the recent debate in East Asia on the possibility of confidence-building and transparency measures suggests that here too non-government actors can contribute significantly to the shaping of security policies. Perhaps of even greater significance, they have had a key role in the process whereby new concepts of what is meant by 'security' and 'region' are accepted, and even taken by granted: thus changing the parameters within which specific policy discussions are held.[27]

ASEAN societies are not, for the most part, liberal democracies on the Western model. But nor are they Soviet-style totalitarian regimes. As part of their process of rapid modernisation over the last two decades, all have experienced a rapid growth in their links with the rest of the world: though business links, education, tourism, and exposure to mass media. The ASEAN process has itself contributed to the growth of international exchange between its members, and has involved a flourishing of ASEAN non-governmental dialogues.[28] The increasing openness of the processes of economic and social change in the region also mean that new generations of officials and politicians are increasingly willing to accept the value of learning from others, both from their counterparts in other ASEAN countries and from broader regional communities of experts.

The influence of non-governmental experts in policymaking is also enhanced, in some cases, by the relatively small number of government officials with the background and experience necessary to engage in the international processes to which their governments are increasingly committed.[29] As a consequence, non-governmental policy entrepreneurs are often called upon by governments to contribute to the preparation of key ASEAN and ARF meetings, and even to act as advisors at the meetings themselves.

Through the 1980s, non governmental organisations had an important role to play in building a transnational network devoted to promoting the idea of regional economic cooperation. Of particular significance was the Pacific Economic Cooperation Council (PECC), founded in 1980 as a result of an Australia/Japanese initiative, and often seen as establishing the basis for the later formation of APEC.[30]

The influence of non-government actors on the security agenda was more restricted until recently. Partly this may have been because, in contrast to the role of private businesses in second track dialogue on economic and trade matters, no similarly autonomous, but powerful, constituency existed in the area of security matters. Of greater importance, however, was that, for most of the first twenty years of ASEAN's existence, security was primarily an internal matter for its member states. There was some cooperation between governments and security services in efforts to address these internal security problems. But the role of non-government actors in these cooperation efforts seems to have been relatively limited.[31]

As a result of recent changes in the security situation in ASEAN states, however, there has been a spreading awareness in defence and foreign policy elites of the regional dimension of their national security policies. In seeking to respond to the new issues which this new dimension has thrown up, governments have often been willing to draw on the work of policy entrepreneurs to help them formulate policy. For example, non-governmental experts have been drawn upon for advice on the contents of Defence Policy Statements and to help formulate responses to transparency and confidence-building proposals made by other ASEAN and ARF participants. Their usefulness to their national governments has been enhanced by their wide range of personal contacts throughout the region: an asset that is of particular importance in the sort of informal dialogue that plays such an important role in the evolution of policy agendas in ASEAN-type processes.

One of the most notable regional examples of the influence of non-government experts in shaping the policy debate is in Australia. Many of the foreign and security policy initiatives of the Labour government that came to power in 1983 were closely associated with academics based at the Australian National University (ANU) in Canberra. Stuart Harris, a professor at ANU concerned with analysing the intersection of political and economic policy, was appointed secretary of the Department of Foreign Affairs, and oversaw its integration with the department of trade in 1987.[32] Academics such as Andrew Mack, founding Head in 1984 of ANU's government-financed Peace Research Centre and subsequently Head of its Department of International Relations, have developed close links with the Ministry of Foreign Affairs and Trade. When the government wanted to conduct a fundamental review of defence policy, it turned to Paul Dibb, then working at ANU's Strategic and Defence Studies Centre (SDSC), to produce a Report, which was in turn the subject of important debates within SDSC and a wider academic community.[33] The SDSC continues to play a key role in the education and training of military officers, not only from Australia but also from the region as a whole.

The role of Malaysia's policy communities in the process of regional integration is disproportionate to both its size and economic and political importance, according to a recent study by David Camroux.[34] Out of an estimated total of twenty-six policy bodies and research institutes in existence in 1993, the most influential and well-connected remains the Institute of Strategic and International Studies. Founded in 1983 by Noordin Soopie, and now hosting a total of fifty researchers, ISIS work covers a wide range of domestic, economic and foreign policy issues. Noordin Soopie is reported to have close links to top Malaysian government leaders, including Prime Minister Mahathir. As well as being ISIS Director, he is chairman of PECC, Malaysian representative on the Eminent Persons Group in APEC, and Malaysian representative on the CSCAP Steering Committee.[35]

Through the deployment of its considerable financial and human resources, ISIS (Malaysia) has been able to play a key role in the establishment of a 'second track' dialogue on security issues. In 1987 it initiated the annual Asia-Pacific Roundtable, which has since become the largest dialogue event in the region. In 1988, it played a leading role in the formation of ASEAN-ISIS, a grouping of strategic studies institutes from all ASEAN member states except Brunei. ISIS (Malaysia) provides the secretariat for ASEAN-ISIS, as well as for the more recently formed Council for Security Cooperation in the Asia-Pacific (CSCAP).

In 1993, two new thinktanks on security issues were established in Kuala Lumpur. The Malaysian Institute of Maritime Affairs (MIMA) has a particular interest in developments in the South China Sea, and both its Director (B. A. Hamzah) and its Research Director (J. N. Mak) have written extensively on confidence-building and security in the region. The Malaysian Strategic Research Centre, headed by Abdul Razak Abdullah Baginda, has former defence Minister Najib as its chairman, and has developed close links with government. In addition, Professor Johan Saravanamuttu has established a Peace Research Centre at the Universiti Sains Malaysia in Penang; and Professor Zakaria Haji Ahmad heads a Strategic and Studies Unit at the Universiti Kebangsan Malaysia, just outside Kuala Lumpur. Overall, the Malaysian strategic studies community remains relatively small. But recent years have seen it become increasingly pluralist in nature, and this trend seems likely to continue as new generations of scholars enter the field.

Indonesia has also played a central role in the development of regional second track dialogue, largely as a result of the work of its well-resourced Centre for Strategic and International Studies. A recent study suggests that CSIS's leading security specialist, Jusuf Wanandi, is 'one of the most pivotal policy entrepreneurs in the Asia-Pacific region'.[36] Wanandi played a particularly important role in the foundation of CSCAP, and is currently joint chair of that organisation.

Policy entrepreneurs also play an important role in other ASEAN countries. In Singapore, members of the Singapore Institute of International Affairs, the Institute of Policy Studies and the Institute of South-East Asian Studies all make an important contribution to the regional security dialogue. In Thailand and the Philippines respectively, the Institute for Security and International Studies (Chulalongkorn University) and the Institute for Strategic and Development Studies play leading roles in contributing to regional dialogue processes.

Policy institutes in China and Vietnam provide a significant contrast with those in ASEAN insofar as they are more clearly directly under the control of central government ministries or party apparatuses. Participation in regional dialogue activities is combined with advisory work for government, training courses for diplomats and the armed forces. Senior personnel are often drawn from, and return to, regular service in the Foreign Ministry.

Even in these cases, however, the increasingly popular practice of sending young researchers abroad for postgraduate education - to the US, Australia, Europe, or other Asian states - is increasing the ability of these institutes to contribute to regional dialogue in ways that go beyond the rhetoric that is often seen as characterising communist diplomacy. As these countries become more involved in dialogue processes, these institutes are likely to play an increasing role, both as more sophisticated exponents of their own governments' positions, and as interpreters of the perceptions of other countries for their own leaderships. Some of the excellent recent contributions to the regional security debate from scholars from these countries demonstrate very clearly that opportunities now exist, within limits, for a freer discussion of ideas than in the past.[37]

In communist countries, as indeed in some non-communist ones, it still remains to be seen how far participants in regional 'second track' processes have real influence on their national policies. Given the closeness of so many Australian and ASEAN participants to policy discussions in their own countries, however, it will be difficult for participants from communist states not to go at least some way to matching this if they are to be seen as making a serious effort to play a part in the process.

The Institutes and individuals involved in 'second track' dialogue on security issues in the Asia-Pacific should not, however, be seen as falling into the same category as the NGO's (non-governmental organisations) that play an increasing role in influencing policy debates on issues such as the environment and human rights. Such organisations exist in Asian countries, as well as in Western Asia-Pacific countries. In some cases - for example in relation to East Timor - they have had some success in mobilising support across national borders in favour of particular, and often awkward, demands on security policy-makers.

While many of those participating in the officially recognised 'second track' share the concerns of these 'grass roots' movements, however, their ability to publicise their concerns is limited by the norms of politeness, equality and solidarity that tend to inform relations between participants in both ASEAN itself and in unofficial, but officially sanctioned, dialogue processes. In contrast to those NGO's who derive their influence above all from their ability to mobilise public opinion behind a particular cause, and thus make things awkward for political leaders, those taking part in debates on regional security seek to influence policy debates behind-the-scenes through persuasion: effectively giving them a position of insiders or semi-insiders in the policy process itself.

This ambivalent positioning of security studies institutes clearly creates problems, especially if frank advice is tempered by a desire to retain favour and access. Yet in this respect, the position of ASEAN institutes may not be so different from that of Western strategic studies and arms control institutes, many of whom maintain extremely close links to governments and produce briefings for them. In the US, for example, many prominent policymakers have come from research institutes concerned with security issues (Defense Secretary Perry comes from Stanford University, Assistant Defense Secretary Nye from Harvard) and may return to them in future. The degree of autonomy does differ between different political systems, and is likely to be greater in countries with more pluralist overall political systems. But the difference between the position of second track participants in ASEAN and Western countries should not be oversimplified. Both face similar dilemmas in maintaining both their relationship with power and their distance from it.

ARF and CSCAP

The expansion of the regional security dialogue process in recent years has been so rapid in recent years that it is difficult even for participants to keep track of all the activities involved. A 1993 survey by Paul Evans discovered 20 separate channels for multilateral discussion of security issues in the Pacific.[38] The Australian Department of Foreign Affairs and Trade, in conjunction with the Strategic and Defence Studies Centre, has produced a calendar of Asia-Pacific regional security dialogue events which shows 89 such events taking place in the second half of 1995 alone.[39]

Of the many channels now open, one of the most important is the series of workshops on the South China Sea, hosted by Indonesia and involving primarily government participants 'in a personal capacity' together with selected academics. Issues are able to be discussed relatively frankly in this forum because governments can disregard the solutions proposed. And the process is currently the only place in which both China and Taiwan are engaged in discussion on security issues. Technical working groups have been established in scientific research, environmental protection, resource assessment and legal matters. There is no sign of a rapid move towards a multilateral solution. But it is hoped that the very existence of the process helps to defuse tension and can, over time, generate a constituency for a negotiated solution.[40]

In order to formalise the second track process as a whole, in June 1993 the leading ASEAN strategic studies institutes, together with institutes in Australia, Canada, South Korea, Japan, and the US, established a Council for Security Cooperation in Asia-Pacific (CSCAP). Modelled loosely on PECC (the second track organisation that plays an important role in supporting the APEC process), CSCAP is widely seen as 'one of the most important milestones in the development of institutionalized dialogue, consultation and cooperation in the Asia/Pacific region since the end of the Cold War.'[41] It has established four working groups charged by producing policy-oriented studies, one of which is currently studying possible CSBM's that might be adopted by ARF.

Although CSCAP sees itself as shadowing the ARF process and responding to requests made by its official committees, the countries represented in CSCAP are not the same as in ARF. There have been particularly difficult debates about whether individuals from Taiwanese institutes should be asked to take part. Those who support this argue that the Taiwanese question is clearly one of the key security issues in the region, and that China should accept that the participation of Taiwanese individuals 'in a personal capacity' in CSCAP should not be seen as in any way altering Taiwan's political status. At the time of writing, however, China was not convinced of this argument and was continuing to insist that it would refuse to take part if Taiwan were included.

As is to be expected for an organisation with links to the policy process, the makeup of the National Committees that together constitute CSCAP has in some countries been the subject of intense politicking. The balance between keeping the process manageable while allowing for a real diversity of views within countries has not always been an easy one. As Desmond Ball has observed:

> 'In many countries, there are personal animosities and institutional rivalries which are resulting in the exclusion of particular individuals, institutes or alternative perspectives from Member Committees. In some countries, governments have unabashedly linked the extent of their financial support and participation to their degree of control over their respective Committees. ... The corollary is also a major concern: it is likely that the strongest Member Committees will be those that toe their official government lines most closely. Unless great care is taken, the Member Committee structure might tend to entrench particular national political positions

> rather than provide a mechanism for frank and open dialogue,
> including dissentient views, about pan-regional issues.'[42]

The continuing relevance of the second track dialogue lies, not in the structural power of those concerned - which is limited - but in their intellectual creativity. The challenge for the individuals and institutes involved is thus how to balance the imperative of staying close to power, yet at the same time helping to move the debate forward by questioning aspects of existing policy and practice. The last five years have seen extraordinary successes as a result of the willingness of key individuals to push new ideas into the policy arena. But, as the debate moves on, the challenge for those involved in the second track process will be how to continue to be both innovative and influential.

Dialogue and Democracy

All governments are, to varying degrees, sensitive about suggestions that openness and accountability in security policy can be of confidence-building value. Even in democracies, national security bureaucracies tend to enjoy much greater autonomy of action from party political pressure than do their domestic policy counterparts. In regimes often seen as 'soft authoritarian', the limited latitude granted for public dissent on issues of social and economic policy is rarely extended to security issues. Few governments find it easy to reveal more information to their parliaments about what they are doing.

Nowhere is sensitivity on the matter of public accountability greater, both in supplier and recipient countries, than on issues surrounding the arms trade. Several of the scandals that have rocked the British government in recent years - including the BMARC exports of equipment to Iraq via Singapore, the 'Pergau Dam' affair, and the events surrounding the Scott inquiry - are a direct result of its attempts to cover up its involvement in the arms trade. Indonesia's import of second-hand German warships in 1993 prompted fierce domestic criticism in Indonesia itself, followed by the closure of several newspapers. A 1992 report on the corruption in the Thai military's procurement provoked fierce controversy in Thailand.[43]

Few would openly defend the practices exposed in these various incidents. Yet none would have seen the light of day without the access to information by non-governmental actors. Such actors also have a more general role in widening and democratising the security debate in their countries. They include a wide range of individuals and organisations, each with distinct roles and perspectives, ranging from campaigning groups 'on the outside' to 'semi-insiders' such as research institutes and former armed forces officers. Together they help promote a more vigorous policy debate which, in turn, helps improve wider regional security.

Finally, given the relationship between transparency and domestic governance, it will be particularly important to address the issue of the extent of civilian involvement in security dialogues. Some commentators have commented on the desirability of involving the military more centrally in the process of regional dialogue in the Asia Pacific, and there is much merit in this argument. Yet a process of dialogue dominated by military to military exchanges between countries where the military is already heavily involved in political and economic affairs is not unproblematic. As Desmond Ball has argued

> '(the) outcome could well be to further entrench the positions of military establishments not only relative to the other actors involved in their respective national security establishments (such as the foreign ministry) but also with respect to shaping the future course of security cooperation in the region. A CSBM process which led to stronger bonds amongst regional military leaders, particularly if unmatched by comparable progress in the political, economic and cultural spheres, would not be an unmixed blessing for the region.'[44]

VII   ARF and confidence-building measures

The last five years have already seen profound changes in the institutional architecture of regional security, with the expansion of ASEAN to include Vietnam and the inauguration of a region-wide security dialogue through ARF. At the beginning of the decade, ASEAN did not explicitly accept that it had a role in discussions of security matters. Now, in both the formal ARF committee structure and in the 'second track', detailed discussions are taking place on a wide range of regional security issues.

One of the areas in which there is hope of progress is in confidence building measures (CBM's). Much of the impetus for giving a high priority to the CBM agenda came from 'second track' bodies in ASEAN. Following their success in persuading their governments to establish the ASEAN Regional Forum, the ASEAN strategic studies institutes issued a joint memorandum in December 1993 entitled 'Confidence Building Measures in

South-East Asia.' In view of the new strategic and security situation in the region, they argued that:

> 'it has become imperative that confidence building measures be introduced into the region with greater vigour. CBM's possess a genuine promise for reducing the chances of unintended conflict and for improving the basic quality of a region's political environment. ... They basically aim at enhancing transparency between states. ... CBM's also seek to make explicit military intentions in order to promote confidence by increasing the flow of information to make relations more predictable, thereby reducing the chances of conflicts and surprise attacks.'[45]

The memorandum went on to argue that the two key variables that should underpin a CBM system are information exchange and operational constraints. With this in mind, it proposed a series of specific measures, including an expansion of existing ASEAN military exercises from a bilateral to a multilateral basis, greater military transparency (including Defence 'White Papers' and a South-East Asian Arms Register, notification of forthcoming military exercises, mutual invitations to force manoeuvres, exchanges of information on military strengths, and the establishment of an ASEAN Peacekeeping Centre.)[46] Many of the same ideas were also endorsed as suitable for the Asia-Pacific region as a whole in a memorandum issued by CSCAP in April 1994, shortly before the ARF summit.[47] CSCAP thinking has since been further developed in its Working Group on CSBM's.[48]

In parallel to, and in close cooperation with, the ASEAN effort, Australian analysts have also been working to develop the agenda of confidence-building measures. In one of the most important early contributions to the debate, Desmond Ball argued in a 1991 monograph for a 'building block' approach to regional security, involving 'a multiplicity of subregional arrangements ... building on the wide range of bilateral and limited multilateral arrangements already in place'. Ball then identified, and discussed in some detail, a number of specific 'building blocks' for regional security, including: much greater transparency with respect to major arms acquisitions programs and strategic objectives; intelligence exchanges; strengthening and expanding existing bilateral defence activities, currently involving ASEAN countries and Australia; and the recently agreed Timor

Sea Zone of Cooperation between Australia and Indonesia. In addition to the ARF process itself (then called the ASEAN PMC process), six new regional regimes were also proposed as possible 'building blocks'. These were: a Maritime Surveillance and Safety Regime; an Avoidance of Incidents at Sea Regime; an Airspace Surveillance and Control Regime; a Southwest Pacific Sovereignty Surveillance Regime; a Technology Monitoring Regime; and an Environmental Security Regime.[49]

Ball's comprehensive survey of the field was complemented by the work of analysts from the Australian armed forces, such as Sam Bateman and Ross Swinnerton.[50] In recognition of Australia's expertise in this area, the Senior Officials' Meeting of the 1993 ASEAN PMC asked Australia to prepare a paper setting out practical proposals for security cooperation in the region. Largely written by Paul Dibb (Head of the Strategic and Defence Studies Centre at ANU and author of the 1986 Review of Defence Policy), the paper was presented to the first ARF meeting in Bangkok in July 1994 by Foreign Minister Gareth Evans. Its ambitious list of 'possible information-sharing areas' included: strategic dialogue, including the exchange of strategic assessments; strategic policy, military doctrine, national military aims; orders-of-battle and main characteristics of major platforms; acquisition plans for new weapon platforms; historical data on weapons acquisitions, including from local production, assembly or imports; data on military exercises (size and composition) and on major deployments or movements; data that will help the monitoring of the movement of illicit drugs and of illegal movements of people, as well as transnational environmental hazards; oceanographic and hydrographic research, information on shipping routes and hazards, mapping and charting; information relevant to the management of potential conflicts over resources exploitation.

The Australian government recognised that everything could not be done at once, and that it was therefore important to start with measures that warranted early consideration because they were 'relatively achievable.' These were identified as:

- limited exchange of military information;

- a regional security studies centre;

- a maritime information data base;

- strategic planning exchanges;

- observers at military exercises;

- peacekeeping training.[51]

After the July 1994 ARF meeting, the work of ASEAN and Australian analysts, together with that of experts from other ARF states, was developed further in a number of 'second track' seminars around the region, including most notably an intersessional seminar in Canberra in November 1994 involving foreign ministry and defence officials and key regional academics from all the ARF countries, and subsequently the Asia-Pacific Roundtable on Confidence Building and Conflict Reduction in Kuala Lumpur in June 1995. A further paper by Paul Dibb, published in July 1995, attempted to summarise this debate and proposed how the most promising measures might be implemented.[52]

The payoff from this activity began to be seen in the results of the second ARF meeting, held in Brunei on 1 August 1995. The Foreign Ministers were anxious to emphasise that 'the ARF process shall move at a pace comfortable to all participants' and that 'the approach shall be evolutionary.' But they also suggested that 'Stage I' of this evolutionary process should be 'the promotion of confidence building', and urged further efforts to 'discuss means of implementing confidence building.' In a significant advance on their 1994 meeting, they urged all participants to

- enhance their dialogues on political and security cooperation;

- submit to the ARF, on a voluntary basis, an annual statement of their defence policy;

- increase high level contacts and exchanges between military academies, staff colleges and training;

- encourage those ARF countries not participating in the UN Register to do so.

In order to develop these proposals further, an Inter-sessional Support Group (ISG) on Confidence-Building was established at inter-governmental level, to look in particular at dialogue on security perceptions and defence policy papers. This would be jointly chaired by Indonesia and Japan. Inter-sessional Meetings (ISM's) would also be held on Peacekeeping (chaired by Malaysia and Canada) and on Search and Rescue Cooperation (chaired by Singapore and the US).[53]

The 1995 meeting revealed that significant differences remained on which confidence-building measures were appropriate to the region, and on the pace at which they should be introduced. Yet there were some indications of convergence between what had been very different 'Western' and 'Asian' conceptions of the confidence-building process. Amongst Western participants, there was an acceptance that an over-formal approach would be counterproductive, and that it was best to proceed in an incremental fashion, building confidence step-by-step. ASEAN's past success helped to convince sceptics that such an approach could be of value. Amongst most Asian governments, on the other hand, there was an increasing acceptance that the value of dialogue could be enhanced by increased sharing of information between countries on their military doctrine and plans, and by backing up general statements of intent with specific evidence. This acceptance was demonstrated most clearly by ASEAN's Concept Paper, presented to the 1995 ARF meeting by ASEAN governments, which accepted the case for specific confidence-building measures to be introduced.

Chapters 7 and 8 will focus on some of the specific confidence-building measures being considered at this stage. The range of measures now under discussion is an impressive one, and it will not be possible to do justice to all of them in one publication. What they all have in common, however, is that none of the ideas now under discussion would have been considered as a serious possibility during the Cold War years. One of the most significant achievements of the regional security dialogue to date has been to make many of these ideas real possibilities.

Notes

1. Michael Haas, *The Asian Way to Peace: A Story of Regional Cooperation*, Praeger, 1989, p. 282.

2. Amitav Acharya, *A New Regional Order in South-East Asia: ASEAN in the Post-Cold War Era*, Adelphi Paper Number 279, International Institute of Strategic Studies, Brasseys, August 1993, p. 36.

3. For example, see K. U. Menon, 'An ASEAN defence community: real or imagined?', *Asia-Pacific Defence Reporter*, April 1991, pp. 28-30; Amitav Acharya, 'The Association of Southeast Asian Nations: "Security

Notes continued

Community" or "Defence Community"', *Pacific Affairs*, 64, 1991, pp. 159-178.

4.   For further discussion, see David D. Dewitt, 'Concepts of Security for the Asia-Pacific Region' in Bunn Nagara and K. S. Balakrishnan (eds), *The Making of a Security Community in the Asia-Pacific*, ISIS Malaysia, 1994, pp. 9-44.

5.   Jusuf Wanandi, 'The Future of ASEAN', *Harvard International Review*, Spring 1994, p. 31.

6.   Carlyle A. Thayer, *Beyond Indochina*, Adelphi Paper Number 297, International Institute of Strategic Studies, Oxford University Press, July 1995, p. 71.

7.   Ted Bardacke, 'ASEAN endorses push to expand to 10 members', *Financial Times*, 15 December 1995.

8.   Andrew Mack and Pauline Kerr, 'The evolving security discourse in the Asia-Pacific', *The Washington Quarterly*, 18, 1, Winter 1995, p. 123.

9.   For a discussion of the problems with the 'Asia-Pacific' concept, see Richard Higgott, 'APEC - a Sceptical View', in Andrew Mack and John Ravenhill (eds), *Pacific Cooperation: Building Economic and Security Regimes in the Asia-Pacific Region*, Allen and Unwin, 1994, pp. 66-97.

10.   Trevor Findlay, 'South-East Asia and the new Asia-Pacific security dialogue', Stockholm International Peace Research Institute, *SIPRI Yearbook 1994*, Oxford University Press, 1994, p. 138.

11.   Guy de Jonquieres and William Dawkins, 'Asian members resist muscular approach', *Financial Times*, 20 November 1995. Perry's suggestions were, however, 'firmly discounted' by US and Japanese officials. William Dawkins and Guy de Jonquieres, 'Seeking to smooth the ruffled feathers', *Financial Times*, 17 November 1995.

12.   Gareth Evans and Bruce Grant, Australia's Foreign Relations, Melbourne University Press, 1991, p. 111.

13.   'A Time for Initiative - Proposals for the consideration of the Fourth ASEAN Summit', *ASEAN - ISIS Monitor*, Issue No 1, July 1991.

Notes continued

14.   Michael Antolik, 'The ASEAN Regional Forum: The Spirit of Constructive Engagement', *Contemporary South-East Asia*, 16, 2, September 1994, p. 123.

15.   Bilveer Singh, 'The 'Najib Initiative' and Confidence-Building in the Asia-Pacific Region', *Asian Defence Journal*, 7/92, pp. 6-13.

16.   Ibid, p. 120.

17.   *Chairman's Statement of the Second ASEAN Regional Forum*, 1 August 1995. Despite the careful wording of this last point, the EU representative at the meeting felt obliged to circulate a written disclaimer. 'ASEAN Regional Forum wins stronger role', *Peace and Disarmament News*, Australian Department of Foreign Affairs and Trade, September 1995, p. 16.

18.   Malcolm Chalmers and Owen Greene, *The United Nations Register of Conventional Arms: Examining the Third Report*, Bradford Arms Register Studies Working Paper, Bradford University, November 1995.

19.   *Chairman's Statement of the Second ASEAN Regional Forum*, p. 2.

20.   For further discussion, see Owen Greene, *Confidence-Building in North-East Asia*, Bradford Arms Register Studies Number 7, Westview, 1996.

21.   Bilson Kurus, op cit, p. 831; N. Ganesan, op cit, p. 465.

22.   'VN eyes AFTA membership', *Vietnam News*, 15 February 1995.

23.   Nikki Tait, 'Indian Ocean grouping faces a big 'Maybe', *Financial Times*, 14 June 1995.

24.   Mark Nicholson, 'Indian 'giant' urged to awaken', *Financial Times*, 11 January 1996.

25.   Peter M. Haas, 'Introduction: Epistemic Communities and International Policy Coordination', *International Organisation*, 46, 1, Winter 1992, pp. 1-35.

26.   Matthew Evangelista, 'The paradox of state strength: transnational relations, domestic structures, and security policy in Russia and the Soviet Union', *International Organisation*, 49, 1, Winter 1995, pp. 1-39. Also see Emanuel Adler, 'The Emergence of Cooperation: National Epistemic Communities and the Evolution of the Idea of Nuclear Arms Control', *International Organisation*, 46, 1, Winter 1992, pp. 101-145.

Notes continued

27.   For a wide-ranging discussion of this issue, see Richard Higgott (ed) 'Special Issue on Ideas, Policy Networks and International Policy Coordination in the Asia-Pacific', *The Pacific Review*, Vol. 7, No. 4, 1994 and Vol. 8, No 1, 1995.

28.   Dewi Fortuna Anwar, *Indonesia in ASEAN: Foreign Policy and Regionalism*, Institute of South-East Asian Studies, 1994, Chapter 6.

29.   A point made in the Indonesian case by Andrew MacIntyre, 'Ideas and experts: Indonesian approaches to economic and security cooperation in the Asia-Pacific region', *The Pacific Review*, 8, 1, 1995, p. 160.

30.   Stuart Harris, 'Policy networks and Economic Cooperation in the Asia-Pacific', *The Pacific Review*, 7, 4, 1994, pp. 381-398. Also see Richard Higgott, 'APEC - A Sceptical View', in Andrew Mack and John Ravenhill (eds), *Pacific Cooperation: Building Economic and Security Regimes in the Asia-Pacific Region*, Allen and Unwin, 1994, pp. 66-97.

31.   Pauline Kerr, 'The Security Dialogue in the Asia-Pacific', *The Pacific Review*, 7, 4, 1994, p. 398.

32.   Richard Leaver, 'The evolution of an Asia-Pacific policy community in Australia', *The Pacific Review*, 8, 1, 1995, p. 181.

33.   Paul Dibb, *Review of Australia's Defence Capabilities, Report to the Minister of Defence*, Australian Government Publishing Service, March 1986; Desmond Ball, *Notes on Paul Dibb's Review of Australia's Defence Capabilities*, Strategic and Defence Studies Centre, Australian National University, Reference Paper Number 143, August 1986. Also see Graeme Cheeseman, *The Search for Self-reliance: Australian Defence since Vietnam*, Longman Cheshire, 1993, pp. 12-24 for a critical appraisal of the Dibb Report and its aftermath.

34.   David Camroux, 'The Asia-Pacific Policy Community in Malaysia', *The Pacific Review*, 7, 4, 1994, pp. 421-422.

35.   Ibid, p. 429.

36.   Andrew MacIntyre, op cit, p. 169.

37.   For example, see Hoang Anh Tuan, 'Vietnam's Membership in ASEAN: Economic, Political and Security Implications', *Contemporary South-East Asia*, 16, 3, December 1994, pp. 259-273; and Sheng Lijun, *China's Policy Towards the Spratly Islands*, Strategic and Defence Studies Centre

Notes continued

Working Paper Number 287, Australian National University, Canberra, 1995.

38.   quoted in Miles Kahler, 'Institution-building in the Pacific' in Andrew Mack and John Ravenhill (eds), op cit, p. 16.

39.   Department of Foreign Affairs and Trade, *Regional Security Dialogue: A Calendar of Asia-Pacific Events*, January 1994 - December 1994.

40.   Mark Valencia, *China and the South China Sea Disputes*, Adelphi Paper 298, International Institute for Strategic Studies, Oxford University Press, 1995, pp. 50-54.

41.   Desmond Ball, 'A New Era in Confidence Building: The Second Track Process in the Asia/Pacific Region', *Security Dialogue*, 25, 2, 1994, p. 171.

42.   Desmond Ball, *CSCAP: Its Future Place in the Regional Security Architecture*, paper prepared for the Eight Asia-Pacific Roundtable, Kuala Lumpur, June 1994. Ball is a founding member of the CSCAP Steering Committee and the chairperson of the CSCAP Sub-committee on Working Groups.

43.   Kenneth Stier and Bao Anyou, 'The Bitter Truth behind Thailand's Khaki Commerce', *Asia Inc*, October 1992.

44.   Desmond Ball, 'Strategic Culture in the Asia-Pacific Region, *Security Studies*, 3, 1, Autumn 1993, pp. 65-66.

45.   ASEAN-ISIS, *Confidence Building Measures in South-East Asia*, Memorandum Number 5, December 1993, pp. 11-12.

46.   Ibid.

47.   CSCAP, *The Security of the Asia-Pacific Region*, Memorandum Number 1, April 1994.

48.   A summary of the work of the Group is contained in Ralph Cossa, *Confidence and Security Building Measures: Are They Appropriate for Asia?*, Pacific Forum CSIS, January 1995; and Ralph Cossa (ed), *Towards a Regional Arms Register in the Asia Pacific*, Pacific Forum CSIS, August 1995.

49.   Desmond Ball, *Building Blocks for Regional Security: An Australian Perspective on Confidence and Security Building Measures (CSBMs) in the Asia/Pacific Region*, Canberra Papers on Strategy and Defence Number 83, Strategic and Defence Studies Centre, Australian National University, 1991.

Notes continued

50.   For example, see Desmond Ball and Sam Bateman, *An Australian Perspective on Maritime CSBM's in the Asia-Pacific region*, Strategic and Defence Studies Centre Working Paper Number 234, Australian National University, 1991; Ross Swinnerton and Desmond Ball, *A Regional Regime for Maritime Surveillance, Safety and Information Exchanges*, Strategic and Defence Studies Centre Working Paper Number 278, Australian National University, December 1993; Ross Swinnerton, 'Confidence-building measures at sea: the challenges ahead in South-East Asia', *The Pacific Review*, 8, 2, 1995, pp. 327-343.

51.   Paul Dibb and Gareth Evans, *Australian Paper on Practical Proposals for Security Cooperation in the Asia Pacific Region*, Department of Foreign Affairs and Trade, April 1994.

52.   Paul Dibb, *How to Begin Implementing Specific Trust-Building Measures in the Asia-Pacific Region*, Strategic and Defence Studies Centre Working Paper Number 288, Australian National University, July 1995.

53.   *Chairman's Statement of the Second ASEAN Regional Forum*, op cit, pp. 4-5.

CHAPTER 7

The UN Register and South-East Asia

I   Introduction

Although not specifically intended as a regional regime, the United Nations
Register of Conventional Arms does have regional significance. It is
intended to address precisely the phenomenon that is of increasing concern
in South-East Asia: the destabilising consequences of build-ups of
conventional arms. Like the Asia-Pacific security dialogue, the Register is a
product of the changes in the international environment since the end of
the Cold War. Neither were possible in the highly polarised conditions of
the Cold War. Both are designed to respond to the requirements of an
environment characterised by uncertainties and concerns rather than by
clearly delineated threats.

The development of the UN Register has paralleled the development of the
Asia-Pacific security dialogue in other ways too. The idea of a Regional
Register of conventional arms was proposed by Malaysian Defence
Minister Najib as early as April 1992: after the UN Register had been
agreed in principle, but before its detailed modalities had been worked
out.[1] The concept of a Regional Register has made little progress since this
time, in part because of the argument that its place has been taken by the
UN Register. Yet, as will be discussed in Chapter 8, there remain many
possibilities for such a Register, not as a replacement for the UN Register
but as a complement to it.

Perhaps of greatest significance, the UN Register was the first specific
information sharing measure on which the participants in ARF could
agree. At their first meeting in Brunei in July 1994, it was agreed that the
Chairman of the ARF, Brunei, working with other ARF participants,
should

> 'promote the *eventual* participation of all ARF countries in the
> UN Conventional Arms Register.'[2]

Before the ARF meeting, participation in the UN Register in the region had
been patchy. In the first round of replies, submitted retrospectively in 1993
relating to transfers during 1992, all the region's major powers - China,
Japan and the US - participated, along with Australia, Canada and South

Korea. But the only ASEAN members taking part were Malaysia, the Philippines and Singapore.

Shortly before the first ARF meeting in July 1994, however, Indonesia responded to the requests from its neighbours by submitting a full return for the Register's second year (relating to its imports for 1993), together with a 'nil' return for 1992. In February 1995, Thailand submitted its first report, relating to its imports of equipment during 1993. In April 1995, Vietnam also joined the Register, submitting a 'nil' return for 1994 only a few months before its formal acceptance into ASEAN.

As a result of this sequence of decisions, 16 of the 19 participants in the 1995 ARF meeting were taking part in the UN Register (the exceptions being Brunei, Cambodia and Laos).[3] This in turn encouraged ARF Ministers to agree to a further strengthening of their commitment to the Register:

> 'The Ministers also agreed ... to take note of the increasing participation in the UN Conventional Arms Register since the first ARF and encourage those not yet participating to *soon* do so.'[4]

The importance of this explicit endorsement of the UN Register by ARF should not be underestimated. It is too early to say what role the information provided to the Register will be able to play in the regional confidence-building process. Even if it proves to be marginal, however, the near-universal participation in the Register in the region marks a highly significant acceptance of the principle of sharing information on conventional arms. Because of the sensitivities involved, progress in releasing further information is likely to continue to be slow. But the precedent set by the UN Register means that the principle of transparency has now been accepted. Future discussions can now focus more on the practical difficulties posed by particular proposals.

This Chapter will review the origins of the UN Register, seeking to explain why it proved popular to ARF participants. It will then examine the information provided to the UN Register by individual countries in the region. Finally, it will point to lessons that may be learnt from this experience for the design and operation of future regional confidence-building measures.

II Development

The idea of an Arms Register can be traced back to the aftermath of World War One, when it was agreed to set up a League of Nations office responsible for receiving, and then publishing, copies of all arms export licences. Between 1924 and 1938, the League also published an annual Statistical Yearbook of the Trade in Arms, Munitions and Implements of War. By 1938, it covered sixty countries, together with 64 colonies, protectorates and mandated territories. However, the data - on values rather than numbers of weapons - were incomplete and mostly non-comparable.[5]

Various attempts were made to revive the Register idea in the 1960s and 1970s. But little progress was made while the international environment was polarised by the Cold War. It was not until 1990 that several developments came together to create the circumstances for the creation of a global Register. First, the apparent success of confidence-building and transparency measures in easing tensions in Europe in the last years of the Cold War helped encourage a belief that CBM's could also play a role in addressing problems in other regions.[6] Second, President Gorbachov's support for a policy of military glasnost, together with the collapse of the Warsaw Pact, meant that the Soviet Union and its former allies now supported increased arms transparency: as evidenced by Soviet Foreign Minister Shevardnadze's support of a UN Register of arms sales in a letter to the UN Secretary-General in August 1990. Finally, concern about the effect of unrestrained arms build-ups in regions of tension came to a head with the Iraqi invasion of Kuwait. After the defeat of Iraq in early 1991, there was a widespread feeling that 'something had to be done' to prevent a similar build-up happening again. It was in this period, leading up to the General Assembly meeting in December 1991, that the agreement to set up a UN Register was reached.

In September 1991, a Group of Experts published a detailed report for the UN Secretary-General on 'transparency in international transfers of conventional armaments.' The Group's membership of eighteen was drawn from a wide range of UN members, including Australia, Canada, Indonesia, Japan, the Soviet Union and the US from the 'Asia-Pacific' region. Chaired by a UK representative, it recommended unanimously that 'a UN system be established to collect, process and publish official standardised information on international arms transfers on a regular basis, as supplied to the UN by Member States on their arms exports and imports.[7]

The Group of Experts' report was followed up by extensive lobbying by both Japan and the European Community in support of the establishment of a Register. Australia and Canada were also active in support of the proposal. The US was initially reluctant. But, in a position that has some similarity with its lukewarm position towards the proposals for Asia-Pacific security dialogue also developing at this time, it eventually felt it had no choice but to go along with an initiative supported by its main allies.

After some revisions to address issues raised by a number of developing countries, a resolution supporting the Register was passed by the UN First Committee in November 1991 by a margin of 106 in favour, 1 against (Cuba) and eight abstaining (including China, North Korea, Myanmar and Singapore). When the vote came to the General Assembly the following month, 150 countries voted in favour, with none against and only 2 abstentions (Cuba and Iraq). However, a number of Member States did not participate in the General Assembly vote, indicating continuing reservations. These included China, Laos, Myanmar and Vietnam.[8] In addition, some of those states that had abstained in the First Committee, but voted in favour in the General Assembly, issued statements expressing some continuing concerns. Notably, Singapore was concerned that the national security interests of member states had to be taken into consideration.[9]

Before the Register could be established, it was necessary to agree in detail the definitions of the categories of weapon systems that should be included, as well as the procedures for submission of information. In order to do this, a Panel of Technical Experts was established under the chair of Ambassador Wagenmakers of the Netherlands. The membership of seventeen was drawn from a broad cross-section of developed and developing countries. Representatives from the Asia-Pacific included officials from Canada, China, India, Japan, Malaysia, Russia and the US.

The Asian states, and in particular China and India, were key to the success of the 1992 Panel, which was effectively a negotiating body acting on behalf of the General Assembly. American and European participation in the Register could be guaranteed, as could that of Japan and (in this pro-Western phase of policy) Russia. The major Latin American countries were also enthusiastic. At the other extreme, most sub-Saharan African countries, although nominally supportive, were unengaged in the process; and encouraging a high rate of participation in the Middle East was clearly going to be an uphill struggle. If the UN Register was to be able to claim to be a global regime, therefore, it was crucial to have the major developing countries of Asia 'on board'. Otherwise it risked becoming a mechanism confined mainly to Northern countries, and thus largely irrelevant.

The 1992 Panel was able to succeed in bringing the largest two Asian powers on board as founding participants in the Register, in large measure because its debates meant that the structure and provisions of the Register were determined through a process of negotiation based on consensus. Concessions were made by all sides and, while the final result may appear rather untidy from a technical point of view, the process served to reassure key developing states - especially China and India - that their arguments had been taken fully into account. For example, in response to Chinese concerns, the Register does not include ground-to-air missiles or their launchers.[10] As a result of an Indian proposal to reduce the lower limit on the calibre of weapons on armoured combat vehicles from 20 mm to 12.5 mm, the coverage of Category II 'armoured combat vehicles' was significantly extended. The two countries did not win all their arguments. For example, China failed in its attempt to add electronic warfare aircraft, air-refuelling aircraft, command and early-warning aircraft to Category IV 'combat aircraft'.[11] But, by making clear that their concerns were being taken seriously, the rest of the Panel were able to bring both China and India to sign a unanimous final report.[12] Their conclusions were subsequently endorsed without opposition by the General Assembly on 15 December 1992.[13]

In order to participate in the Register, countries were asked to report on numbers of weapons exported and imported during the previous calendar year under seven categories:

I. Battle tanks

II Armoured combat vehicles

III Large calibre artillery systems

IV Combat aircraft

V Attack helicopters

VI Warships

VII Missiles and missile launchers

Detailed definitions for all seven categories are given in Table 7.1. Although the titles of the first five categories are identical to those limited by the Conventional Forces in Europe (CFE) Treaty, the definitions used for Register purposes are significantly broader (a source of continuing confusion for some CFE participants). The 'warship' category includes all vessels armed or equipped for military use of 750 tonnes or above, as well as those of less than 750 tonnes which are equipped to launch missiles or torpedoes with a range of 25km or more. The seventh category - 'missiles and missile launchers' - conflates both missiles with a range of 25km or more and launchers for such missiles not included in one of the other six Register categories (but excluding ground to air missiles).

The Register makes no presumption that possession or transfer of conventional arms is illegitimate, and does not define in what circumstances a build-up of such arms is destabilising. Rather, by making the process of arms acquisition more transparent, it provides a framework within which other mechanisms, at a global or regional level, can be used to discuss the implications of the data provided. In contrast to regimes such as 'successor to CoCom' and the Missile Technology Control Regime, developing countries are accepted as having equal status with developed states, and have identical responsibilities and rights. As a result, the Register is less commonly perceived as an instrument of North-South domination than are these other regimes.[14]

An additional noteworthy feature of the Register is that the information provided by states to the UN is publicly available, thus facilitating public debate as well as inter-governmental discussions. As a result, Register data can be scrutinised by members of national parliaments, research institutes, journalists and others interested in the subject. It is thus a welcome contribution to promoting the role of public scrutiny in monitoring the trade in major conventional weapons.

The central achievement of the Register so far has been to establish, on a global scale, the principle that states have a responsibility to be transparent, albeit to a limited degree, in relation to their transfers of conventional arms. States have a right to maintain conventional arsenals sufficient for self-defence, but it is recognised that this right has to be circumscribed by the responsibility to exercise this right with regard to the

Table 7.1 Categories of equipment to be used in reporting transfers to the UN Register

I. Battle Tanks. Tracked or wheeled self-propelled armoured fighting vehicles with high cross-country mobility and a high level of self-protection, weighing at least 16.5 metric tonnes unladen weight, with a high muzzle velocity direct fire main gun of at least 75mm calibre.

II. Armoured combat vehicles. Tracked, semi-tracked or wheeled self-propelled vehicles, with armoured protection and cross-country capability, either: (a) designed and equipped to transport a squad of four or more infantrymen, or (b) armed with an integral or organic weapon of at least 12.5mm calibre or a missile launcher.

III. Large calibre artillery systems. Guns, howitzers, artillery pieces, combining the characteristics of a gun or a howitzer, mortars or multiple-launch rocket systems, capable of engaging surface targets by delivering primarily indirect fire, with a calibre of 100mm and above.

IV. Combat aircraft. Fixed wing or variable-geometry wing aircraft designed, equipped or modified to engage targets by employing guided missiles, unguided rockets, bombs, guns, cannons, or other weapons of destruction, including versions of these aircraft which perform specialised electronic warfare, suppression of air defence or reconnaissance missions. The term 'combat aircraft' does not include primary trainer aircraft, unless designed, equipped or modified as described above.

V. Attack helicopters. Rotary-wing aircraft designed, equipped or modified to engage targets by employing guided or unguided anti-armour, air-to-surface, air-to-subsurface or air-to-air weapons and equipped with an integrated fire control and aiming system for these weapons, including versions of these aircraft which perform specialised reconnaissance or electronic warfare roles.

VI. Warships. Vessels or submarines armed and equipped for military use with a standard displacement of 750 metric tonnes or above, and those with a standard displacement of less than 750 metric tonnes, equipped for launching missiles with a range of at least 25 kilometres or torpedoes of a similar range.

VII. Missiles and missile launchers. Guided or unguided rockets, ballistic or cruise missiles capable of delivering a warhead or weapon of destruction to a range of at least 25 kilometres, and means designed or modified specifically for launching such missiles or rockets, if not covered by categories I through VI. For the purposes of the Register, this category:(a) also includes remotely - piloted vehicles with the characteristics for missiles as defined above; (b) does not include ground-to-air missiles.

interests of others. Extension of the principle of transparency into the area of conventional arms represents an important addition to the obligations that form part of this responsibility.

The UN Register did not appear out of a vacuum. But, until the Register was established, it was not universally accepted that this principle was relevant beyond the particular context of Europe, whose security (and arms control) dynamic was, until 1990, overwhelmingly defined by the bipolar confrontation between two antagonistic military alliances. By extending the principle of conventional arms transparency to a global level, the Register represented an acceptance of the value of the transparency principle even in the absence of a particular threat or power balance.

Whatever the other benefits of the Register, the acceptance of this new principle has been of value in itself. Symbols matter in international politics, as they do domestically, and the creation of the Register symbolised a new degree of commitment to the principle that the trade in conventional arms is a legitimate matter of international interest.

III   Participation in the Register

An assessment of the initial achievement of the Register, however, must rest not only on the principle it embodies but also on the extent to which this principle has been accepted on a global level. Here too the record of the Register's first three years is reasonably impressive. With only 122 of the 188 states asked to take part having replied so far to the request for data, participation has not yet become a universally-accepted obligation comparable, for example, with the Nuclear Non-Proliferation Treaty or Chemical Weapons Convention.[15] In each year of the Register, participation has risen modestly: from 82 in December 1993 for the first year, to 86 in December 1994 for the second year and 90 in December 1995 for the third year. But only 68 countries have submitted replies for all three years, and 66 countries have never submitted any information.[16]

Yet these figures underestimate the extent of participation amongst countries that are active participants in the arms trade. Amongst the top 25 exporters for 1990-1994 listed in the annual survey of the Stockholm International Peace Research Institute (SIPRI), all but one country (North Korea) provided information to the Register in 1995. Amongst SIPRI's top 25 importing states for the same period, 18 provided data for 1994. Of the remaining seven importers, two (Egypt, and Iran) have provided data in the past, but have now suspended participation. Three have never taken part

(Saudi Arabia, Kuwait and the United Arab Emirates). The government of Afghanistan has made clear its inability to provide information due to its lack of control over much of its own territory.[17] And Taiwan was not asked to provide information because it is neither a member of the UN or a recognised observer state. Although there have been substantial exports to Taiwan over the last three years, notably from France and the US, there have been no reports of such exports in the UN Register. It appears that the exporters in question are excluding exports to Taiwan from their replies on the grounds that it is not a recognised state.[18]

Looking at the different regions of the world, the only region in which Register participation is higher than in Asia is **Europe** (outside the former Soviet Union), with 31 out of a possible 38 states providing information in 1995. (See Table 7.2) Three states of former Yugoslavia - Croatia, Yugoslavia (Serbia and Montenegro) and Slovenia - provided unconvincing 'nil' reports. The only states not reporting were Albania, Andorra, Bosnia, Macedonia, Monaco, San Marino and the Holy See.

Participation in the Register amongst the 15 republics of the **former Soviet Union** was significantly lower, despite their common membership of the transparency regimes of the Organisation of Security and Cooperation in Europe (OSCE). Participation increased significantly, from 5 to 9, in 1995. But, as a result of a prolonged internal dispute, Russia only submitted its reply after the annual Secretary-General's report on the Register was published. Given the current reaction within Russia against many of the international commitments into which it entered in the early 1990s, there must be some uncertainty whether it will continue its participation in the Register in future years.[19]

Participation in the **Americas** also increased significantly in 1995, with 19 out of a possible 35 countries taking part. Most of the countries with larger defence budgets - including Argentina, Brazil, Chile, Mexico and Peru, as well as Canada and the US - are regular participants. But many of the smaller countries in the region have, at best, reported only on an irregular basis. Finally, participation in both the **Middle East** and **sub-Saharan Africa** has declined over the last year. Only 8 out of a possible total of 66 countries provided replies in 1995, bringing the average global rate of Register participation down sharply. With both Egypt and Iran apparently dropping out, the only states of any significance in the international arms trade that continued to participate from these two regions are Israel and

South Africa. Iraq, Kuwait, Saudi Arabia, Syria and the United Arab Emirates - five of the world's biggest arms importers over the last decade - have so far given no indication of a willingness to take part.

While participation was falling away in the Middle East and sub-Saharan Africa, however, it was consolidating in **Asia and Oceania**, particularly amongst ARF countries. As Table 7.3 shows, 12 out of the 15 'local' ARF countries (as well as 'external' ARF participants Canada, the European Union, Russia and the US) took part in the Register in 1995: leaving only Brunei, Cambodia and Laos as the only ARF countries not participating in the global Register. As Table 7.4 shows, 10 out of 17 non ARF countries in this region also took part, including India and Pakistan.

Nor is the fact that it took countries such as Indonesia, Thailand and Vietnam more than two years to submit their first reply to the Register entirely a negative sign. For it reflects the fact that the Register is more than another rhetorical commitment. It takes time for governments to carry out the practical steps necessary for the preparation of Register returns, and they have to overcome resistance - especially from defence ministries - to the very idea of releasing any information on military matters. On the evidence of the Register's first three years, however, this cultural adjustment is gradually being achieved, at least within the ranks of ARF participants. As more ARF countries join the Register, the universality of the norm of transparency in this area is reinforced and it becomes correspondingly more difficult for other states to resist the pressure to join.

This initial success is particularly encouraging because it represents a real and substantial change in attitude towards transparency in several of the countries involved. None of the data provided is sensitive in the sense that it can be seen as compromising the national security of the countries concerned. But most of it is information which was not previously published. Many Asian countries periodically provide gross figures on defence budgets for the purposes of national planning and parliamentary accountability. The practice of revealing detailed figures on conventional arms, however, has been much less widespread, and its adoption as a result of the UN Register - albeit only in relation to transfers - thus represents a significant step in the direction of greater openness.

Table 7.2 Participation in the UN Register by region

Region	1992 replies by December 1993	1993 replies by December 1994	1994 replies by December 1995
Europe	30	31	31
Asia & Oceania	18	20	22
America	14	16	20
Former Soviet Union	5	5	9
Sub-Saharan Africa	8	11	6
Middle East	7	3	2
Total	82	86	90

Source: Malcolm Chalmers and Owen Greene, 'The UN Register of Conventional Arms: the third year of operation', in J. B. Poole and R. Guthrie (eds), *Verification 1996: Arms control, peacekeeping and the environment*, VERTIC/Westview Press, 1996.

Table 7.3 Register replies for Asia & Oceania (ARF countries)

	Reply for 1992 by December 1993	Reply for 1993 by December 1994	Reply for 1994 by December 1995
Australia	*	*	*
Brunei Darassalam			
Cambodia			
China	*	*	*
Indonesia		*	*
Japan	*	*	*
Laos			
Malaysia	*	*	*
New Zealand	*	*	*
Papua New Guinea	*		*
Philippines	*	*	*
South Korea	*	*	*
Singapore	*	*	*
Thailand			*
Vietnam			*
TOTAL	9 out of 15	9 out of 15	12 out of 15

Table 7.4 Register replies for Asia & Oceania (Non-ARF Countries)

	Reply for 1992 by December 1993	Reply for 1993 by December 1994	Reply for 1994 by December 1995
Afghanistan		*	
Bangladesh			
Bhutan		*	*
North Korea			
Fiji	*	*	*
India	*	*	*
Maldives	*	*	*
Marshall Islands		*	*
Micronesia			
Mongolia	*	*	*
Myanmar			
Nepal	*	*	*
Pakistan	*	*	*
Samoa		*	*
Solomon Islands	*		*
Sri Lanka	*		
Vanuatu	*	*	
TOTAL	9 out of 17	11 out of 17	10 out of 17

Note: Cook Islands, Kiribati, Nauru, Tonga and Tuvalu were not UN members as of 1 January 1995. They were therefore not asked to provide information for the UN Register.

IV   The Register as a process

Process is often as important as content in the formation and operation of international regimes, and nowhere is this clearer than in the case of the UN Register. For the key to the high level of participation in the Register in the Asia-Pacific region has been that, in contrast to treaty-based arms control regimes, the UN Register is characterised by a degree of informality and flexibility in several key respects:

* First, the Register is a **voluntary regime**. Countries are requested to provide data on their transfers of conventional arms, but it is accepted that some countries may take longer than others to meet this request. Even if governments have made a commitment to the Register in principle, it can take time to persuade domestic interests - in the armed forces and in arms companies in particular - that national interests are not being compromised. As more countries in a particular region join, this argument tends to lose its force amongst those who remain reluctant to participate. The 1995 ARF statement suggests that informal pressure on Brunei, Cambodia and Laos (together with aspiring ARF participants such as Myanmar) to join the Register may increase in future. But the nature of the Register process is such that this peer pressure can be exerted in the context of an appreciation that some governments may need to be given more time than others to meet those norms.

* Second, although the minimum requirement for participation is reasonably clear (despite there being no formal definition of participation), replying states have considerable **flexibility** as to how much more information on their transfers they wish to provide, over and above this minimum. For each transfer reported, states are asked to indicate the country of origin or destination, together with the Category into which the weapon system falls (for example, 'Armoured Combat Vehicle or 'Combat Aircraft'). But it is left up to states to decide whether to provide any description of the weapon transferred (for example, 'V150 Commando' or 'Mig 29'). This 'differential transparency' helps maximise the number of countries participating in the Register by allowing each country to decide, within limits, the level of openness with which it is comfortable.

ARF countries have used this flexibility. Australia, Indonesia, Malaysia, New Zealand, the Philippines, South Korea and, to a more limited extent, Canada and Russia have all provided some description of the weapon systems reported to the Register. By contrast, China, Japan, Singapore, Thailand and the US have provided no such information. Even the countries of the European Union (also a ARF participant) differ in their use of this part of the Register, with 12 member states providing descriptions of the weapons transferred and two (France and the UK) not doing so.[20]

* Third, as a result of the political compromise that made the establishment of the Register possible, states are invited to provide 'available background information' on their **military holdings, procurement through national production and relevant policies.** But the UN does not specify the form in which this data should be provided, nor does it publish the data that is submitted. The Register does provide, for the first time, a structured opportunity for states to provide this data if they so wish. The information is not included in the annual report, but it is available for public consultation in the UN in New York.[21]

Because of the more voluntary nature of the request for 'available background information', less than half of the states taking part in the Register have provided data on military holdings. A large number of states are likely to continue to have severe reservations about providing data in this area. Nevertheless, the number of countries providing such data has increased between 1993 and 1995 (from 25 to 29), and the principle of global information exchange in this area has begun to be established. Most of the states providing such information in 1995 are developed countries (including ARF participants Australia, Canada, Japan, New Zealand, and the US).[22] But some developing states, including Argentina, Brazil, Mexico and Armenia, also provided data under this heading.

* Fourth, the main institution involved in the Register - the UN's **Centre for Disarmament Affairs** - is used to facilitate participation rather than police or enforce it. It is responsible for receiving the replies of national governments, answering enquiries from governments, and preparing the publication of data received. It has organised a series of regional workshops in order to educate national officials as to the nature and requirements of the Register (including one in Japan in February 1993). It plans to hold further such workshops in 1996. However, it is not empowered to seek clarification of national replies, or to seek explanations for the lack of replies, far less to investigate discrepancies between the replies of importing and exporting states. It is left to national governments to decide what action, if any, to take in response to problems that may arise in the interpretation of Register data.

* Fifth, the process of **verification** is decentralised. States are not asked to furnish any documentation to demonstrate that their replies are truthful,

and the UN has no mandate to check national replies for accuracy. But, because there are two parties to every international transfer, it is possible to cross-check many of the replies and identify discrepancies as requiring further study. Moreover, a wide range of non-governmental sources regularly publish data on arms transfers, and it is therefore possible to use these as another source of corroboration of government replies. Undoubtedly, the lack of a more refined verification system allows some transfers to go unreported. But it would have been impossible to persuade a majority of UN member states to accept the degree of intrusion necessary to verify Register replies.

V   Implementation Problems

Initial problems in compiling national replies were widely anticipated.[23] Even in major Western states, the information necessary to complete the exports section of the return to the UN had not previously been easily available. Governments issued licences to companies authorising particular transfers. But, until the Register was established, no central record was maintained on whether and when these licences were used.

In addition, many of the officials directly involved in the Register also found that considerable effort was required in order to learn the detailed requirements of the Register, apply the categories and procedures laid down by the UN to their own particular circumstances, and set in place systems for gathering the information required. Their problems were increased by the fact that, in many cases, the officials involved did not themselves have a full understanding of the rationale for the Register or the history behind the development of its categories and definitions. In defence ministries with no history of publishing any information on their procurement plans, the culture shock was even greater.

In addition to their high level of Register participation, ASEAN members have demonstrated a relatively high quality of replies compared with some other developing regions. But considerable implementation problems remain. In many cases, the official(s) responsible for the Register also have responsibility for many other matters (for example, other UN matters), and may spend much of their time advising Ministers on matters of greater immediate importance. Yet the UN Register requires countries to set up an annual cycle of activity, and not simply the single burst of activity often required for the signature and ratification of other global security regimes. Before a reply can be submitted, the officials involved have to gather the relevant data, vet it for security implications, discuss it on an interdepartmental basis, and ensure its timely dispatch to the UN. At each stage, there are temptations to 'shortcut' the process, even at the cost of compromising the quality of the reply.

The potential for error in any bureaucracy means that Register replies will never be completely free from error. Yet, after three years of operation, it is disappointing that more institutional learning has not taken place, and that more progress has not been made at national level in streamlining procedures for collecting and producing Register replies. Even a cursory glance at the third year replies reveals several cases where the Register guidelines have not been followed. Given this record even in those cases where cross-checking is possible (for example where both exporter and importer have reported), it is likely that there are many more cases where the guidelines have not been followed, but where this is not immediately evident.

Perhaps the most obvious symptom of the Register's implementation problems has been the worryingly high level of discrepancies between the replies of exporting and importing states. Thus, out of a total of 159 separate exports reported to have taken place in 1994 by exporting states, 60 were to states not participating in the Register and could not therefore be cross-checked. Out of the remaining 99 exports, however, only 52 of the exporters' replies marched those of the importing states. Some of the 47 recorded discrepancies were relatively small in nature, but many were not. For example, whereas Israel reported importing 3 armoured combat vehicles, 6 artillery pieces, 53 combat aircraft, 2 warships and no helicopters from the US in 1994, the US reported exporting 450 armoured combat vehicles, 6 artillery pieces, no aircraft or warships and 4 helicopters.[24]

Some exporters have a better record in this regard than others. Germany, the world's second largest exporter according to the Register, reported 25 separate exports for 1994, of which 20 matched exactly the replies of importing states, 2 did not match and 3 were to non-participants. By contrast, only 8 of the 33 exports reported by the US were matched by the replies of the recipient countries, with 17 failing to match and 8 going to non-participants.[25]

The discrepancy between the exports reported by the US and imports reported by its recipient countries was also a problem in the first two years of the Register, and was raised as an issue with the US in a series of bilateral discussions. As a result, the US subsequently submitted some corrected data relating to 1993 in the form of a Corrigendum to the UN.[26] It remains to be seen whether the US will submit a similar set of corrections to its third year reply.

The Register does not need to be 100% perfect in book keeping terms to be of value. Indeed, in those cases where consistency between the replies of importing and exporting states appears to be a result of consultation rather than of convergence between independent estimates, perfect matching may not be entirely reassuring. Nevertheless, it is clear that the current degree of mismatching between the replies of exporters and importers could, if not tackled, progressively undermine the credibility of the Register (and, by association, similar regionally-specific measures) as a useful contribution to international confidence-building. Not only will it undermine the credibility of the data for transfers between Register participants. It will also call into question the care with which the data for exports to non-participants has been prepared. Since some of the countries of greatest regional concern - such as Myanmar and North Korea - are not yet Register participants, this is of considerable importance.

There is no single explanation for the problem of widespread discrepancies. Rather, it is the result of a combination of factors, some bureaucratic in nature and some related more broadly to the degree of detail which countries have been willing to provide in their replies. The examples used relate mainly to the Asia-Pacific region, but similar cases can often also be found in other regions.[27]

Starting with those factors of lesser significance, but of some nuisance value, the covering note which Australia provided with its reply for 1993 reported that Singapore and Brunei were required by Australian Customs to obtain an export licence to remove some of their own military equipment from Australia following exercise and training activities. The UN guidelines on the Register make it clear that, since this equipment was never under Australian control, Australia was correct not to report its transfers. But it does serve as a reminder that national governments cannot use unaltered Customs data for compiling Register replies.

Second, there have been continuing problems about how to treat weapon systems that are not intended for military use by the recipient country, but which, from the exporting state's point of view, constitute exports of weapon systems according to the Register definitions. Thus, the UK reported the export of 8 armoured combat vehicles to Australia in 1992, adding a note to the effect that these were 'obsolete equipment for museums.' The Australian reply for 1992 did not acknowledge that this import had taken place, but did note in a covering letter that

> 'Not listed ... are one battle tank, one armoured combat vehicle and one large calibre artillery piece ... imported from Kuwait solely for the purpose of display at the Museum of the School of Armour'.

A similar, though more serious, example of the same problem arose in 1993. The US reported the export of a warship to Australia, but Australia did not report an import of a warship in its standardised form, instead adding a note that it had imported

> 'One DDG-class warship, which was not commissioned into the Royal Australian Navy and never will be, and is now in the process of being dismantled for spares.'

Whether this is the same warship as the one exported by the US cannot be established from the Register replies. Even if it is, the Australian note raises the important issue of whether the transfer of weapon systems should be reported only if, and when, they are commissioned into service in the armed forces of the recipient country. This would be a departure from the current practice of most exporting states, as we shall see later in this section, not least because exporting states do not usually track what happens to weapon systems once they have been transferred into the custody of another state. It is perhaps in recognition of its own uncertainty as to whether it should have included this transfer in its imports form that Australia added its note. But it does raise the possibility that other, unexplained, discrepancies could also be a result of importing states failing to include those imports that are for purposes (such as break-up for spares or scrap, museum display, use with police forces, or storage as attrition reserves) other than immediate deployment with operational units.

The problem of defining exactly when a transfer takes place is one that both the 1992 UN Panel of Experts and the 1994 UN Group of Experts were unable to resolve. The most that the 1994 Group could agree was that countries should append explanatory notes to their standardized forms, 'indicating their national criteria used for determining when a transfer had occurred.'[28]

In response to this request, some exporting states did provide further information. Canada stated that it assumed that a transfer took place when a weapon system was physically transferred, and South Korea stated that (for exports) it used the date of departure from Korea. The US used the 'transfer of ownership title between the US and another country'. Both the UK and France used two criteria: 'transfer of title to and control over the equipment' in the case of the UK, and 'departure of equipment from the exporter's territory' and 'transfer of title' in the case of France. However neither of these two countries made clear whether one of their two criteria took priority over the other.[29]

These differences in definitions can create discrepancies which, although manageable over a period of years, can initially be confusing. For example, the US reported the export of 20 missiles and missile launchers to Singapore in 1993, while Singapore reported the receipt of only 8. In 1994, however, Singapore reported the receipt of 12 missiles and missile launchers from the US, while the US reported no further exports in this category to Singapore. The discrepancy between the two replies could be a result of the two countries reporting two quite different transfers (without any descriptions of the missiles being included, it is difficult to know). But it seems more likely that Singapore may have used a definition of time of transfer (perhaps the date on which its armed forces take physical possession) that is different from the one used by the US (transfer of title).

A further set of problems results from the common practice of late submission. Countries are requested to submit data on their exports and imports during the previous calendar year by 30 April. Yet, as of 12 May 1995, only 40 countries had provided information on their transfers for 1994 (including ARF participants Canada, Indonesia, Japan, New Zealand, South Korea, Singapore, US and Vietnam, together with 11 EU members).[30] Over the next five months, a further 44 states reported, giving a total of 84 replies provided to the UN in time for the annual Register report to go to the UN publishers on 13 October. ARF participants replying during this period included Thailand (30 June), China (3 July), Australia (17 August), Malaysia (9 October), and all four remaining EU members. A further three states replied in late October and early November, too late for inclusion in the annual Report, which is timed so that it can be available for the start of the UN First Committee meeting in early November. These included ARF participants Papua New Guinea (30 October) and Russia (8 November).[31]

In terms of the Register's contribution to confidence-building, there are clearly costs involved in having a delay of almost a year between a transfer taking place and its being published or, in some cases, even reported to the UN. Indeed, as a consequence of such concerns, some have suggested that Register reporting be more regular that it is at present. At the present stage of development of the Register, however, the wish for prompt information will have to be balanced against both the importance of accuracy and the UN's understandable desire to maximise the annual 'headline' figure for participation by publishing the annual Register report as late as possible.

One of the most striking features of the replies from South-East Asian countries is that many have chosen not to adhere strictly to the UN definitions of weapon categories when submitting their replies. This may not matter too much in those case where countries provide additional information on systems that fall below the Register's thresholds and make it clear in their replies that they are doing so. For example, both governments involved have reported the transfer of nine Kondor minesweepers from Germany to Indonesia despite the fact that, with a tonnage of 414 tons, these vessels fell below the 750 tonnes threshold set in the Register.[32] Many of the imports reported by both Malaysia and the Philippines also appear to fall outside the Register categories. For example, Malaysia's report of the import of 29,906 items in the 'artillery' category in 1994 appears to refer to artillery ammunition rather than artillery pieces.

The provision of additional information in this way provides a welcome additional element of transparency and might, in time, help to pave the way for an expansion in the Register's coverage. But it can also create problems. When one or both of the countries concerned in a transfer have not provided descriptions of the items concerned (as is the case with ASEAN members Singapore and Thailand), such flexibility would make the interpretation of replies more difficult. A comparison of the Singaporean and Thai replies with publicly available data, together with the replies of exporters, suggests that these two states have kept more strictly to the Register definitions than their ASEAN colleagues. But there may be some cases where discrepancies between importer and exporter replies are a result of different interpretations of the Register definitions. For example, France has included the export of 8 attack helicopters to Singapore in its reply for 1993, but Singapore has made no matching return, either for 1993 or for 1992 or 1994. A recent publication from SIPRI and the Malaysian Institute of Maritime Affairs reports that 10 AS-555 Fennec helicopters were supplied to Singapore by France, with the estimated date of delivery being 1992. The same publication also reports that these helicopters were 'assembled in Singapore'.[33] Since countries are not obliged to report procurement through national production in their Register replies, it is therefore possible that Singapore may have decided that local assembly should not be included under 'imports' while France decided that it should be.

Many of the problems caused by different interpretations of the Register categories could be resolved if participants included brief designations for the weapons transferred. The provision of such information would enable others to distinguish between transfers of systems that do fall within the Register categories (typically, 'heavier' or more combat-capable systems) from those which fall below Register thresholds. It would also make it easier to identify the causes of discrepancies between exporter and importer replies when they occur.

Yet, even when weapon designations are included, the ease with which countries ignore the Register guidelines by including additional systems does create some uncertainty as to whether, in respect of other transfers, countries may not also be applying a degree of flexibility as to whether to report transfers that do fall within the Register categories. On balance, this problem may be offset by the advantages that accrue from countries reporting more than is strictly necessary. But it does illustrate the way in which 'differential transparency', if taken too far, can corrode the confidence placed on the data provided.

In response to this catalogue of problems, it is sometimes argued - more frequently in foreign ministries than in defence ministries - that the political commitment of countries to the Register is more important than the technical proficiency of their replies. Whilst this may be true in the initial stages of a regime's development, however, it is less sustainable over time. Even if individual discrepancies are manageable in themselves, in combination they can create a climate in which the Register guidelines themselves are taken less and less seriously. The current Register provides a valuable balance between clear guidelines and flexibility in interpretation and implementation. If the balance swings too far towards the latter, however, the resulting confusion may significantly undermine its contribution to confidence-building.

The central lesson that need to be drawn from this discussion, which is of particular relevance to the consideration of other possible confidence-building measures, is that as much attention need to be paid to the practicalities of military information exchange mechanisms as to the principles. Carrying them out cannot be left to junior officials who are overwhelmed by other work, and often lack the time to undergo proper training or briefing. Much of the responsibility in this regard lies at national level. But there will also be a need to have international arrangements in place to facilitate a steady improvement in Register implementation. The experience of other international information exchange regimes, in both the military and non military spheres, suggests that this is best done by the creation of a small secretariat with a specific responsibility for helping national officials to understand in detail the information requirements of the regime.

In the case of the UN Register, this secretariat already exists in the form of the Centre for Disarmament Affairs. However governments have so far been reluctant to provide it with the authority and the resources necessary to enable it to be effective.

VI   SIPRI's 'Second Track' Register

Many aspects of the arms trade are not covered by the UN Register. It does not include any information on the value of weapons transferred. Nor, for most countries, does it provide data on military holdings. Estimates for these do exist: the publications of the US Congressional Research Service and the US Arms Control and Disarmament Agency (for estimates of the value of the arms trade), together with the work of the International Institute of Strategic Studies and Jane's Information Group (for estimates of military holdings).[34] For the purpose of cross-checking Register data on the transfers of major conventional weapons, however, the most valuable source is the Stockholm International Peace Research Institute (SIPRI). It is also worth discussing the SIPRI Register in some detail because it illustrates some of the ways in which independent data collection and analysis can complement and enhance an intergovernmental process.

The annual SIPRI Yearbook, which was first published in 1968, draws on an extensive database of material, drawn from a wide range of open sources, to produce a 'Register of the trade in and licensed production of major conventional weapons' that are 'on order or under delivery, or for which the licence was bought and production was under way or completed' during the previous calendar year.[35] The SIPRI Register has a wider coverage than the UN Register in several crucial respects, for example through its inclusion of licensed production and the category of 'guidance and radar systems'. Yet in its essential structural characteristics - retrospective reporting on numbers of major weapons delivered or produced in the previous calendar year - it is very close to its UN counterpart.

This is hardly surprising. The Director of the UN Office for Disarmament Affairs during the Register's formative years in the early 1990s was Provoslav Davinic, who had himself co-authored an influential SIPRI study on the arms trade with the Third World in 1971. The then leader of SIPRI's arms transfers research project, Herbert Wulf, was one of the two consultants to the UN Panel of Governmental Technical Experts that drew up the detailed guidelines for the UN Register in 1992.[36] From the beginning, the design of the UN Register was therefore strongly influenced by the SIPRI experience.

The SIPRI Register is of value to the UN Register in several ways. First, and perhaps of greatest importance, its existence has meant that much of the information that countries are asked to provide to the UN is already publicly available in a readily-accessible format. This has helped to erode resistance to the UN Register by persuading governments that much of the information they are being asked to provide is already in the public domain. Second, it has also provided a useful cross-check on UN Register data, so that independent analysts can query UN Register replies if they do not include transfers that have been reported by SIPRI and appear to fall within the UN guidelines. Third, the SIPRI Register has provided a degree of detail on specific transfers - for example on weapon descriptions - that is often not available in the UN replies. As a result, the SIPRI Register provides a means for filling in the 'gaps' in the replies of countries that have chosen only to report the number, but not the model, of imported arms. Such a matching of the UN and SIPRI Register entries will not be entirely accurate. But, as Appendix 1 shows, the existence of the SIPRI database compensates, at least to some extent, for the failure of some South-East Asia governments - like Singapore and Thailand - to provide model specifications for their imports.

Before its establishment, it was often argued that, although the UN Register might be significant as a political gesture, it would add little to what was already publicly known about the arms trade. The experience of the Register's first three years suggest otherwise. Detailed comparisons suggest that the UN Register continues to add a significant amount of knowledge that had not been previously been published by SIPRI.[37] For example, a study of the UN Register replies for 1994 reveals some 59 transfers reported to the UN that were not listed by SIPRI as having taken place in 1994.[38] Transfers reported to the UN Register for 1994, but not to SIPRI, were particularly noticeable in the case of exports to countries in conflict (such as Algeria, Angola, Cambodia, Mexico, and Nigeria) and countries in sub-Saharan Africa. Of the 26 separate exports to sub-Saharan Africa reported to the UN Register, only 3 were included in the SIPRI Yearbook for the year in question, with SIPRI having particular difficulty in tracking exports from Russia and the ex-communist countries of Central and Eastern Europe.

Compared with other regions, however, SIPRI's coverage of arms transfers to South-East Asia is relatively good. It is not always possible to know for sure that one is correctly matching UN and SIPRI entries, especially when the UN data does not include weapon descriptions. But the only significant omission from the 1995 SIPRI Yearbook appears to be the 1994 transfer to Cambodia of 40 T-55 tanks and 26 OT-64 armoured personnel carriers from the Czech Republic, along with 50 T-55A tanks from Poland. In most other cases, SIPRI has already indicated that knowledge of the transfer in question was in the public domain.

Where the UN Register is clearly an improvement on the SIPRI Register, however, is in its ability to provide more precise information on the size and timing of transfers. SIPRI figures on the numbers of systems on order and delivered, and the dates of delivery, often have considerable margins of error attached to them. By contrast, even allowing for the problems associated with the UN reporting system, the UN Register often provides more accurate information on these aspects. As Ian Anthony, the current leader of SIPRI's Arms Transfers project, has commented:

> 'One of the main gains anticipated from the UN Register was that it would clarify the scale and timing of transfers whose broad outline was already known from public sources. One of the perennial problems for the SIPRI register is determining in which year the deliveries of any given system took place and at what intensity. The Register did go a considerable way to providing this information.'[39]

Since the publication of the UN Register, SIPRI has been active in developing further ways in which its data can be used in regional confidence-building discussions. Most recently, in cooperation with the Malaysian Institute of Maritime Affairs, it has published historical data from the SIPRI archives on transfers to ASEAN countries for the period 1970-94 as a means towards developing regional confidence and consensus in favour of increased transparency in the arms trade.[40]

With the debate on confidence-building in the region now developing rapidly, the MIMA/SIPRI project is a timely and valuable initiative. Improvements in the availability of information through such projects can help encourage further transparency on an intergovernmental level and, in the absence of any other form of verification, act as a valuable cross-check on the accuracy of officially-provided information.

Yet, however reliable 'second track' data becomes, official data declarations will continue to be key to confidence-building processes. As Ian Anthony argues:

> 'the UN Register can provide a basis for dialogue between governments, which SIPRI data never could. If governments which have volunteered information to the UN Register are subsequently questioned about the reasons for any given import or export they must deal with the substantive issues at stake in the case in question. Questioned on the basis of information published by SIPRI, however, governments can avoid issues of substance by challenging the validity of the data.'[41]

VII   The Replies from the Region

Beneath the unanimous support by the countries of the region for the Register in principle, and the recent attainment of near-universal participation in it, there are continuing differences between governments over how far they have felt able to go in supplying information on their own procurement and forces to the Register. These in turn suggest where some of the most interesting regional debates on transparency might be over the next few years.

Australia and New Zealand

In keeping with their image as the countries most enthusiastic about increased transparency, Australia and New Zealand were the only countries in the South-East Asia/ Pacific region that provided any 'available background information' on their military holdings and procurement through national production. In each of the first three years of the Register, Australia enclosed copies of its *Defence Annual Report,* together with

Australia's Strategic Planning (for 1992), *Strategic Review* (for 1993), and its *Defence White Paper* (for 1994). For 1992, New Zealand provided the annual report of its Defence Force, together with a policy paper entitled *The Defence of New Zealand*. For 1993 and 1994, New Zealand also provided details of its military holdings and procurement through national production, based on the seven Register categories.

In Australia's case, perhaps the most significant aspect of its 'available background information' - not least if one is trying to gauge the limits of regional transparency measures - is what it chose not to include. Most OECD countries (including ARF participants Canada, Japan, New Zealand, and the US, as well as 11 of the EU's 15 member states) provided information for both military holdings and national procurement in a standardized form, using the UN Register categories designated for the reporting of transfers. But Australia did not. Some of the relevant information on Australian holdings and national procurement can be obtained from reading the detailed policy documents and reports sent to the UN, along with some of the other defence documents produced by the Australian government. But none of these documents provide a comprehensive listing of Australia's military holdings in the seven Register categories. There are clearly some aspects of its military holdings which the Australian armed forces have been unwilling to disclose.[42]

One of those aspects is almost certainly Australia's stocks of missiles, which have been reported to be at such a low level that US re-supply would be required in order to sustain high intensity military operations.[43] The influential Australian analyst Desmond Ball recently suggested that, as a result of such sensitivity, which Australia shares with many of its ASEAN neighbours, too much transparency in this area could undermine the perception of national self-reliance in defence, and have destabilising rather than reassuring results:

> 'The effect of transparency is different for countries with more 'defensive' as opposed to 'offensive' defense postures, as well as for those countries more dependent on arms imports rather than indigenous production. It can expose vulnerabilities (in both intelligence collection and force structure capabilities). Uncertainty about the capabilities of potential adversaries sometimes serves to enhance deterrence (or induce caution).

In addition, particular problems and sensitivities obtain in the Asia-Pacific region. The widespread and extensive acquisitions over the past decade notwithstanding, many countries still maintain only very limited stockpiles of some critical weapon systems and ordnance. For example, the holdings of precision guided missiles (PGMs) by the Royal Australian Air Force are so small that they 'would not last one day of intensive operations at the higher level.' Thailand has only sixteen Harpoon anti-ship missiles. A full public listing of stocks of these systems could undermine the credibility of many defense postures in the region, thus diminishing regional resilience.'[44]

Australia is not alone in its reluctance to reveal the size of its missile stocks in its Register reply. In the Register's first year, Canada was the only country to provide data on its holdings of missiles and missile launchers (MML) by type (845 AIM 7 Sidewinders and 784 AIM 9 Sparrows). But in the second year it reduced its level of transparency in this area by providing only an aggregate figure: 1960 missiles and missile launchers. France, Germany and Japan only provided data on their holdings under the first six Register categories, and failed to provide any information on their MML holdings. The figures for total MML holdings provided by Italy (916), the Netherlands (16320 Army and Navy only), the UK (32853) and the US (120331) include such a wide variety of munitions as to be extremely difficult to interpret.[45] A few countries have declared that they do not possess any MML (including New Zealand). But, at least in the Register's first two years, there was no country that was willing to reveal meaningful data on its missile stocks.[46]

Despite these reservations, Australia has proved more willing than some of its OECD colleagues to provide detailed information on its annual imports of missiles. Although careful not to break down its missile imports precisely by type, it did specify that its imports of 82 MML over the first three years of the Register included Harpoon, Sparrow and Standard missiles, as well as 2 Mk 13 missile launchers for its frigates. (See Appendix 1).

It could be argued that, over time, the provision of data on annual imports of missiles would enable a picture of total military holdings to be developed: thus effectively undermining the purpose of the refusal to provide MML holdings data. Yet any attempt to estimate MML holdings on this basis in, say, 10 years time would also have to estimate Australia's initial missile holdings (as of 1992), losses of missiles due to attrition, training and retirement, and the composition by model of the annual figures provided. While Australia's Register replies on missile imports will therefore help analysts over time to build up a general indication of the size of its missile stockpile, it will only be able to do so within quite wide margins of error: thus, Australian defence planners hope, balancing the requirements of deterrence with those of confidence-building.

The Philippines and Malaysia

The Philippines and Malaysia were participants in the UN Register from the beginning, and have also been willing to provide more information than is strictly necessary. Both have included descriptions of the weapons they have imported, and neither appears to have been particularly sensitive about its handling of missile imports. The relatively permissive attitude to transparency in these two countries seems to be related to the relatively high degree of civilian control of defence policy in comparison with other ASEAN members, as well as to a political commitment to the process of confidence-building.

In both cases, however, the value of the high degree of transparency displayed may have been somewhat dissipated by the fact that the Register definitions of weapons categories have been largely disregarded in the compilation of national replies. Solely on the basis of the numbers of imports reported under each Register category, for example, an outside observer might surmise that, in 1994, Malaysia was responsible for 96% of reported imports of artillery pieces world-wide, and the Philippines was responsible for 75% of total reported imports of missiles and missile launchers world-wide. In 1993, the Philippines appears to be the world's second largest importer of warships (with 13 vessels), only marginally behind Indonesia's import of 14 vessels in the same year.

This does not make sense, and the explanation is clear. Both Malaysia and Philippines have chosen to include in their replies a wide range of items that do not fall within the Register categories. The large Malaysian import of artillery in 1994 appears to be a result of the inclusion of artillery shells, rather than artillery pieces.[47] The large 1994 Philippines import of MML is a result of the import of 10,680 'RX MTR HK 40/56'. 12 of the 13 'warships' which the Philippines reported as imports in 1993 were in fact only patrol boats. And the import of 504 Starburst missiles from the UK (delivery of which was due to begin in October 1993) was not reported by the UK because the 'Missiles and Missile Launchers' category in the Register specifically excludes ground-to-air missiles.

Moreover, Malaysia also appears to have used orders, rather than deliveries, as the basis for reporting imports. This accounts for the fact that Malaysia reports the import of 3 artillery pieces (155 mm) and 28 Hawk aircraft from the UK in 1993, yet the UK does not report having exported these weapons to Malaysia until 1994.[48] It explains why Malaysia's reply for 1993 included the import of 8 F/A-18D aircraft from the US, (together with associated missile systems) despite the fact that open sources suggest that they are not due to be delivered until 1997.[49] It also explains why Malaysia's reply for 1994 includes the import of 18 Mig 29 aircraft from Russia, although open sources suggest that delivery did not take place until 1995.[50]

It is an indication of the Malaysian government's strong commitment to greater military transparency that it has been willing to include detailed descriptions of its weapons imports even before they have been delivered. The value of Malaysia's initiative in including deliveries in its reply would have been greatly enhanced if it had provided this data as a supplement to the data on deliveries that the standardized forms are designed to hold, rather than as an alternative to it.

The approach taken by the Philippines and Malaysia in their Register replies is not without its problems. But it can be seen as an example of the benefits of having a confidence-building regime that allows a certain degree of flexibility in interpretation even as it maintains some clear minimum guidelines. Both countries have serious security concerns, and both remain relatively weak in military terms compared with some of their neighbours. Yet both countries have been willing, in the first three years of the UN Register, to go beyond what is strictly necessary, and have thereby established precedents which could be of value in future confidence-building measures, as the next Chapter discusses.

Singapore

Singapore was the third ASEAN member to be a founding participant in the UN Register. In contrast to other ASEAN members, however, it had expressed its initial reservations about the Register through its abstention in the November 1991 vote in the UN First Committee,[51] and through a statement that the Register 'would have to take into account the national security interests of member states.'[52] Singapore's security concerns were also reflected in the fact that, unlike Malaysia and the Philippines, it chose not to include any weapon descriptions or designations. Singapore has done what is required by the Register, but it has not used it as an opportunity for providing more information than is requested.

Yet this rather minimalist approach to the Register has to be seen in the context of the considerable detail included in the Singapore government's biennial statement of its defence policy, which is the most detailed such statement from any of the ASEAN countries. *Defence of Singapore 1994-95* does not provide data on the numbers of weapons in Singaporean armed forces' stockpiles. But it does detail the types of weapons that Singapore possesses, and those it has recently acquired: allowing most of the 'gaps' in Singapore's Register reply to be filled in from a Singapore government source. It is therefore the one import that cannot be calculated in this way - the import of 20 missiles and missile launchers from the US in 1993-94 - that may do most to explain Singapore's reluctance to provide more data for the Register itself. Like other states in the region that rely heavily on small stocks of precision-guided munitions (including Australia), Singapore may feel that its security interests constrain the extent to which it can reveal details of its imports in the Register's MML category, even if there is no real obstacle to doing more in the other six categories.

Singapore has clearly taken the process of completing its Register replies very seriously. In most cases, there is a close correspondence between its replies and those of its two main suppliers, the US and France. But its replies have clearly been compiled independently, as can be seen by the differences with France on the timing of artillery imports and with the US on the timing of missile imports. The decision not to report the import of helicopters from France in 1993 is probably the result of the fact that they were locally assembled in Singapore, and therefore can be seen as falling outside the remit of the transfers Register. Singapore is also one of the very few countries to report an import from a country not taking part in the Register: 8 combat aircraft imported from Jordan in 1994.

There has been some regional interest in whether Singapore will include the full squadron of F-16 aircraft it is buying from the US in its Register reply, since some of these aircraft are due to be retained in the US for training purposes. The 1992 UN Group of Experts was quite clear that such an arrangement should indeed count as a transfer for the purposes of the Register.[53] Moreover, by making transfer of title the sole criterion for its own reply, the US should also have no problem in reporting this transaction. But Singapore's delay in reporting imports of missiles from the US suggests that it may be using a different criterion, such as the physical entry of weapon systems into Singapore territory. With the F-16's due to be transferred to Singapore in 1995 and 1996, this is an issue that may well have to be resolved early in 1996. If Singapore decides not to report these aircraft in its next replies, but the US does, it may elicit unjustified suspicion that it is seeking to conceal its acquisitions. On the other hand, there would clearly be difficulties involved in its changing its definition of a transfer in order to accommodate a single case. However Singapore decide to treat this case, it would therefore be helpful for its reply to state clearly the definition of transfer that is being used and highlight any transfers (such as the F-16 purchase) that may have been omitted because of the way in which such a definition works.

Overall, Singapore's record of participation in the Register's first three years suggests that it has put aside many of its initial reservations and has become a serious and committed participant: a process that was undoubtedly aided by its place as the only ASEAN member on the 1994 UN Group of Experts charged with examining the implementation and development of the Register. The detail provided in its annual defence policy statement suggests that Singapore may be willing to take part in further developments in military transparency. But, perhaps more than some of its ASEAN partners, it is also likely to ask hard questions about any possible security implications of such transparency.

Indonesia

Indonesia failed to submit a Register reply in 1993, and might never have done so without the momentum towards a regional security dialogue that was building through 1993 and 1994. When it did reply, moreover, it was only to reveal the modesty of its procurement efforts. For 1992, it submitted a 'nil return', and for the next two years the only (albeit substantial) transfer reported was the import of 27 'warships' from Germany: part of a 39-vessel deal involving most of the navy of the former German Democratic Republic. This modest reply was not a result of concealment. With the exception of Germany, none of the major supplier states reported any exports to Indonesia in the Register's first three years, and the only other transfer reported (which Indonesia did not confirm) was the export of 12 artillery pieces from Slovakia in 1993. No other transfers were reported by SIPRI as having taken place during this period.

By reporting the import of vessels that fell outside the Register 'warship' category (the Condor minesweepers and the demilitarised Frosch landing craft), and by including the designations of these vessels rather than simply giving the gross numbers involved, Indonesia may have made a deliberate decision (like Malaysia and the Philippines) to supply more information than the minimum required. It is equally possible, however, that it simply decided to replicate as closely as possible the reply made by its supplier, in this case Germany. It will be interesting to see whether Indonesia will continue to be as transparent in relation to future imports, particularly in those cases - like the impending (1996-97) import of 24 Hawk 100/200 aircraft from the UK - where the exporting state does not normally report weapon descriptions.

A greater source of concern regarding Indonesia's position came in November and December 1994, when Indonesia joined a group of non-aligned countries, as well as China, in expressing opposition to the draft resolution on the Register's development tabled on 2 November by a group of 78 countries, including the EU states, Japan, Australia, Singapore, Malaysia and Cambodia. The dissenting states wanted (a) the Register to be expanded to include weapons of mass destruction, (b) no convening of another Group of Experts to review possible Register expansion, and (c) 'transparency in armaments' to be dropped from the agenda of the Conference on Disarmament. Significant concessions were made by the sponsors of the original resolution to address these concerns (for example, a postponement of the next Group of Experts from 1996 to 1997). But these revisions were not enough to secure adoption by consensus.

A series of votes followed on the various clauses and sub-clauses in the draft resolution.[54] In the final General Assembly vote on 15 December 1994, a revised version of the original resolution was adopted by 150 votes to none, with 19 abstentions and 15 countries not taking part in the vote.[55] Indonesia was one of the 19 countries abstaining. (Other abstentions in the region were North Korea and Myanmar. Not taking part were Laos and Vietnam. China and Cambodia voted in favour of the final resolution).

Indonesia's stance at this session of the UN was of concern for two reasons. Firstly, it might have been the first step towards Indonesian withdrawal from Register participation altogether. Of the 34 countries that had abstained or failed to take part, only 6 (Cuba, India, Iran, Indonesia, Jordan and Mexico) had been Register participants in 1994. There was a real concern that Indonesia might join the majority of this group (as Iran and Jordan did) and fail to provide a Register reply in 1995: thereby dealing the new regime a serious blow.

Second, it was significant that Indonesia was the only ASEAN member not to support the final resolution. ASEAN members often stress that they derive strength from their solidarity in UN discussions, and its endorsement by the ASEAN Regional Forum in July 1994 had appeared to give the Register a regional seal of approval. But Indonesia decided to give more weight, on this occasion, to its ties with fellow members of the Non-Aligned Movement. This particular vote does not appear to signal a more general realignment in Indonesia's international position. Nor has it led to a withdrawal from the Register. But it does indicate that, despite its tradition of 'talking softly' in ASEAN discussions, Indonesia's position on these issues will continue to have to be monitored carefully.

Thailand

Thailand was the last of ASEAN's original members to join the UN Register, submitting its first reply on 27 February 1995. The delay may be due to the evolving balance of power between the civilian and military arms of the government, a balance in which access to information on military procurement plays an important part. But the decision to submit information for the Register, which followed by only a few months the decision to issue Thailand's first ever 'white paper' on defence policy, appears to indicate that the armed forces are willing to make at least some concessions in the direction of greater accountability and openness.

The replies for 1993 and 1994 received so far have tended to confirm open sources that suggest that Thailand is the biggest importer of conventional arms in ASEAN. In contrast to many of the imports reported by Malaysia and the Philippines, most reported Thai imports appear to fall within the Register guidelines and have been confirmed by exporter replies.

Thailand does indicate that the warship imported from the US in 1994 is HTMS Phuttrayotya Chulalok, formerly a US Navy Knox class vessel. With this single exception, however, it has chosen not to enclose weapon descriptions in its reply. As a result, some parts of the Thai reply are difficult to interpret. First, the identity of the 90 missiles and missile launchers imported from China in 1993 is not revealed, and the import has not been confirmed by China. Second, Thailand has reported the import of 72 combat aircraft from the Czech Republic - 36 in 1993 and another 36 in 1994 - while the Czech Republic has confirmed the shipment of only 36 aircraft (the L-39Z combat-capable trainer) in total. Since most open sources suggest that the total order was only 36, the most likely explanation appears to be clerical error on the part of the Thai government. Such an error was perhaps made more likely by the fact that the reply for 1994 was actually submitted only four months after the (very late) reply for 1993.

Finally, the Thai replies did not confirm the import of the warships which China reports as having exported to Thailand: 2 in 1992 and 1 in 1994. The most plausible explanations appear to be that (a) they have not yet been accepted into Royal Thai Navy service because they are still being fitted with new weapon systems and electronics; (b) because of this refitting, the Thai authorities may consider these vessels to constitute 'procurement through national production', and thus not the subject of Register reporting. Without any explanation for their omission being included with the reply, however, it is not possible to confirm either explanation.

In contrast to Singapore, the lack of detail in Thailand's reply is not primarily a result of security concerns. Rather it reflects the highly sensitive and corrupt nature of the Thai procurement process. It has been common for one part of the government not to know what other parts are doing, and the issue of access to military procurement information is a key domestic political issue. The issue of Thai participation in the Register, or indeed other transparency measures, is therefore likely to be decided most of all on the basis of domestic political factors rather than external security concerns. The fate of regional transparency measures may depend, in this case, most of all on the future evolution of military/civilian relations.

Others

There is less to say about the other countries of the region. Prompted in part by its imminent acceptance as an ASEAN member, **Vietnam** finally joined the Register in April 1995, with the task of convincing sceptical military chiefs made somewhat easier by the fact that the first reply (for 1994) was a 'nil return'. In future years, some imports, such as the purchase of 6 Su-27 aircraft from Russia in 1995, should be reported. So the reply for 1995 should provide a better indication of how far Vietnam will be willing to go in providing system descriptions.

The final participant from the region is **Papua New Guinea**, which submitted a nil return in the Register's first year, but then failed to reply in

1994. In 1995, it again failed to meet the deadline for publication in the annual Register report. But, on 30 October, it replied to the UN by submitting a 'nil return' for the years 1993, 1994 and 1995. In its reply, the Papua New Guinea government explained that:

> 'Papua New Guinea does not have in its inventory any of the ... weapon systems (in the seven Register categories). ... the Papua New Guinea Defence Force is a relatively lightly armed force compared to other regional countries with large and sophisticated weapons systems. Furthermore, Papua New Guinea does not manufacture, let alone export, such lethal weapons.'[56]

This reply is not surprising, given what is known of Papua New Guinea's defence force. The UK did report the export of a single armoured combat vehicle to Papua New Guinea in 1992, and Australia reported (though not on the standardized form) the export of an obsolete Saracen armoured vehicle 'for use by a private company as secure transport for cash, securities and bullion'. But these replies do little more than illustrate the continuing uncertainty about how to report transfers of weapon systems to clients that do not intend to use them as such. They do not undermine the essential point that Papua New Guinea (despite having a population larger than either New Zealand or Singapore) is at present not a participant in the regional arms equation.

Of the four countries in South-East Asia that remain outside the Register, two - **Brunei** and **Laos** - are of rather limited importance in the regional balance of power. Brunei's level of arms acquisitions may increase in future if current plans for new corvettes and/or combat aircraft come to fruition. But the main benefit from their joining the Register would be political, given ARF's aim of achieving universal regional participation.

Cambodia, by contrast, is a significant importer of conventional arms, acquiring 90 battle tanks and 26 armoured combat vehicles in 1994 alone (according to replies from Poland and the Czech Republic). These acquisitions do not constitute a threat to neighbouring states as they are clearly aimed at strengthening the government's position against the rebel Khmer Rouge forces. But they do underline the importance of bringing the country into the UN Register as soon as possible.

The most significant non-participant in the region, however, is **Myanmar**. As a result of large scale shipments of Chinese arms, SIPRI has estimated that over the five years 1990-94 its arms imports totalled $1042 million (at

1990 prices). This made Myanmar the world's 32nd largest arms importer: ahead of both Singapore and Malaysia, though behind Australia, Thailand and Indonesia.[57] Figures from the US government's Arms Control and Disarmament Agency paint a similar picture, estimating total Myanmar arms imports for the four years 1990-93 at $796 million (at 1993 prices): ahead of Indonesia and Malaysia, but slightly behind Singapore.

China did report the export of 12 combat aircraft to Myanmar in 1992, and there is no reason to believe that it would conceal future exports that fell within the Register categories. Yet the limited size of these exports is difficult to reconcile with independent estimates of Myanmar's arms acquisitions. SIPRI reports a total of 36 combat aircraft delivered in 1994.[58] In August 1995, the International Institute of Strategic Studies reported the delivery of 150 Chinese Type-85 armoured personnel carriers 'during the last twelve months,' together with possible orders for 30 aircraft, 20 helicopters, 60 armoured combat vehicles and 50 artillery pieces.[59] The recent delivery of APC's could be reported by China in its reply for 1995. Nevertheless, Myanmar's own participation in the UN Register would help to reduce regional uncertainty about the size and nature of these arms acquisitions, and would be taken as a positive indication of the regime's willingness to respond to regional concerns about its military build-up.

VIII A Regional Forum on the UN Register?

The UN Register has got off to a promising start in its first three years of operation. The relatively high, and increasing, rate of participation in the Asia Pacific region may be one of the first fruits of efforts to deepen the level of security dialogue in the region, and of the greater degree of regional self-confidence in general. As the region moves towards near-universal participation, discussion is likely to turn increasingly to whether further measures can be developed in order to increase the extent to which the UN Register is used and to complement it with further measures that are distinctly regional.

It is sometimes argued that transparency and confidence-building measures need to be devised at regional level, and tailored to regional peculiarities, in order to be relevant. There is, after all, a limit to what can be achieved in a global forum of almost two hundred states facing a wide variety of concerns and with very different cultures and political systems. On the other hand, countries often find it easier to accept a more distant source of authority than one that is closely linked to neighbouring states. UN peacekeeping missions often try to avoid recruiting troops from adjacent states for this reason. In the area of arms control, while regional agreements do exist (such as the South Pacific Nuclear Free Zone), the most far-reaching verification measures are those agreed at global level (for example in relation to the Nuclear Non-Proliferation Treaty and the Chemical Weapons Convention). In other global regimes many countries take part because participation is seen as being part of being a responsible member of the international community. Similarly, it facilitates participation in the UN Register that it does not require governments to be convinced that the rules set out are appropriate for their particular circumstances, or even that there is a problem relating to conventional arms in their region in the first place.

One of the proposals actively under discussion in the region is a Regional Arms Register, first proposed by Malaysian Defence Minister Mohamed Najib bin Tun Abdul Razak in 1992, and often included in lists of possible regional transparency measures. The Australian paper prepared for the 1994 ARF meeting suggested that the idea of such a Register was a 'promising area.'[60] And the ASEAN Concept Paper prepared for the 1995 ARF meeting includes 'further exploration of a Regional Arms Register' in its list of proposals for exploration over the medium and long term.[61]

With the successful establishment of the UN Register, it is now widely agreed that a Regional Register would have to complement, not replace, the global regime. In order to know what the role of a Regional Register might be, therefore, the countries of the region need to consider whether there are particular aspects of transparency in arms that are not included in the UN Register and which they would like to have included in a regional regime. Mention is often made of particular classes of weapon systems that are not included in the UN's seven categories but might nevertheless be of considerable significance to Asia-Pacific regional stability.

Yet the establishment of concerns about the coverage of the existing Register is not enough in itself to make the case for a new Regional Register. It is also necessary to consider whether these concerns can more effectively be addressed using the existing UN framework, or whether they might require a separate regional framework. As earlier sections of this Chapter have discussed, the UN Register provides a flexible framework, within which different states can choose to exercise varying degrees of transparency. Before deciding to establish a Regional Register, therefore, it is necessary to ask whether enough has yet been done to utilise the scope that already exists for increasing levels of transparency within the UN framework.

A discussion of possible alternative means of improving regional transparency also needs to take account of the significant difficulties that would be involved in negotiating and establishing a separate Regional Register. If successive UN Group of Experts, on all of which the US, Japan, China and ASEAN were represented, could not reach consensus on expanding the Register's requirements further, a similarly diverse, if somewhat smaller, group of countries may find it no easier to reach agreement on a regional level. Moreover, in drawing up the boundaries of the new Regional Register, negotiators will have to address the highly sensitive issue of what the boundaries of the 'region' actually are. For example, should procurement of the North American and European states involved in ARF be included in the Register, even if the systems in question are deployed entirely in and around the Atlantic? Or should the Asia-Pacific be redefined to include only the Western seaboard of the Pacific Ocean? On such issues, diplomats can undoubtedly find creative solutions. But the cost of doing so, in terms of time and effort expended, could be considerable. Before embarking on the path towards a Regional Register, therefore, there needs to be some expectation that the result is a significant contribution to confidence-building.

Such considerations suggest that the immediate priority in this area is not a Regional Register itself, but the establishment of a set of processes - a 'Regional Forum on the UN Register' - through which countries can discuss their UN Register replies. In some cases, these processes might be best started at a subregional or even bilateral level. The key would be to find what is the best way to tie the UN Register more clearly into the regional security dialogue, rather than seeing it as a worthwhile but 'stand alone' initiative.

Organised regional discussions on the UN Register could serve a variety of purposes,. They could obtain additional information (for example on forward plans, weapon models, and defence doctrines) over and above that provided by the UN. They could be used to provide a more solid mutual understanding of weapons purchases and plans as an additional input into the broader discussions on defence doctrine that are also being developed through ARF. In addition to broader discussion of the policy underlying states' acquisitions, they could provide an opportunity for a more technical discussion of the content of Register replies, in which officials responsible for the Register could share their experiences and spread best practice.

As part of this process, the states of the region could agree to provide more to the UN than the minimum required. Considerable flexibility exists within the UN framework for countries to provide more data than the minimum normally seen as being required. One possibility for discussion might be to find ways in which to persuade those ARF members who are at present less transparent in this respect to consider whether they could do more. Such an approach might yield more in terms of transparency, especially in the short term, than an attempt to create a whole new regime. Through a process of consultation and mutual example, states might hope to gradually lever up national levels of transparency. Officials could discuss why different countries have chosen different ways to reconcile the requirements of transparency and military secrecy within the Register framework. They could, for example, discuss the relative merits of Japan's approach to reporting military holdings (which involves reporting only the first six Register categories and thus avoiding awkward problems with the reporting of missile holdings) with that of Australia (which does not report military holdings as such, but includes much relevant data in its annual White Paper). ASEAN states, for their part, could discuss why some of them - Philippines, Indonesia, and Malaysia - have felt able to include weapon descriptions in their Register replies, but others - Thailand and Singapore - have not.

It is sometimes thought that the UN Register is only a Transfers Register, and that a separate Regional Register is therefore necessary for procurement through national production and military holdings. Thus, for example, the Australian government paper for the 1994 ARF argues that ARF officials should examine the Regional Register proposal, including

> 'whether - and, if so, how - it should handle existing military equipment holdings and domestic production - two important areas that are not so far addressed by the UN Register.'[62]

Yet the UN Register does include specific provision for the submission of information on military holdings and domestic production. As part of the compromise involved in the Register's establishment in 1992, member states were invited to provide 'available background information' on their military holdings, procurement through national production and relevant policies. In order to emphasise the more voluntary character of this invitation, it was agreed that the information provided would (unlike that on transfers) not be published, and no standardised definitions or forms were provided for the submission of this data. But the information provided is publicly available for consultation at the library of the UN Centre for Disarmament Affairs; and the military holdings and national procurement data for the first two years has already been published in the Bradford Arms Register Studies series.[63] In 1995, 29 states provided some information on military holdings, including ARF members US, Australia, New Zealand, Canada, Japan and most EU members. The UN Register therefore already provides a framework for the provision of national procurement and military holdings data without the need to establish a new regional Register for this purpose.

There are other ways in which a process of discussions around the UN Register could be used to encourage a 'levelling up' of transparency in the region. ARF countries could follow the UN's suggestion that they include with their replies a clear explanation of the definitions of transfers that they are using, thus making it easier to resolve some of the discrepancies between the replies of importing and exporting states. Governments could also follow the Australian example, and regularly include copies of their statements of defence policy as 'available background information'.

Following the precedent set by Malaysia and the Philippines, and to some extent Indonesia, ARF countries might also be able to use their UN replies as a way of reporting additional systems and orders for weapons. This would not be so easy to fit within the existing UN Register framework, and some consultation with the Centre for Disarmament Affairs might be necessary to ensure that the information provided was published. Given the UN's sympathy and support for regional transparency initiatives, however, it may be possible to find some way for the countries of the region to use the UN Register in this way.

In addition to measures designed to improve the quality of replies and the extent to which they are used in intergovernmental dialogue, more could also be done to improve the general accessibility of Register data. At present, the only official sources for Register replies are the basic, and limited circulation, documents produced by the UN General Assembly, which are then supplemented by a series of even more obscure corrigenda and addenda. Non-governmental organisations play a valuable role in disseminating Register data, but their work tends to focus on analysis of the global data.[64]

As part of an effort to increase the availability of Register data, ARF countries could consider publicising and distributing their Register replies in their own countries. For example, a useful first step might be for ARF members to agree to include Register replies in their annual defence policy statements, thus emphasising the links between two parallel transparency exercises. Such a step would be relatively easy to implement because it would only involve the republication of information that is already, in any case, in the public domain. It would not only help increase awareness of the existence of the Register and the data it contains. It would also be a small step towards encouraging countries to produce defence statements that include concrete, and nationally-derived, data.

In addition to national publication of national replies, it might also be useful to have a single publication that brings together all the replies from the region, together with all the reports of transfers to (and from) the region made by extra-regional states. Such a publication would encounter a number of political sensitivities if it was conceived as an official document. The question of which countries should be included in the 'region' would be of particular sensitivity. At this stage, therefore, it might be better for such a publication to be undertaken by a 'second track' organisation such as CSCAP. It need not necessarily be published as a free-standing document. It could, for example, form part of the 'regional strategic outlook statement' that Paul Dibb has recently proposed.[65] It need do no more than reproduce the data provided to the UN that relates to the region, including any 'available background information' on holdings and procurement that countries have chosen to submit. But it could be used as an opportunity to commission a series of independent studies of the trends which the data suggest.

Finally, intergovernmental regional discussions could be used as a means of exchanging ideas on the future development of the UN Register. The UN is due to hold another major review of the operation and development of the Register during 1997, and a new Group of Experts will therefore be appointed in late 1996 or early 1997. The ARF was well represented (by Australia, Canada, China, Japan, Russia, Singapore, United States, as well as three EU members) on the last Group of Experts in 1994. But these countries appear to have acted largely without consultation with those Asian countries that were not represented on the Group. Now that regional mechanisms for the discussions of confidence-building measures are developing, they could be used to discuss whether it is possible to develop a common regional consensus on the issues in advance of the global discussions.

Developing a regional consensus may be most feasible at the ASEAN level. The ASEAN countries have been represented on all three UN reviews in this area: by Indonesia in 1991; by Malaysia in 1992; and by Singapore in 1994. So, on a rotational basis, either Thailand or the Philippines seems quite likely to be included in the 1997 review. ASEAN countries have not always been able to sustain a common position on the Register in the past, as the Indonesian decision to break ranks at the December 1994 General Assembly illustrates. But, with their growing experience of actually operating the UN Register at regional level, ASEAN may be able to make a useful contribution to the UN debate.

More ambitiously, one might speculate about the possibility of an ARF consensus on the future direction of the UN Register. There is little doubt that, if such a consensus were possible, ARF could play a determining role in the next review. With very few countries from sub-Saharan Africa and the Middle East now participating in the Register, countries from these regions are likely to have little leverage in determining where the Register should go next. ARF could therefore play the sort of leading role in the development of global transparency measures that Europe sought to play at the beginning of the decade. At a minimum, the development of Asia as a strong source of ideas and experience in confidence-building measures could allow it to play an equal role with the traditionally predominant NATO/EU/OSCE axis.

At present, the chances of a common ARF position on the development of the Register appear remote. The divisions that led to the failure of the 1994 Group of Experts to reach consensus were, most of all, divisions between the region's major powers: with the US on one side, China on the other, and Japan and Australia seeking some compromise between the two. On the other hand, states from the region might be able to bring some of the lessons from ARF confidence-building to the UN process. Through such a link, it is possible that new ways of using the UN Register more effectively for purposes of regional confidence-building may be found.

IX   Conclusions

The high rate of regional participation in the UN Register may be one of the first results, in terms of confidence-building measures, of the intensified regional security dialogue that has been taking place (most of all through the ARF process) since 1993. It is still too early to say whether the Register is having any positive impact in the region and further measures may be needed before maximum benefit can be gained from existing data. But it is already possible to point to at least two lessons from the regional experience so far that are of relevance for both the UN Register itself and for possible regional measures.

First, the variety of Register replies received from states in the region illustrates the scope that exists within the existing Register for encouraging all countries to aim towards emulating regional 'best practice'. The quality of replies in the region is already reasonably high by global standards. Yet, within the existing Register framework, Singapore and Thailand could emulate their neighbours by providing more detailed weapon descriptions. Malaysia and the Philippines could distinguish more carefully between systems that fall within the Register categories and those that do not. Australia could consider whether it might not be able to provide data on its military holdings in a more systematic way, as both Japan and New Zealand decided to do in 1994.

Second, implementation matters. Agreement in principle to transparency and information exchange measures is crucial. But, in order to establish a regime that can build trust and that can live through the ups and downs of international relationships, it is necessary to have efficient systems for the regular production of data. Even in the case of the UN Register, widely regarded as being modest in its requirements, ambiguities in interpretation of definitions and failings in national administration could, if not addressed, undermine the perceived utility of the data provided. If the Register is to be used as a model for future exchanges of military information measures, it is vital that the administrative, as well as the security, implications of proposals are carefully considered.

Notes

1.   Bilveer Singh, 'The 'Najib Initiative' and Confidence-Building in the Asia-Pacific Region', *Asian Defence Journal*, 7/92, pp. 6-13.

2.   *Chairman's Statement, First Meeting of the ASEAN Regional Forum*, 25 July 1994, Bangkok, p. 3. My italics.

Notes continued

3. In addition to the 12 countries detailed in Table 7.3, ARF participants Canada, the European Union, Russia, and the US all provided replies for the Register.

4. *Chairman's Statement of the Second ASEAN Regional Forum*, 1 August 1995, Bandur Seri Begawan, p. 5. My italics.

5. Malcolm Chalmers and Owen Greene, *Taking Stock: the UN Register After Two Years*, Bradford Arms Register Studies Number 5, Westview Press, 1995, pp. 15-16.

6. For example, see Aabha Dixit, 'India-Pakistan: are commonly-accepted confidence-building structures relevant?', *Security Dialogue*, 26, 2, 1995, p. 193.

7. United Nations, *Study on ways and means of promoting transparency in international transfers of conventional arms*, UN General Assembly document A/46/301, September 1991, paras 154-155.

8. For a complete listing, see Malcolm Chalmers and Owen Greene, *Implementing and Developing the United Nations Register of Conventional Arms*, Peace Research Report Number 32, Department of Peace Studies, Bradford University, May 1993, pp. 88-93.

9. Herbert Wulf, 'Appendix 10F: The United Nations Register of Conventional Arms', Stockholm International Peace Research Institute, *SIPRI Yearbook 1993*, Oxford University Press, 1993, p. 536.

10. However, it does include surface-to-air missiles launched from ships.

11. Herbert Wulf, op cit, p. 539. Herbert Wulf was an expert advisor to the 1992 Panel. Also see Edward J. Laurance and Herbert Wulf, 'Appendix 14D: The 1994 review of the United Nations Register of Conventional Arms', Stockholm International Peace Research Institute, *SIPRI Yearbook 1995*, Oxford University Press, 1995, p. 564.

12. UN Panel of Technical Governmental Experts, *Report on the Register of Conventional Arms*, General Assembly document A/47/342, 14 August 1992.

13. For further details of this period, see Malcolm Chalmers and Owen Greene, *Taking Stock*, op cit, pp. 15-30.

Notes continued

14.   For a recent discussion of the negotiations on a successor to CoCom, see Owen Greene, *Developing a Successor to COCOM*, Saferworld, London, September 1995.

15.   The UN had 185 members as of 1 January 1995. Switzerland and the Holy See have observer status at the UN and were also asked to provide information for the Register (Switzerland did so, the Holy See did not). Yugoslavia was suspended from the UN at this time, but provided information.

        As of 12 October 1995, 182 states (183 if Taiwan is included) had acceded to the Non-Proliferation Treaty. *US Arms Control and Disarmament Agency Fact Sheet*, October 12, 1995. As of 4 October 1995, 159 countries had signed the Chemical Weapons Convention, of which 40 had ratified it. *US Arms Control and Disarmament Agency Fact Sheet,* 4 October 1995.

16.   For a detailed analysis of participation figures, see Malcolm Chalmers and Owen Greene, *Taking Stock*, op cit, pp. 33-55; Malcolm Chalmers and Owen Greene, 'The UN Register of Conventional Arms: the third year of operation', in J. B. Poole and R. Guthrie (eds), *Verification 1996: Arms control, peacekeeping and the environment*, VERTIC/Westview, 1996.

17.   See Malcolm Chalmers and Owen Greene, *Taking Stock*, op cit, p. 40.

18.   Ibid, pp. 48-49.

19.   Malcolm Chalmers and Owen Greene, *The UN Register of Conventional Arms: the third year of operation*, op cit.

20.   EU members providing weapon descriptions in their 1995 replies were Austria, Belgium, Denmark, Finland, Germany, Greece, Ireland, Italy, Netherlands, Portugal, Spain, Sweden. Those not doing so were France and the UK. Luxembourg did not export or import any major conventional weapons during 1994.

21.   The data on holdings and national procurement for 1992 has been published in Malcolm Chalmers and Owen Greene, *Background Information: an analysis of information provided to the UN on military holdings and procurement through national production in the first year of the United Nations Register of Conventional Arms*, Bradford Arms Register Studies Number 3, Westview Press, 1994. Malcolm Chalmers and Owen Greene, *Taking Stock,* op cit, contains full details of the data provided for the second year of the Register.

Notes continued

22. 12 of the EU's 15 member states also provided 'available background information' on military holdings. The only exceptions were Finland, Ireland and Luxembourg. *United Nations Register of Conventional Arms: Report of the Secretary-General*, General Assembly document A/50/547, 13 October 1995.

23. For example, see Malcolm Chalmers and Owen Greene, *Implementing and Developing the United Nations Register of Conventional Arms*, op cit, pp. 45-46.

24. Malcolm Chalmers and Owen Greene, *The United Nations Register of Conventional Arms: Examining the Third Report*, Bradford Arms Register Studies Working Paper, November 1995, pp. 14-17.

25. Ibid, p. 15.

26. *United Nations Register of Conventional Arms: Report of the Secretary-General: Corrigendum*, General Assembly document A/49/352/Corr. 1, 8 November 1994. A further minor adjustment was made in *United Nations Register of Conventional Arms: Report of the Secretary-General: Corrigendum*, General Assembly document A/49/352/Corr. 2, 3 February 1995. For more details, see Malcolm Chalmers and Owen Greene, *Taking Stock*, op cit, pp. 69-77.

27. For further details, together with references, see Appendix 1.

28. Malcolm Chalmers and Owen Greene, *Taking Stock*, op cit, p. 271.

29. *United Nations Register of Conventional Arms: Report of the Secretary-General*, General Assembly document A/50/547, 13 October 1995. The date refers to the cut-off date for the inclusion of national submissions. The document was actually released on 31 October.

30. Data provided by UN.

31. These late replies were published in *United Nations Register of Conventional Arms: Report of the Secretary-General*, General Assembly document A/50/547/Add. 1, 13 November 1995.

32. *Jane's Fighting Ships 1993-94*, 1993, p. 300. Vessels with a standard displacement of less than 750 metric tonnes should be included if they are equipped to carry missiles or torpedoes with a range of 25 km or more. This is not thought to be the case for the Kondor class vessels.

Notes continued

33.   Bates Gill, J. N. Mak and Siemon Wezeman, *ASEAN Arms Acquisitions: Developing Transparency: A MIMA-SIPRI Report*, Malaysian Institute of Maritime Affairs, August 1995, p. 51. This important clarification was not included in the last *SIPRI Yearbook* to mention the transfer, *SIPRI Yearbook 1993*.

34.   For a discussion of different data sources, see Malcolm Chalmers, Owen Greene, Edward J. Laurance and Herbert Wulf (eds), *Developing the United Nations Register of Conventional Arms*, Bradford Arms Register Studies Number 4, Westview Press, 1994, especially chapters by Ian Anthony (SIPRI), Andrew Duncan (IISS), and Tim Mahon (Jane's Information Group).

35.   *SIPRI Yearbook 1995*, op cit, p. 513.

36.   Edward J. Laurance, Siemon T. Wezeman and Herbert Wulf, *Arms Watch: SIPRI Report on the First Year of the United Nations Register of Conventional Arms*, SIPRI Research Report Number 6, Oxford University Press, 1993, pp. 13-15.

37.   Malcolm Chalmers and Owen Greene, *Taking Stock*, op cit, pp. 62-69; Malcolm Chalmers and Owen Greene, *Examining the Third Report*, op cit, pp. 12-13; *ibid*, pp. 39-50. Also see John Sislin and Siemon Wezeman, *1994 Arms Transfers: A Register of Deliveries from Public Sources*, Monterey Institute of International Studies, March 1995.

38.   Based on a comparison with John Sislin and Siemon Wezeman, *op cit.*, published specifically in order to facilitate comparisons with the UN Register. The subsequent *SIPRI Yearbook 1995*, op cit, does include 10 of these transfers, but was finalised after the first Register replies had been submitted to the UN.

39.   Ian Anthony, 'What is required to have a useful transfers Register?' in Malcolm Chalmers, Owen Greene, Edward J. Laurance and Herbert Wulf (eds), *Developing the United Nations Register of Conventional Arms*, op cit, p. 103.

40.   Bates Gill, J. N. Mak and Siemon Wezeman, *ASEAN Arms Acquisitions: Developing Transparency: A MIMA-SIPRI Report*, op cit.

41.   Ian Anthony, op cit, p. 89.

42.   For details of the information on military holdings and procurement through national production provided to the Register, see Malcolm Chalmers and Owen Greene, *Background Information*, op cit, pp. 23-70; Malcolm Chalmers and Owen Greene, *Taking Stock*, op cit, pp. 210-263.

Notes continued

43. Gary Brown, *Australia's Security: Issues for the Next Century*, Australian Defence Studies Centre, 1994, p. 70.

44. Desmond Ball, 'Arms and Affluence: Military Acquisitions in the Asia-Pacific Region', *International Security*, 18, 3, Winter 1993/4, p. 108. The quote is from former RAAF Chief of Staff Air Marshal David Evans.

45. Malcolm Chalmers and Owen Greene, *Taking Stock*, op cit, p. 87.

46. At the time of writing, 'available background information' on the third year of replies had not been studied.

47. The number has been further increased by the inclusion of shells of calibre well below the 100mm threshold of the Register definition.

48. The UK reply was slightly different. It reported that only 24 aircraft were delivered rather than 28.

49. Bates Gill, J. N. Mak and Siemon Wezeman, op cit, p. 68; also see *SIPRI Yearbook 1995*, op cit, p. 431.

50. *SIPRI Yearbook 1995*, ibid, p. 431.

51. *Report of the First Committee*, A/46/673, 29 November 1991. The resolution was carried by 106 votes to 1 (Cuba), with eight abstentions (China, North Korea, Iraq, Myanmar, Oman, Pakistan, Singapore, Sudan). Cuba, China, Pakistan and Singapore have all subsequently participated in the Register.

52. Herbert Wulf, 'Appendix 10F: The United Nations Register of Conventional Arms', op cit, p. 536.

53. *Report on the Register of Conventional Arms: Report of the Secretary-General*, General Assembly document A/47/342, 14 August 1992, paragraph 11.

54. For details, see Malcolm Chalmers and Owen Greene, *Taking Stock*, op cit, pp. 120-122 and pp. 283-288.

55. Excluding Yugoslavia, which was barred from the General Assembly at this time.

56. *United Nations Register of Conventional Arms: Report of the Secretary-General*, General Assembly document A/50/547/Add. 1, November 1995.

Notes continued

57.   *SIPRI Yearbook 1995*, op cit, p. 494.

58.   Ibid, p. 534.

59.   International Institute for Strategic Studies, *The Military Balance 1995-1996*, Oxford University Press, 1995, p. 153.

60.   Paul Dibb and Gareth Evans, *Australian Paper on Practical Proposals for Security Cooperation in the Asia Pacific Region*, Department of Foreign Affairs and Trade, April 1994, p. 11.

61.   ASEAN, *The ASEAN Regional Forum: A Concept Paper*, 1995. Also see Paul Dibb, *How to Begin Implementing Specific Trust-Building Measures in the Asia-Pacific Region*, Strategic and Defence Studies Centre Working Paper Number 288, Australian National University, July 1995, p. 10.

62.   Paul Dibb and Gareth Evans, op cit, p. 11.

63.   Malcolm Chalmers and Owen Greene, *Taking Stock*, op cit; Malcolm Chalmers and Owen Greene, *Background Information*, op cit.

64.   For examples of reports detailing the 3rd year replies, see Edward J. Laurance and Tracy Keith, *Research report: An Evaluation of the Third Year of Reporting to the United Nations Register of Conventional Arms*, Monterey Institute of International Studies, 31 October 1995; 'Chronicling an Absence of Restraint: the 1995 UN Arms Register, *BASIC Papers*, British American Security Information Council, 3 November 1995; Malcolm Chalmers and Owen Greene, *The United Nations Register of Conventional Arms: Examining the Third Report*, Bradford Arms Register Studies Working Paper, November 1995.

65.   Paul Dibb, op cit, pp. 12-13.

CHAPTER 8

Confidence-building measures

I Introduction

The establishment of the ARF process has encouraged a wide-ranging discussion of confidence-building possibilities in the region, and the high level of participation in the UN Register is one result. The purpose of this Chapter is to discuss some of the other possibilities. The Chapter starts by an examination of the idea of annual defence policy statements. It then discusses proposals for greater military-to-military cooperation, for example in joint exercises and operational transparency measures. Finally, it returns to the Register idea by examining the possible role of a Regional Arms Register.

II Statements on defence policy

One of the more interesting ideas to emerge from the regional dialogue on confidence-building in recent years has been the proposal that all states should produce regular public statements of their defence policy, explaining the basis of their defence policies and outlining the main features of their defence provision.

The proposal for annual statements - sometimes misleadingly called 'Defence White Papers' - has gained considerable momentum over the last couple of years as countries throughout the region considered whether, and how, to take up the concept themselves. The concept was given a regional stamp of approval by the ARF meeting of August 1995, in which Ministers agreed

> 'for the ARF countries to submit to the ARF or ARF-SOM, on
> a voluntary basis, an annual statement of their defence policy.'[1]

The idea of annual statements on defence policy is not a new one. **Australia** has a long tradition of publishing detailed reports on its defence policy for parliament, and its annual Defence White Papers are recognised as being the most comprehensive in the region.[2] **Singapore** also produces a detailed statement on a biennial basis, the latest of which was produced in August 1994.[3] Because of its strong parliamentary system, the **Philippines'** armed forces have submitted detailed (and publicly available) modernisation plans to Congress,[4] and production of a defence policy paper is under consideration. **Thailand's** Ministry of Defence produced its first statement in May 1994, and a second statement was due to come out in late 1995.[5] In 1994, Major-General Dato Nordin Yusof and Abdul Razak Abdullah Baginda co-authored a book 'intended to commemorate the achievement and contribution of **Malaysia's** Armed Forces towards safeguarding the nation's sovereignty and its strategic interests.'[6] The book contains the same range of material found in other ASEAN policy statements, for example on the structure and equipment of the three Malaysian services, relationships with ASEAN neighbours, and Malaysia's role in UN peacekeeping. Although not an official statement of government policy, it was published by the Malaysian Armed Forces and was co-authored by the Assistant Chief of Defence Staff and the head of an influential Malaysian thinktank with close links to the Ministry. It can probably be considered as a 'trial run' for a government policy document in the near future.[7] **Indonesia** released its first report on its defence and security policy on 17 August 1995, 'to promote wider understanding of Indonesia's defence and security policy in support of ... mutual understanding with other nations, particularly neighbouring nations.'[8] Finally, prompted by its membership of ASEAN and ARF, officials in **Vietnam** are actively discussing the possibility of a defence policy statement.[9]

Perhaps of greatest significance, however, are the tentative signs that **China** may also be moving towards greater openness. Since early 1993, there were persistent reports that China was preparing to produce a statement on its defence policy.[10] After much speculation about a vigorous debate within the Chinese government about what should go into it, the first Chinese defence policy statement - entitled 'China: Arms Control and Disarmament' - was finally published in November 1995.[11] As expected, the detail included was rather limited. But it did contain commitments that China had no plans to increase its defence spending unless its security was threatened, and that it would station no troops on foreign soil.

The last two years have therefore seen the region move towards near-universal adoption of the idea of a defence policy statement. Some of the credit for this achievement must go to the efforts made by Australia, as one of the first regional countries to have a White Paper. Over the last three years, it has devoted substantial effort to bringing key defence ministry officials to Canberra to explain the mechanics of how Australia goes about production of its White Paper. By doing so, it has helped to reassure those governments who had felt that a policy statement needed to contain a level of detail that they would not be willing to accept. Rather, Australian officials emphasised that a defence policy statement was intended as a flexible framework which countries could use in a variety of ways depending on their own particular circumstances.[12]

The flexibility involved in the publication of defence policy statements has been the key to its success so far. In some cases, the information provided has been very limited in scope. But, by endorsing the principle of publication on an annual basis, ARF has built into the process a mechanism for gradual improvement in quality. Governments do not have to endorse 'top down' definitions of what they should be revealing. But, once the principle is accepted, advocates of greater transparency within governments do have a vehicle for pressing their case on a regular basis. Thus, for example, publication of the second (1995) Thai statement was delayed because early drafts were reported to be a significantly more open than the first statement in 1994. Those elements within the Thai government who are resistant to a more open statement may win the argument this year. Even if they do, however, it illustrates the way in which the ARF's endorsement of annual statements - like its support of the UN Register - can have real force in obliging governments to take transparency much more seriously than before.

The policy statement concept has been easier for ARF governments to accept in part because each country can go at its own pace, and is not obliged to accept any verification of what it is saying. Its value lies as much in its discussion of policy thinking and threat analysis as in the specific facts and figures involved. Over time, the practice of annual publication should allow readers to discern trends in thinking and use this as the basis for regional dialogue.

Yet, even if most of the ARF countries are now producing regular statements, they are of variable quality. In contrast to the UN Register, no guidelines on minimum content are available. The first statement from Thailand, for example, contains virtually no data on the size or equipment of its armed forces, and contains only a short section on the defence budget. By contrast, both the Indonesian and Singaporean statements provides a significant amount of detail on personnel numbers, procurement plans and force organisation.

All statements on defence policy will contain significant 'silences' and omissions, and it takes time for countries to learn how to maximise openness without endangering operational security. Variations in national levels of transparency are in part a result of differences in national political/military cultures. In general, however, countries with some experience of producing statements are likely to be more confident than those who are just publishing their first statement. With reports now due on an annual basis, there is an expectation that the quality of reports will improve over time.

In order to accelerate this process, it has recently been proposed that it would be a useful exercise to try to develop guidelines on what should be included in policy statements. The CSCAP working group on confidence-building measures is studying what the content of such guidelines might be, with a view to developing 'minimum standards of openness' and 'uniform outlines' for defence policy statements.[13]

The agreement of minimum guidelines can, as in the case of the UN Register, provide a useful standard against which ARF members measure their own performance. They can help 'lever up' levels of openness, encouraging governments to consider emulating the example of more open neighbours, and facilitating regional discussion of what specific measures would have the greatest confidence-building value.

Many proposals have already been made for the content of defence data exchanges, many of which might suitably form part of the discussion on policy statement guidelines. The most common suggestions include:

- national understandings of the strategic environment and how it affects national defence thinking;

- concepts underlying national defence and security policy, including the relationship between national defence and the regional security dialogue;

- national orders-of-battle, such as numbers and roles of squadrons, regiments and naval vessels (such data is less sensitive, and more widely available, than details of weapons holdings);

- military personnel numbers, perhaps together with data on paramilitary forces and civilian support staff. Data might also be included on issues such as recruitment policy, pay and conditions, and training;

- a report on major operations since the previous report, including participation in UN peacekeeping missions, involvement in regional exercises, and larger national exercises;

- a report on acquisitions, including recent procurement and planned acquisitions. Such a report could include a commentary on the country's latest UN Register reply.[14]

Perhaps the issue on which transparency and defence policy statements could be of greatest value is defence spending. Data on current defence budgets do not, in themselves, provide a proxy indicator for military capability. The efficiency with which countries convert spending into capability varies too much for such a simple translation to be made. But defence spending figures are of particular importance in the confidence-building process because they can help - especially once trends can be discerned over time - to illuminate national priorities and concerns. Countries increasing the priority given to defence spending (compared with other parts of the government budget and/or total GNP) tend to be more worried about security than those who are cutting defence's share. Countries that are worried about their own security are often in turn a source of concern to others.

The potential benefit from defence budget transparency is perhaps most obvious in the case of China. Other ARF participants often express concern at the level and growth in Chinese defence spending. Yet the possibility of a meaningful dialogue on the subject is limited by the lack of Chinese budgetary figures that command any confidence amongst other states. As a result of these problems, Japan, the US, and ASEAN members have all been urging China to become more transparent in this area.

The first, and most obvious, step towards greater defence budget transparency would be to urge all ARF participants to include details of their current defence budget in their annual defence policy statement. In addition, they might be asked to provide data on the trends in real defence spending, and defence spending as a proportion of GNP, over the last few years. Most ARF countries already publish this data in some form, principally in the form of budgetary reports to parliament. It should, therefore, be possible to use the defence policy statement as a means of making this data more available for the regional dialogue process.

Steps of this sort, while useful, will not be enough. For one of the biggest sources of concern about defence budgets - seen most clearly in the case of China, but also a problem in several other cases - is that the real meaning of official defence budget figures can be difficult to interpret without a detailed technical explanation. Published defence budgets sometimes exclude items that in other countries would be included in defence spending. In some cases, these exclusions may be a result of deliberate attempts to conceal the level of defence spending from parliament, public and/or other states. Yet exclusions are often as much a result of differences in national accounting systems as of deliberate attempts at concealment. Even within Western Europe, there is a big variation in what is included in national defence budgets, as can be seen by comparing national figures with defence spending calculated on the standardised NATO definition. In 1994, Germany's defence spending using its own national definition was 47.2 billion marks: 19% less than the 58.1 billion marks calculated on the NATO definition. By contrast, the UK's defence spending in 1994 on a national basis was almost exactly the same (£22.77 billion) on a national basis as on a NATO basis (£22.71 billion). The difference is a result, not of Germany's lower level of transparency in military spending compared with the UK, but of the differences in national systems for accounting for various support costs.

In the same way, almost every ARF country, including China, publishes an official defence budget figure that makes sense in terms of its own national accounting system. But the coverage of different countries' defence budgets varies considerably because each chooses its own way of accounting for various items. Amongst the most common items that are the subject of different treatments in different countries are: military pensions; pensions for civil servants who worked previously in the defence ministry; income received by the armed forces as a result of economic activity, including the sale of surplus weapons; spending on police and paramilitary forces (such as the coastguard); spending on national intelligence services; subsidies paid directly to national arms industries; and arms imports financed by payment in kind rather than cash.

If further progress is to be made, therefore, it will not be enough to ask countries to become more transparent. It will also be necessary to provide more specific guidelines as to how they should do so. It is unrealistic to expect the countries of the region to adopt a standard definition of military spending if this involves major changes in their systems of government accounts. The countries of NATO have not done so even after forty years of close military cooperation. The states of ARF, with their much bigger variation in governmental and socio-economic systems, are not about to do so either. But it may be possible - perhaps initially through 'second track' discussions, then through discussions in ARF itself - to work towards an agreement on a regional definition of defence spending which countries could then use alongside their own national definition. Once such a definition were developed, countries could then be requested to provide data on their defence spending on both a national and a standard basis in their policy statements, perhaps with an accompanying technical commentary.

Achieving agreement on a common definition will not be easy, but the differences are often more technical than political in nature. Even if a common definition is not possible at first, it may be possible to encourage states to be more explicit about what is and is not included in their defence budgets.

There is likely to be no shortage of ideas for the content of annual defence policy statements. As with the UN Register, however, the process of discussing the statements will be as important as their content. The fact that most ARF countries now produce such statements is itself a step forward. But it will be just as important that mechanisms are set up for regular consultations over their contents, both before and after their publication.

Governments will never be entirely open about their concerns in public statements of policy, especially when the expression of those concerns could be seen as implying distrust of fellow ARF members. It is one of the paradoxes of confidence-building that it sometimes requires participants to be more willing to openly express their fears, even if this means being willing to express a lack of confidence in each other. But the process of openly discussing the assumptions behind contingency planning has to be handled with care if contingencies are not to be perceived as threats. The possible consequences of greater openness were seen in Indonesia's reaction to the shift in Australian defence policy in the late 1980s towards a more explicit policy of defence against an attack launched from the north. Australia was right to pursue a policy of maximum openness towards its neighbours on the assumptions underlying its defence policy, and relations with Indonesia have not been harmed in the long run. But the episode does illustrate that, as written policy statements become more honest and revealing, processes of dialogue and explanation are likely to become more, not less, important.

III   Extending the spiderweb

One of the most long-standing forms of military confidence-building in the region is military exercises, already discussed in Chapter 2. It is also an area of considerable promise, with many proposals to build on, and extend, the 'spiderweb' of defence relationships between ASEAN countries and between individual ASEAN members and Australia. The experience of such measures is widely judged to be a successful one, building trust between the militaries of the different countries, and helping each to understand the concerns of others. For example, in 1988, the Royal Australian Navy initiated a biennial conference - the Western Pacific Naval Symposium - that brings together representatives of the navies of the ASEAN states, the US, Japan, South Korea, China, Papua New Guinea, Australia and New Zealand. Topics under discussion have included the Law of the Sea and SLOC protection, as well as the scope for information sharing in areas such as piracy, fisheries infringements, search and rescue and maritime pollution.[15]

Through its subordinate workshops, the WPNS has begun to produce tangible results, such as a Maritime Information Exchange Directory, a WPNS Tactical Signals Handbook and a WPNS Replenishment at Sea Handbook.[16] In addition, through the Pacific Area Senior Officers' Logistics Seminar (PASOLS) series, practical cooperation in logistics - exchanging logistics doctrine, procedures, documentation and experience - has been under way for some time. Its confidence-building has been enhanced by the existence of a standing secretariat.[17]

The extension of this process is not specifically mentioned in the 1995 ARF document, but it is a common theme in the literature on regional confidence-building. For example, Desmond Ball suggests efforts to extend the size and scope of existing bilateral exercise programmes, to develop more multilateral programmes, and to allow regional observers at major military exercises 'not just for a couple of days of carefully orchestrated activity, but for a sufficient period to understand the purposes of the exercises (and) the operational concepts being tested.'[18]

A complementary suggestion is that of prior notification of major exercises. Bilveer Singh has suggested that:

> 'If such CBM's are in existence in sea, then the problem, for example, caused by Indonesia-Malaysia joint exercise called MALINO DARSARA in August 1991 could have been avoided. The Singapore leadership maintained that there was

no prior notification and that the joint exercise was timed to apply political pressure on the vulnerable republic. That the exercise was timed to climax with the republic's National Day made it all the more ominous.'[19]

More ambitiously, it has been suggested that ARF countries might soon be able to take advantage of the Open Skies Treaty to extend transparency in the region.[20] The Treaty is currently expected to come into force in late 1996, with 27 participants from former NATO and Warsaw Pact states. Central to the Treaty is the provision that members are given rights to overfly the territory of other member states, with certain restrictions on the types of equipment carried, in return for providing reciprocal rights for flights over their own territory. Most of the information thus revealed is available in any case to powers - such as the US - with access to satellite intelligence. But it can provide considerable additional information for states without these resources. In contrast to other East/West treaties, the Treaty's area of application covers the whole territory of both Russia and the US, and includes provision for new members to join, subject to the agreement of existing participants.[21]

At first, the main interest in Open Skies membership is likely to be in North-East Asia, where Japan may be interested in learning more about Russian deployments in the region.[22] Over time, however, it is possible to envisage a gradual extension of the regime to encompass other parts of the region. Swinnerton suggests, for example, that the Open Skies approach could be used in maritime areas open to dispute, such as the Spratlys.[23]

The chances of region-wide accession to the Open Skies Treaty in the near future seem small, not least in China. But recent developments suggest that a more evolutionary approach to military transparency is already having some successes. In the absence of a clear set of obligations established by treaty, some countries are likely to participate more in the process of greater openness than others. But, as both the experience of the UN Register and of the defence policy statement idea suggest, the trend towards greater transparency appears to be affecting all but the most intransigent regional states.

While the relatively informal and uneven nature of regional transparency has clear advantages in relation to the publication of information, however, caution is needed in assessing the confidence-building value of joint exercises and training. The purpose of exercises is to prepare armed forces for possible conflicts, and joint exercises are thus based on the possibility of the armed forces of different countries fighting together against a common foe. While such exercises undoubtedly build confidence between the participants, they may have a less comforting effect on those countries not included, especially if they have reason to believe that they are considered as a potential opponent.

The 'spiderweb' of exercises that has developed within ASEAN, and increasingly with Australia and the US, involves all member states to some extent. Concerns continue to be expressed when neighbouring states exercise separately (for example Singaporean concerns about Malaysia/Indonesia exercises). But these concerns tend to be mollified because, if individual exercises are viewed in the context of the spiderweb as a whole, nobody feels left out of the process.

Over the coming years, the defence spiderweb in South-East Asia is likely to develop further with multilateral exercises becoming more common, and with an increased level of participation from new ASEAN member Vietnam. While this process is broadly to be welcomed for its confidence-building value within South-East Asia, it may have less welcome side-effects if it is perceived to be an attempt to build ASEAN, rather than Asian, security resilience. If China is invited to take part in regional exercises and refuses, the problem will be of its own making. But the more developed the South-East Asian process becomes, and the nearer it gets to areas of Chinese interest, the more important it will be that efforts are made to draw it in.

This does not mean that the dual function of joint military activity - confidence-building between participants, deterrence towards (some) non-participants - is invalid. The balance of power will continue to be one of the keys to regional security, and the solidarity of the smaller states of ASEAN can be a stabilising feature in that balance. But it does illustrate that what may be presented as confidence-building measures can in reality have a more complex character. Measures to build confidence within ASEAN could, under some circumstances, reduce confidence between ASEAN and China.

The key to confidence-building between ASEAN and China will be in the South China Sea. Many possible compromise solutions to the Spratlys disputes have been suggested, both by ASEAN and Chinese commentators.[24] Whatever solution is acceptable to all parties will almost certainly have to include a series of military confidence-building measures, for example guaranteeing free passage through disputed areas, limiting military deployments in the area, and providing for pre-notification of major movements. One possible precedent for a settlement is the Timor Gap Treaty between Indonesia and Australia, which leaves sovereignty issues to one side in order to jointly exploit the natural resources of the disputed region. Yet even in the absence of a formal settlement of this sort, some more limited confidence-building measures might play a role in reducing the potential for conflict.

Perhaps the most important confidence-building measure would be a clear acceptance by all parties that they must exercise self-restraint pending the results of negotiations. Such restraint would involve a clear commitment on China's part to refrain from actions similar to its February 1995 seizure of Mischief Reef. But it might also involve other participants - such as Malaysia, Philippines and Vietnam - suspending current plans for development in the area, such as Malaysia's plans for development of the tourist facilities on Swallow Reef. Such an agreement will not be easy. But the stakes are high for all countries concerned. Modest confidence-building measures could provide a useful first step towards creating the political conditions for a more far-reaching settlement.

IV Maritime peacetime cooperation

A large part of the work of ASEAN navies is concerned with policing missions, such as protecting offshore oil exploration, combating piracy, drug smuggling and waste dumping, and defending fish stocks against illegal fishing. While these missions essentially involve the use of national armed forces against private individuals, however, the individuals involved are often citizens of neighbouring states. As such, many of these issues can become a source of inter-state tension, even threatening to embroil national armed forces.

The issue of illegal fishing is particularly sensitive. In November 1995, for example, the Malaysian Navy killed two Thai fishermen who were fishing illegally in Malaysian waters. While the Thai government did no more than get the Malaysians to return the bodies and pay for funeral expenses, Thai fishermen threatened to blockade Thai ports to force their government to do more. In response, the Malaysian and Thai prime ministers held a meeting on the topic on the periphery of the December 1995 ASEAN summit in Bangkok. It is hoped that the result will be the establishment of a bilateral fisheries committee between the two states.[25]

In addition to specifically military confidence-building measures, there have therefore been proposals in recent years for ways to promote confidence through greater cooperation between regional navies in their peacetime roles. As the waters of South-East Asia become increasingly crowded, and competition for their natural resources becomes fiercer, the need for cooperation also increases.

Perhaps the biggest obstacle to more rapid progress in this area is the continuing existence of sovereignty disputes in the region, not only between ASEAN members and China, but between ASEAN members themselves. For it is difficult to institute effective cross-border cooperation without at least some implicit agreement on where the borders are. But there may be some areas on which countries will be willing to set aside issues of sovereignty in pursuit of common security concerns, and in the process perhaps pave the way for dispute settlement.

As a first step in this direction, the 1995 ARF summit authorised an Intersessional Meeting on Search and Rescue Co-ordination and Cooperation, to be chaired jointly by Singapore and the US.[26] In addition, ASEAN's Concept Paper for the summit has suggested that areas in which progress might be possible in the medium term include:

- maritime information data bases;

- cooperative approaches to sea lines of communication, beginning with exchanges of information and training in areas such as search and rescue, combating piracy and drug control;

- mechanisms to mobilise relief assistance in the event of natural disaster;

- establishment of an ASEAN relief and assistance force and a maritime safety unit;

- conventions on the marine environment (dumping of toxic wastes, land-based sources of marine pollution);

- sea level / climate monitoring system;

- explore the idea of joint marine scientific research;

- maritime surveillance.[27]

This is an ambitious agenda, even if only ASEAN states (perhaps along with Australia) are initially involved. The fact that such ideas are now being seriously discussed, however, is itself a sign of the increased priority being given to the confidence-building agenda in the region. It remains to be seen whether this initial momentum can be translated into concrete progress over years to come.

V   A Regional Register

As Chapter 7 suggested, the UN Register has already started to make a contribution to the process of regional confidence-building. In the short term, its establishment has delayed serious consideration of a Regional Arms Register. For many of the functions previously proposed for the regional Register are already being fulfilled by its UN counterpart. Yet, given that there are limits to the extent to which regional states can use the existing UN Register for specifically regional ends, there may be a case for considering separate but complementary regional arrangements for the exchange of military information. Indeed UN Secretary-General Boutros Boutros-Ghali has gone so far as to argue that:

> 'Regional registers of conventional arms should now be the
> next step. They have the advantage of allowing the categories
> of weapons to reflect the security concerns felt in the region.'[28]

The idea of 'added value' is central to the discussion of a possible regional Register. The UN Register already includes most of the weapons of concern in the region because of their possible role in offensive operations, and there is no point in replicating arrangements that already exist. Rather the purpose should be to develop measures which are relevant to the concerns of countries in the region but have not, for whatever reason, become part of the UN Register. Thus the 1994 Group of Experts on the development of the UN Register commended regional initiatives to increase military openness and transparency, but cautioned that they

> 'should complement and not detract from the operation of the
> universal and global United Nations Register of Conventional
> Arms'[29]

In considering the nature of a regional Register, questions of both content and process need to be discussed, both of which are important in confidence-building terms. On content, it is not hard to identify areas where a regional Register could in principle add to the data provided in the UN Register. It may nevertheless be helpful to sketch out some examples of the sort of measure that might find its way onto the agenda.

The most commonly discussed suggestion is the inclusion of additional systems, not included in the UN Register's seven categories, in reported imports and exports of weapons. For example, China's suggestion (in the 1992 Panel of Experts) that transfers of airborne early-warning and tanker aircraft should be reported to the UN Register might be taken up on a regional level. Other possibilities might include combat support helicopters, ground-to-air missiles, and warships that fall outside the thresholds set in the UN Register.[30] Some of these systems have already been included on an ad hoc basis in regional replies to the UN Register (for example, by Indonesia, Malaysia and the Philippines). Including them formally in a regional Register would put such transparency on a more institutionalised and universal basis.

Second, data could be exchanged on procurement through national production. It is anomalous that arms-importing countries are obliged to reveal their entire procurement programme, while those that produce their own weapons are not. At present, transparency in this area is likely to be more difficult for China, which produces most of its own major weapon systems, than for ASEAN states, which do not. But the development of indigenous arms industries, notably in Singapore and Indonesia, means that domestic arms production, including production under licence, is likely to become increasingly important even within South-East Asia itself. Establishing a regional norm of transparency in respect of national production would help ensure that this process could be discussed alongside the issues surrounding international transfer of arms.

Third, the countries of the region could agree to exchange data on their military holdings. There is likely to be considerable resistance to providing data for all seven Register categories, with missile holdings being of particular sensitivity because of the small stocks which many countries carry. One possible compromise might be to agree, as a first confidence-building step, to exchange details of inventories of more visible systems such as warships, combat aircraft and helicopters. Once a framework for transparency in holdings had been established, countries might then be ready to gradually increase the information they would be willing to provide in this area, taking into account both their own security concerns and the levels of openness displayed by their neighbours.

Fourth, in addition to the UN Register's requirement for post-notification, data could be provided to a Regional Register on systems under order, for example detailing all the systems ordered in the previous calendar year. A possible model for such a data exchange could be provided by Malaysia's replies to the UN Register. The apparent ease with which Malaysia has been able to provide details of its weapon orders placed during 1993 and 1994 suggests that there may be no insuperable reason why it cannot be provided on a more systematic basis (by Malaysia and others) in future.

Thus there is no shortage of areas where a regional Register could play a useful role in adding to the transparency already provided by the UN equivalent. However, the success of the regional Register concept also requires agreement on the process through which it would be created, and through which agreement on its content might be reached.

The first question would be to decide on the mechanism through which the countries of the region should go about reaching a consensus on the nature of a regional Register. Since the aim of a regional Register is to fill the gaps left by the UN Register, it first requires regional consultation on the UN Register itself. A natural product of these discussions might then be the development of a collective view of those areas where the UN Register is inadequate, and thus where a regional Register might be of particular value. It might then be the task of an ARF committee or Group of Experts to develop a consensus on what should go into the Register.

The central problem faced in reaching such a consensus would be to reconcile the differing approaches of ARF countries to transparency. In the 1994 UN Group of Experts, China was one of the countries that was most insistent on resisting further transparency in national procurement and military holdings, and this resistance would have to be overcome if progress was to be made towards greater transparency on these issues on a regional basis. China may possibly be less resistant to increased transparency in other areas, such as adding new types of military systems or weapons under order. But China is not the only ARF country that might decide to object to a particular component of a Register. A successful result to such negotiations is possible, given a will to compromise between the major states concerned. But it would not be easy.

In addition to agreeing on the content of a regional Register, the geographical scope of the Register has to be agreed. Since the concept is being discussed within the ARF, it is often assumed that the countries covered would be those in the Asia-Pacific proper, defined as the countries of South-East Asia, North-East Asia, (probably) Australasia and (probably) India. It might also be argued that an ARF Register should encompass the territory of all ARF participants, including Canada, the European Union, Russia and the US. As in the Organisation for Security Cooperation in Europe, however, it is likely that the forces of 'external' participants (in OSCE's case, the US, Canada and Russia) may only be considered part of the region if they are actually stationed in the region (that is East Asia) itself.

Given the difficulties that might be anticipated in reaching agreement between 20 or more countries, one possibility might be to look to develop the idea of a regional Register on a smaller scale, perhaps through the development of an ASEAN Register. Such a Register could help to build confidence between ASEAN members. More importantly, it could help establish a foundation upon which a wider Register could eventually develop, perhaps through the accession of other states to an ASEAN Register framework.

In a recent analysis of the prospects for a regional Register, Mohamed Jawhar Hassan (Deputy Director of Malaysia's Institute for Strategic and International Studies) has suggested that regional Registers have several 'inherent shortcomings':

> 'Unlike a global register which enables comparisons of exports and corresponding imports, such comparisons would be more difficult for regional registers where exports to countries outside the region and imports from them are involved. Since outside states will not be reporting, it would be difficult to check tallies.

> Whether regional registers will be published ... will also require consideration. Participating regional states may object to outside states having access to more detailed information regarding their arms situations without reciprocal action. If the decision is against making available the contents of the register to outside states, then the question of confidentiality will have to be addressed. This may well mean that the register will only be made available to participating regional governments and will not be accessible to their citizens, hence curtailing its value a little.

An arms register for the Asia Pacific region also raises the question of its depository and administration. Who will tend to the maintenance of the register? The ASEAN Regional Forum is the obvious candidate, but it will have to establish an institution for this purpose and equip it with the necessary resources and expertise.[31]

None of these problems are so serious that they would, in themselves, prevent a regional Register being of value. But, in all three cases, Jawhar has raised issues that would have to be addressed in the design of a Register.

Most of the arms imports into East Asia come from Western Europe, Russia and the US, and it should be possible to elicit their cooperation as associate partners in a regional Register. But other states not represented in ARF are also involved in supplying military technology and arms to the region (such as Israel and South Africa). It is not clear how far a regional Register would include exports from East Asia to other regions since, arguably, these exports are of little concern to the security of the region itself. If such exports were to form part of a regional Register, however, there would be no means of cross-checking China's reports of its exports to the Middle East and South Asia.

The issue of confidentiality could become important if the type of data provided to a regional Register were so sensitive as to be of real operational value to a potential opponent. It seems highly unlikely, however, that agreement could be reached for the inclusion of such data in a Register covering the whole of East Asia. The main external security threats felt by the countries of East Asia are, in almost every case, from other East Asian states or (in the case of North Korea and China) from the US. Once countries have been persuaded to provide data to other ARF countries, therefore, there is unlikely to be a significant problem in it being available, even on an asymmetric basis, to non-ARF states.

Confidentiality might become more of an issue if a regional Register were established on a more limited basis - such as ASEAN-only or ASEAN-plus-Australia. In this case, countries might be prepared to exchange data between themselves that they would not be willing to provide to China without reciprocation. Even in the case of an ASEAN Register, however, the potential consequences of confidentiality would have to be carefully considered. Not only would secrecy mean that the regional Register could play no role in promoting greater accountability in defence policy: arguably one of the most important ways in which military information exchange can contribute to confidence-building. It might also create the perception that the countries involved are co-operating against those not involved (such as China). All measures designed to build regional resilience within a limited group of countries contribute to some degree to deterrence of aggression from outside. But an ASEAN Register is less likely to be viewed as part of a strategy of collective defence if it is both publicly available and open to expansion, in due course, to include other states.

The experience of the first three years of the UN Register, not least in the Asia-Pacific region, suggests that a secretariat may be needed in order to develop a regional equivalent. A regional Register will want to allow a considerable degree of flexibility to participating states about the pace at which they fulfil its requirements. But this very flexibility and lack of precision will make it all the more important that an organisation exists that is charged with maintaining the regime itself, reminding states of their commitments and helping to identify the potential for further development. Such tasks cannot be left solely to an intergovernmental committee or to a national ARF secretariat that rotates annually. It requires an organisation that is able to learn and develop over time, responsible to the states of the region as a group, but with a degree of independence from the day-to-day concerns of individual states.

One possibility might be to give this role to a regional Transparency Secretariat, working under the direction of the chair of the ARF Senior Officials' Meeting, and composed of a small number of military and civilian officials. Such a secretariat could act as a repository for information provided through regional confidence-building measures, advise governments on practical aspects of implementation, and report regularly to ARF on progress made.[32]

However valuable such a secretariat would be, it is unlikely to be created solely for the purposes of a regional Register. In its absence, a possible second-best solution might be to use the UN itself as a quasi-secretariat for the regional Register. Regional Register replies could be submitted as regional supplements to UN Register replies, and held by the UN. The information provided in these supplements could then be collated and published, either by the UN or by a regional (possibly second track) organisation.

It remains to be seen whether a consensus can be reached on what should be included in a regional Register. In assessing the value of such a Register, however, attention should not concentrate solely on the confidence-building effect of increased information exchange over and above that available through the UN Register. Just as important, the very act of creating a regional Register would be a powerful symbol of the region's increasing self-confidence in security matters. It is often argued that one of Asia's most serious problems is that it is 'underinstitutionalised' in security terms. By helping challenge this view, a regional Register could have a useful confidence-building effect.

VI   Conclusions

The progress in developing confidence-building measures in East Asia over the last few years has been a result of a convergence of approaches between two models of confidence-building - the 'European' model and the 'Asian' model - that previously seemed irreconcilable. The more European states have come to accept the value of informal dialogue, flexibility and evolution over formal treaty-based approaches to arms control. For their part, Asian states, especially in ASEAN itself, have increasingly accepted that dialogue needs to be accompanied by concrete measures of confidence-building between states. The result has been a flurry of new proposals, some of which have been discussed in this Chapter, and many of which could be implemented over the next few years.

Any one of the confidence-building measures discussed here will seem limited if considered in isolation. Even in combination, they are a complement to, not a substitute for, other means of keeping the peace. States will continue to have to pursue resolution of the many disputes (territorial and otherwise) which underlie regional tensions; and they will remain aware of the need to maintain a balance of power in the region so that no one single state can hope to achieve regional hegemony by force of arms. Yet confidence-building measures can help prepare the ground for conflict resolution and can help the balance of power to operate at lower levels of tension and expense. If they achieve either one of these objectives, the efforts now under way will have been worthwhile.

Notes

1.   *Chairman's Statement of the Second ASEAN Regional Forum (ARF)*, 1 August 1995, p. 5.

2.   Ministry of Defence, *Defending Australia: Defence White Paper 1994*, November 1994.

3.   Ministry of Defence Public Affairs, *Defence of Singapore 1994-95*, August 1994.

4.   Robert Karniol, 'Philippine Navy lines up for 1996 changes', *Jane's Defence Weekly*, 9 September 1995.

5.   Ministry of Defence, *The Defence of Thailand 1994*, May 1994.

6.   Major-General Dato Nordin Yusof and Abdul Razak Abdullah Baginda, *Honour and Sacrifice: The Malaysian Armed Forces*, Malaysian Armed Forces, Ministry of Defence, 1994.

7.   Interviews, Kuala Lumpur, February 1995.

8.   Ministry of Defence and Security, *The Policy of the State Defence and Security of the Republic of Indonesia*, October 1995.

9.   Interviews, Ministry of Foreign Affairs, Hanoi, February 1995.

10.   Discussions with author, Beijing, November 1993. Also see Ji Guoxing, *Maritime Security Mechanisms in the Asia-Pacific Region*, Centre for International Security and Arms Control, Stanford University, 1994, p. 19; Banning Garrett and Bonnie Glaser, 'Multilateral Security in the Asia-Pacific Region and its Impact of Chinese Interests: Views from Beijing', *Contemporary Southeast Asia*, 16, 1, June 1994, p. 31.

11.   'China assures region on arms', *Financial Times*, 17 November 1995.

12.   Interviews, Canberra, July 1994.

13.   Ralph Cossa, *Confidence and Security Building Measures: are they appropriate for Asia?*, Pacific Forum CSIS, January 1995, p. 9.

14.   Paul Dibb and Gareth Evans, *Australian Paper on Practical Proposals for Security Cooperation in the Asia Pacific Region*, Department of Foreign Affairs and Trade, April 1994, pp. 3-4 contains a similar list.

15.   Desmond Ball, A New Era in Confidence Building: The Second Track Process in the Asia/Pacific Region', *Security Dialogue*, 25, 2, 1994, pp. 165-167.

Notes continued

16.   Jack McCaffrie and Sam Bateman, *Maritime Confidence and Security Building Measures in Asia-Pacific: Challenges, Prospects and Policy Implications*, paper presented at International Conference on Marine Policy, Maritime Security and Ocean Diplomacy in the Asia-Pacific, Seoul, September 1994, p. 8.

17.   Russ Swinnerton, *Military Transparency: Preoccupied with the Too-Hard Basket? A Survey of Transparency, Trust- and Confidence-Building Measures in the Asia-Pacific,* paper presented to CSCAP working group on CSBM's, Singapore, April 1995, p. 10.

18.   Desmond Ball, *Building Blocks for Regional Security: An Australian Perspective on Confidence and Security Building Measures (CSBMs) in the Asia/Pacific Region*, Canberra Papers on Strategy and Defence Number 83, Strategic and Defence Studies Centre, Australian National University, 1991, pp. 35-50.

19.   Bilveer Singh, 'The 'Najib Initiative' and Confidence-Building in the Asia-Pacific Region', *Asian Defence Journal*, 7/92, pp. 6-13.

20.   Russ Swinnerton, 'Confidence-building measures at sea: the challenges ahead in South-East Asia', *The Pacific Review*, 8, 2, 1995, p. 338. Shannon Selin, *Asia Pacific Arms Buildups Part Two: Prospects for Control*, Institute of International Relations, University of British Columbia, Working Paper Number 7, November 1994, pp. 35-36.

21.   Stockholm International Peace Research Institute, *SIPRI Yearbook 1995*, Oxford University Press, 1995, p. 824.

22.   For a more detailed discussion, see Owen Greene, *Confidence-Building in North-East Asia*, Bradford Arms Register Studies Number 7, Westview Press, 1996.

23.   Russ Swinnerton, *Confidence-building measures at sea*, op cit, p. 340.

24.   For a useful discussion of compromise solutions proposed by Chinese experts, see Sheng Lijun, *China's Policy Towards the Spratly Islands*, Strategic and Defence Studies Centre Working Paper Number 287, Canberra, 1995, pp. 19-25. Also see Mark Valencia, *China and the South China Sea Disputes*, Adelphi Paper Number 298, International Institute for Strategic Studies, Oxford University Press, 1995, pp. 50-67.

Notes continued

25.   Ted Bardacke, 'Fish war crisis brings Thai and Malaysian PMs to the table', *Financial Times*, 14 December 1995.

26.   *Chairman's Statement of the Second ASEAN Regional Forum*, op cit, p. 4.

27.   Paul Dibb, *How to Begin Implementing Specific Trust-Building Measures in the Asia-Pacific Region*, Strategic and Defence Studies Centre Working Paper Number 288, Australian National University, July 1995, p. 10.

28.   Boutros Boutros Ghali, Address of the Secretary-General to the Advisory Board on Disarmament Matters, *The Disarmament Agenda of the International Community in 1994 and Beyond*, United Nations, 1994.

29.   *Report on the Continuing operation of the United Nations Register of Conventional Arms and its further development*, Report of the Secretary-General, United Nations General Assembly document A/49/316, 22 September 1994, paragraph 38.

30.   For a detailed discussion of possible expansion of UN Register categories, see Malcolm Chalmers and Owen Greene, 'Further development of the Register reporting system' in Malcolm Chalmers, Owen Greene, Edward J. Laurance and Herbert Wulf (eds), *Developing the United Nations Register of Conventional Arms*, Bradford Arms Register Studies Number 4, Westview Press, 1994, pp. 51-85.

31.   Mohamed Jawhar Hassan, 'An Asia Pacific Arms Register: Utility and Prospects', in Ralph Cossa (ed), *Towards a Regional Arms Register in the Asia Pacific*, Pacific Forum CSIS Occasional Papers, August 1995, pp. 39-46.

32.   Russ Swinnerton, *Military Transparency: Preoccupied with the Too-Hard Basket?*, op cit, p. 14.

CHAPTER 9

Beyond Confidence-Building

I   Confidence-building measures: progress so far

Since 1992, considerable progress has been made in strengthening the institutional mechanisms for cooperative security in the region. ASEAN has accepted an explicit security role, and is expanding to include the whole of South-East Asia. The 'spiderweb' of defence relations between ASEAN members has developed further, bolstered and encouraged by Australia and the US. ASEAN is now playing a leadership role in a broader regional security forum (the ARF), through which some of its members' concerns regarding wider regional developments can be addressed.

It is too early to make a definitive assessment of the achievements of the ARF. But the priority given to confidence-building measures in the second ARF summit suggests that a significant evolution in attitudes towards transparency in military affairs is beginning to take place. Until recently, it was often suggested that transparency measures were alien to the 'Asian' way of doing things. While such arguments are still heard, however, most governments in the region now accept the principle that military transparency can contribute to confidence-building. Even China, with its long tradition of government secrecy, became a full participant in the United Nations Register in 1993 and, in November 1995, published its first annual statement on defence policy. Progress seems likely to be gradual and focused on measures that can be implemented in a flexible way. But, in large measure because of ASEAN's active support for the concept, ARF countries have now committed themselves to taking specific steps to put this principle into practice. As a result, there is a growing expectation that further developments in confidence-building and transparency will take place over the next few years.

One of the most notable features of South-East Asian governments in recent years, especially in those countries that have enjoyed the greatest economic success, has been their willingness to try new ideas, learn from their mistakes, and generally adopt a pragmatic approach to policy.[1] This has been especially noticeable in economic matters, but it also helps explain the willingness of regional leaders to try new ideas in the area of confidence-building and security. ASEAN states are anxious to retain a measure of control over the regional process, not least through their leadership role in the ARF. But they also accept that the future of the Asia-Pacific region - as of their own societies - depends on an ability to draw pragmatically on both European and Asian traditions. As senior Singaporean official Kishore Mahbubani has suggested

> 'The Asia-Pacific region is developing a unique 'corporate culture' on regional security: an unusual blend of East and West. It combines both Western concepts (for example, of national sovereignty as well as regional organisation) and Eastern attitudes on managing differences. The best current model is found in South-East Asia.'[2]

In part, the increased focus on confidence-building measures in recent years results from a shift in security concerns from internal problems (which are not so amenable to such measures) to external problems (that are). ASEAN countries are particularly concerned at the way in which the lack of transparency in Chinese security policy is contributing to regional uncertainty. By engaging China in a process of intensified dialogue and confidence-building, modelled on the ASEAN process that has been so successful in containing Indonesia over the last 25 years, they hope to be able to manage regional change through cooperation rather than by recourse to arms.

While the driving force for the confidence-building process is the fear of future conflict, however, the process has only been made possible because regional confidence has already improved considerably. In the 1980s, both the US and the Soviet Union maintained permanent bases in the region, contributing to fears that the region might once again become a theatre for major war. ASEAN was engaged in a bitter confrontation with Vietnam over its occupation of Cambodia. Not least, despite the uneasy alliance between ASEAN and China over the Cambodian issue, neither Malaysia nor Indonesia had diplomatic relations with Beijing, in part because of continuing concerns over China's relations with insurgency movements within their own borders.

Since the end of the Cold War, however, the Soviet Union (now Russia) has ceased to be a player in South-East Asia security. Vietnam has joined ASEAN, and Laos, Cambodia and Myanmar will soon follow. Despite continuing concerns over the South China Sea, diplomatic and economic relations with China continue to develop and improve.

The growing importance of confidence-building measures in the Asia-Pacific, therefore, is not so much a response to an increase in tension as a recognition that, in conditions intermediate between peaceful tranquillity and intensive confrontation, the region could go either way. Countries in the region are not so optimistic about the future that they see no risk of conflict. The continuing growth in arms spending throughout the region illustrates that clearly. But nor are relations between them so tense that dialogue is impossible. With some exceptions (such as relations between the two Koreas), there is a willingness to talk and to seek ways of preventing an increase in regional tension. Most of all, there is a sense of common interest in the region's recent economic success: a success which major armed conflict would quickly halt in its tracks.

An immediate and dramatic increase in military openness in the region is not anticipated. The aim of confidence-building measures at this stage is more about securing a gradual change in the security culture of region than about finding ways to improve the management of specific crises. Over time, it is hoped, greater openness will strengthen and modernise security decision-making in the countries of the region, as well as improving the quality of the regional security dialogue. But this process is bound to take time, and confidence-building measures cannot be expected to deliver miracles.

Moreover, while the process of confidence-building in the military arena is important, it is only one part of a total package of measures designed to prevent conflict. The development of other regional institutions, such as APEC, also has a vital role to play in developing trust and confidence between states. The many bilateral and multilateral security relationships in the region also have an important role to play in reassurance and deterrence. Indeed many of the 'confidence-building' measures now being discussed between the medium powers of the region - such as joint exercises, officer exchanges, and logistics cooperation - also have a deterrent function vis-à-vis larger outside powers.

Transparency and confidence-building measures, by themselves, do not stop any acquisitions or limit any budgets. As a result, the concern is often expressed that

> 'it is not hard to envisage a coming decade of continued security dialogue and continued arms build-ups, neither seeming to have much to do with the other.'[3]

The pace of the arms build-up is not the only indicator of tension. Military spending levels are a result of many factors, of which threat perception is only one. It is therefore possible to envisage continuing increases in military spending in the region even as relationships improve and disputes are settled. Other things being equal, however, arms build-ups do increase tension between states, making it more difficult to maintain a balance of power at low levels, and generating concerns as to the motives behind them. Some of these concerns can be alleviated through a process of transparency and dialogue. For example, greater transparency and explanation may shed light on when China is planning to acquire an aircraft carrier, and why some states are increasing the proportion of their GNP spent on defence. But talking without action will not be enough. If the security dialogue process is to be effective, it will also have to be accompanied by changes in behaviour to take account of the concerns expressed.

II   Arms control

The need for 'action' has led some to suggest that dialogue must form the basis for arms control: that is limits on the weapons and/or forces held by regional states. Certainly, this would be seen as the logical next step within the approach to controlling the arms race advocated by many liberal Western thinkers, who see limits on forces and weapons as central to a future of 'Cooperative Security'. For example, the 1994 Brookings Institution study *Global Engagement: Cooperation and Security in the 21st Century*, many of whose authors (including Defense Secretary William Perry) subsequently became leading officials in the Clinton Administration,[4] provides clear guidelines for what this organising principle requires in the field of arms control:

> 'Cooperative security contemplates an expanding network of generally applicable limitations on weapons systems and force structures. The limits will be defined primarily by agreement rather than strategic interaction.'[5]

The Brookings study falls squarely within the mainstream of the 'Western' model of arms control, with pride of place given to formal treaties, and with 'strategic interaction' (defined as 'unilateral responses to the moves of other actors') seen as having little if any positive role to play in achieving the goals of arms reduction and war prevention. Within this framework, in which achievement is measured by the content of formal agreements, free-standing transparency measures - of the sort now being considered in ARF

- tend to be characterised as a weak compromise that fails to directly stop the deployment of a single weapon, fails to forbid any specific activity, and is at best only an interim measure designed to pave the way for disarmament. Limits on the military capabilities which states may possess or acquire are seen, by contrast, as 'real' arms control. Transparency is acknowledged as having an important role within cooperative security, but characteristically only as a necessary element in a control regime, rather than for its direct trust-building effects.[6]

The greatest success of this approach has been in relation to weapons of mass destruction. An indefinite extension of the Nuclear Non-Proliferation Treaty (NPT) was agreed in 1995, with all but a small handful of the world's states now signatories. The Chemical Weapons Convention (CWC), due to enter into force in 1996, will enforce the prohibition of an entire class of weapons. Negotiations are under way to strengthen the verification and enforcement provisions of the Biological Weapons Convention. All three regimes have as their basis the enforcement of international norms prohibiting particular classes of weapons.[7] In line with the Brookings model of Cooperative Security, all involve legally binding commitments, strict verification, and strong mechanisms for collective enforcement.

The formal basis of these regimes, together with the existence of a comparable regime for conventional weapons in Europe (the Conventional Forces in Europe (CFE) Treaty), has led some commentators to unfavourably contrast the informality of the 'Asian' approach to arms control with this more formal 'European' tradition, with the implicit suggestion that Asian 'culture' is the main obstacle to a more direct, and more effective, policy of regional arms limitation.

Yet this line of argument is unconvincing. ASEAN states are not averse to enforceable arms control treaties in principle. All ASEAN members are signatories of the NPT and the CWC. The 1995 ARF summit strongly supported a proposed Comprehensive Test Ban Treaty, and urged both China and France to end testing immediately. In December 1995, leaders of all ten South-East Asian states signed the South-East Asia Nuclear Weapons-Free Zone Treaty, and urged all five recognised nuclear weapons states to accede to it.[8] Through these actions, ASEAN states have recognised that a clear and enforceable norm of non-possession of weapons of mass destruction contributes to regional security.

In contrast, however, the option of limiting conventional arms through formal treaty is not being seriously considered.[9] The fundamental obstacle to such a step is not cultural. Nor is it concern over the intrusive inspections that such a regime would require (though this would be a problem). Instead, the obstacle is more fundamental, and derives from the reality that a conventional arms treaty - in contrast to one dealing with weapons of mass destruction - can only limit, not prohibit, such weapons. Even if the possibility of war between states has been ruled out, states will require weapons in order to maintain internal order and enforce the law. Moreover, as long as any individual state fears the possibility of attack by other states, geography will set minimum limits on the level of forces it needs to defend its territory. This minimum can change over time as a result of technological and doctrinal development. But it will remain relatively independent, within rather wide margins, of the level of forces possessed by other states: thus effectively setting a lower limit (that is different for different countries) for structural arms control. As Michael Moodie has suggested:

> 'Problems in developing a conceptual framework for conventional arms control are compounded by the fact that arms control theory has been developed almost exclusively by theorists of nuclear strategy. Nuclear and conventional war, however, are very different phenomena. Nuclear warfare is defined in terms of firepower. Conventional war is a combination of firepower and manoeuvre .... In nuclear war, geography is a secondary consideration and topography almost irrelevant. In conventional war, they count - sometimes dramatically.'[10]

The CFE Treaty, signed in November 1990, was an impressive achievement for conventional arms control. It imposed limits on the five most important categories of conventional arms over most of the European continent. It required steep reductions in the arsenals of many of its 22 participating states (subsequently to rise to 29 with the break-up of the Soviet Union). Not least, it involved a level of mandatory information exchange and verification that was unprecedented in its intrusiveness. It thus seemed to suggest that, despite its formidable complexity, conventional arms limitation treaties were possible if the political will existed.[11]

Yet the CFE Treaty was a consequence not of the bipolar confrontation but of its end. It played a vital role in providing additional assurance to

NATO members that unilateral Soviet reductions could be verified and that they would not be reversed. It may also have helped provided political 'cover' for the Soviet leadership against domestic criticism. But it would never have been agreed by the Soviet Union if it were still concerned with conventional parity.

The possibility of applying the CFE model to situations of continuing conflict should not be ruled out, particularly when the conflicts in question have a primarily bilateral character. For example, it could be argued that the changing balance of conventional forces between North and South Korea, and the arms race between them, is relatively self-contained, with both countries' force planning only modestly affected by the actions of other powers in the region. Even in this case of intense bipolar confrontation, however, the potential role of external forces (especially US forces) in the peninsular balance of power is likely to prove a source of dispute and stalemate given the mistrust between the different parties. Moreover, the complex nature of conventional forces is such that there would be a tendency to focus, not on those forces of greatest military value, but on those that can most easily be measured and which are seen to have a degree of symbolic value.

Similarly, the application of the CFE 'bean-counting' concept to East Asia as a whole would run the risk of creating the false impression that China, with its massive arsenals of conventional weapons, now has overwhelming military superiority in the region. Once the roles and quality of the forces concerned are taken into account, however, most analysts would accept that China remains only one of several major military powers in the region. If recent trends continue, China's relative military position seems likely to improve over the next 15 years. But, because of the accompanying shift from quantity to quality, this is likely to be accompanied by a reduction in the size of its forces.[12] A conventional arms control regime for the region that focused on numerical reductions on weapons without taking account of qualitative factors would thus ignore the main issues in the region.

By providing additional reassurance to those who fear a return to the past, conventional arms control treaties can play a useful role in the process of ending long-standing conflicts. But they probably have limited application at the earlier stages of conflict resolution processes. They are too rigid to play a role in actively managing the balance of power, and it is difficult to see how a relatively mechanistic concept of military 'balance' can be applied to the sort of multipolar framework that is typical of East Asia. The circumstances in which conventional arms control treaties can play a role are therefore much more limited than are the opportunities for confidence-building and transparency measures. Even when they are relevant, their contribution may be less profound than is often suggested.[13]

The limited applicability of formal treaties to the problem of controlling conventional arms does not mean that the possibility of mutual force reductions *per se* must be abandoned as idealistic and impractical. It does imply that it must be explored indirectly rather than through an attempt to formulate a grand treaty framework. The complex nature of conventional force balances, often involving substantial asymmetries, means that mutual confidence-building is more likely to come from a process of gradual and progressive mutual restraint rather than from a single major treaty.

III   Mutual restraint

Perhaps the most developed academic discussion of the concept of mutual restraint came in the literature on Graduated Reciprocation in Tension Reduction (GRIT), a concept first advanced by Charles Osgood. Osgood argued that an arms race is 'a kind of graduated and reciprocated, unilaterally-initiated, inter-nation action' and the idea of GRIT is to produce a reciprocal sequence of unilateral actions in the reverse direction.[14] During the 1980s, it was given influential support by Kenneth Adelman, Director of the US Arms Control and Disarmament Agency under the Reagan Administration:

> 'Few fields of human endeavour display as great a gap between what is hoped for and what has been achieved as strategic arms control. ... Another approach, and to me the most promising ... is arms control through individual but (where possible) parallel policies: i.e. arms control without agreements (treaties in particular) ... Adopting this approach of individual, parallel restraint could help avoid endless problems over what programs to exclude, which to include and how to verify them ... Being less formal, such arrangements could be more easily modified if circumstances change than can legally binding treaties.'

Adelman goes on to quote in support of his views a 1933 speech by Winston Churchill, in which he contrasted what he deemed the glaring deficiencies of formalised disarmament negotiations with the oft-hidden benefits of 'private interchanges' in normal diplomatic intercourse, such as

> ' 'If you will not do this, we shall not have to do that,' 'If your program did not start so early ours would begin even later' and so on.'

> ... 'a greater advance and progress towards a diminution of expenditure on armaments might have been achieved by these methods than by the conferences and schemes of disarmament which have been put forward at Geneva.'"[15]

This approach emphasises that, in conditions of considerable tension, the primary purpose of initial measures of restraint is not the achievement of significant changes in the military balance. Rather, it is to begin to challenge the assumptions that contribute to confrontation: 'breaking the ice' of distrust as a first step towards a more cooperative relationship. While Western leaders and commentators tend to judge the success of dialogue in terms of concrete results, their ASEAN counterparts focus on the role of dialogue as a means towards creating conditions of 'comfort' between leaders, which can then be followed by moves to address mutual concerns. They argue, from their own experience in other contexts, that to attempt to reach agreement before establishing trust may be ineffective. In societies where law is a more flexible concept, personal connections play a more critical role than in Western societies, and business negotiators have to accept that the ability to enforce contracts may be limited even within the framework of domestic law. Without a mutual commitment to the relationship, therefore, any agreement between states is of little value. As a 1988 survey of the arms control debate in South-East Asia suggests

> 'Arms control measures work better in Asia if they involve informal arrangements rather than formal documents, and aim to build mutual confidence rather than reduce weapons.'[16]

These 'informal arrangements' are not only hypothetical. Several of the region's states already exhibit considerable degrees of defensive reassurance in their military postures, in some cases as a result of deliberate policy decisions. Despite being Asia's strongest power in economic terms, and despite many American voices urging greater 'burdensharing', Japan has exercised considerable caution in structuring its armed forces ever since its defeat in 1945. In order to reassure its neighbours, it has declined to purchase some of the key offensive weapon platforms: aircraft carriers, bombers, long range missiles and, most of all, nuclear weapons. Its self-restraint has helped to preserve the regional balance of power at lower and safer levels than would otherwise have been possible.[17]

A similar policy of 'self-containment' is evident in the case of Indonesia.[18] Since the New Order regime under Suharto came to power in 1966, it has sought to reassure its neighbours of its defensive intent, both through its membership in ASEAN and through a reorientation of its armed forces towards a clearly defensive, and inward looking, role. Moreover, what is true of Indonesia is also true to some extent of other ASEAN states. The preoccupation of the armed forces of the Philippines, Malaysia and Thailand with counter-insurgency warfare has left them with limited capability for power projection or invasion. Even if current procurement programmes continue, it will take some time before more substantial offensive capabilities can be created. Not least, in terms of its impact on regional security, is the 'defensivity' in China's defence posture. China does not yet possess aircraft carriers or longer range bombers, and its maritime power projection capabilities remain extremely limited.

Other countries in the region are concerned that China's self-restraint is more a result of past poverty than of deliberate self-containment. Now that China is becoming richer, and it no longer needs to give priority to defending its northern frontier with Russia, some fear a long term trend towards a more offensive military posture, designed to make China the regional hegemon in the 21st century. If China pursues such a path, it is feared, it will force other larger powers - including Japan and Indonesia - to follow suit, acquiring offensive capabilities of their own. The delicate balance of reassurance on which the security of South-East Asia is currently based would be eroded, and the risks of conflict increased.

In determining whether any of the major powers of the region are shifting towards more offensive postures, it will be important to watch key procurement decisions - for aircraft carriers, frigates, strike aircraft, main battle tanks, and so on - as well as developments in other aspects of military capability, such as training, communications and logistics. Improved transparency in procurement policy can help provide a system for alerting countries to what others are doing, as well as providing channels through which to express concerns. But it will remain up to the leaders of the key countries involved to decide how to respond to those concerns.

As armed forces become better-resourced and more technologically sophisticated, there is continuing pressure for them to acquire more versatile, and thus potentially more offensive, weapons systems. The difficulties involved in resisting this pressure can be seen in the case of Australia. Despite being, by virtue of its geography, one of the most secure countries in the region, Australia has also maintained the region's most potent offensive strike capability in the form of two squadrons of F-111 aircraft. The roles of the aircraft include attacking airfields and troop concentrations, as well as more general 'infrastructure' targets, on enemy territory. Recent reports suggest that Australia is also considering a future acquisition of sea-launched cruise missiles in a similar role.

The offensive elements in Australia's military posture have at times been a source of concern for Indonesian military planners, whose contingency planning must allow for the possibility of future Australian support for separatist movements in Timor or West Irian. But, in the context of Australia's overall policy of regional engagement, its capabilities for force projection also have a positive element, namely their contribution to ASEAN's ability to resist aggression from the north. The December 1995 security treaty between Indonesia and Australia will have further strengthened this perception.

After Australia, the regional country with the most developed capabilities for long range offensive capabilities is Singapore. As in the case of Australia, Singapore's commitment to forward defence needs to be viewed in the context of an overall security posture that is clearly defensive. It is difficult to seriously believe that Singapore would attack its neighbours unless it believed it was itself under imminent threat. Moreover, like Australia, it has no serious territorial disputes with its neighbours.[19] If Singapore and Australia were the only countries in the region to possess major offensive capabilities, therefore, the prospects for a regional offensive arms race would be rather limited.

Unfortunately this is not the case. Australia and Singapore are ahead of the game because of their higher levels of arms spending and greater technological sophistication. But other countries are following their example. Ball summarises the nature of the problem that may result:

> 'The 'offensive' character of some of the new weapons systems being acquired is also cause for concern. Many of the new acquisitions (such as the maritime strike aircraft, modern

surface combatants, and submarines, all equipped with anti-
ship missiles) involve strike capabilities with offensive
connotations. Unfortunately, for many countries, they provide
the most cost-effective basis for self-reliance; in some cases,
such as that of Australia, a viable posture of self-reliance
would not be possible without some minimal strike
capabilities. Yet these capabilities are the most likely to
generate counter-acquisitions. In these circumstances, it is
imperative that regional mechanisms be established to reduce
the prospects of the various defence modernisation programs
degenerating into a regional arms race.'[20]

Once a particular class of weapons is introduced into the region, it
becomes hard to persuade those countries still without it that it would be
destabilising for them to emulate their neighbours. It is sometimes
suggested, therefore, that governments should explore mutual restraint
rules in which all would agree not to be the first to introduce a particular
system into the region.

The main difficulty is that many of the most obvious candidates for such
rules are systems that are already in service, or will soon be in service, with
at least one regional state. Even if the US is excluded from the comparison,
Australia already possesses strike aircraft, Australia, China and Indonesia
have submarines, Thailand is planning to buy an aircraft carrier, and China
has a limited number of intercontinental range ballistic missiles. So blanket
bans on the introduction of any of these systems would be difficult to
enforce.

South-East Asian governments may be willing to restrain their own
acquisitions if they have assurances of restraint from others, even if the
result falls short of strict balance. Given their current strategic concerns,
however, it is unrealistic to expect such a process to go far without also
taking into account trends in Chinese forces. Intra-ASEAN factors play a
key role in arms acquisitions in South-East Asia. Even if these factors could
be taken into account in a process of mutual restraint, however, South-East
Asia states would also want to ensure that ASEAN restraint did not tip the
regional balance of power in China's favour.

Yet China's planners, for their part, cannot design capabilities solely on the
basis of preserving some sort of balance with ASEAN and Australia. They
also need to take account of the forces of Taiwan, South Korea, and Japan.
Even if they eschew the aim of challenging US maritime supremacy in the

region, this is a formidable task. It means that the prospects for moderating the pace of the arms race in South-East Asia are bound to depend, to some extent, on what happens in North-East Asia. It helps explains why, unwieldy though it may sometimes appear, the ASEAN Regional Forum is an appropriate forum for the discussion of confidence-building measures and arms restraint.

IV   Supplier regimes

Much of the Western debate on restraining the arms race in the developing world revolves around the possibilities for greater supplier restraint. It is often suggested that the recent arms build-up in East Asia has been encouraged by Western companies, anxious to compensate for the decline in their domestic markets. Indeed, the UN Register itself was, in large measure, an attempt to respond to the calls for greater restraint in the light of the revelations of supplies to Iraq during the 1980s.

In the case of South-East Asia, moreover, supplier restraint could be highly effective. In contrast to more self sufficient countries, such as China, the modernisation programmes of ASEAN states remain heavily reliant on imports from a small number of supplier states.[21] Despite the growth of indigenous arms industries, the desire of ASEAN governments to acquire the most sophisticated weapons available has probably increased dependence on imports in recent years. If the US, Western Europe and Russia were to act together, therefore, they could make a real impact on the pace of the local arms build-up.

Supplier controls already have some impact on the pattern of transfers to the region. Many countries restrict exports to Indonesia because of its occupation of East Timor, with Portugal, Sweden, Belgium and Italy all having complete arms embargoes. Britain, one of Indonesia's larger arms suppliers, restricts the supply of equipment that could be used against civil populations and has asked for, and been given, assurances that its Hawk aircraft would not be used for internal security purposes in East Timor or elsewhere in Indonesia.[22] Germany refuses to supply modern Leopard battle tanks to the region, and in 1992 it prevented its shipyard from bidding for the Thai carrier contract.[23] 1995 saw a vigorous debate within the US government over the proposed sale of Advanced Medium Range Air-to-Air Missiles (AMRAAM) to Thailand, largely because its export policy stipulates that it will not export a weapon to a region if it is destabilising or would introduce a significant new capability into the theatre.[24]

Most of all, supplier restraint has had a significant impact on China's military modernisation programme in recent years. In addition to embargoes on arms exports from the US and the EU, the US has successfully applied pressure on Russia to deny requests for the export of long range Backfire bombers and aircraft carriers to China. Although some arms exports from Russia to China continue - most recently in the form of Kilo class submarines and Su-27 fighters - reports suggest that Russia has turned down Chinese requests for state-of-the-art missile systems. Some reports suggest considerable Israeli involvement in the supply of military technology to China, but these cannot be confirmed.[25] The China case suggests that, even in the case of a country with a high degree of defence self-reliance, supplier restraint can make a difference.

The prospects for a more co-ordinated approach by suppliers should be enhanced by the December 1995 agreement to establish a successor to CoCom, the Cold War organisation charged with restricting technology exports to the Soviet Union. The new regime (entitled the 'Wassenaar Arrangement' after the Dutch town where it was signed) is being formally inaugurated in April 1996 in Vienna, the site of its secretariat. Initially, it has 28 members, including Australia, Japan, the US, all EU members and Russia. It is aimed primarily at controlling the export of arms and dual-use goods to Iran, Iraq, North Korea and Libya.[26] But it also provides mechanisms for consultations between its members over exports to other 'countries of concern,' including China. Henceforth, it will be the main forum for consultation over possible restrictions on the supply of military technology and arms to regions of tension.

In current circumstances, the Wassenaar Arrangement is unlikely to be used as a mechanism for restricting exports to South-East Asia, with the possible exception of Myanmar. Even if the human rights situation in Indonesia deteriorated further, pressures for tougher supplier action against ASEAN states are likely to be overridden by the perceived need to balance Chinese power. This could change if an ASEAN state were to decide to pursue policies that ran clearly counter to Western strategic interests: for example if Indonesia were to seek regional dominance by force. Short of such an eventuality, however, the main impact of supplier regimes on ASEAN over the next few years is likely to be to ensure that they continue to have access to military technologies that are denied to China.

Indeed, rather than becoming the target of supplier regimes, it is more likely that some ASEAN states may be asked to become participants in the Wassenaar Arrangement in their own right. Since the end of the Cold War, the main participants in supplier regimes, both for weapons of mass destruction and (in the case of the Wassenaar Arrangement) for conventional weapons and dual-use technology, have been the old group of 'developed' states. Just as membership of the OECD is starting to change, however, so too is the membership of the suppliers' club. Wassenaar Arrangement founding members will include, in addition to the original CoCom states, the Czech Republic, Hungary, Poland, Russia and Slovakia. Applications for membership are expected from South Korea, Argentina, South Africa, Bulgaria and Romania.[27] The continuing technological development of newly industrialising countries means that the spread of technologies with military applications cannot be limited by the action of the old developed states (or even the old developed states plus Russia) alone. It also requires the progressive incorporation of middle income Asian states in supplier regimes, as and when they are ready to fulfil the obligations of those regimes.

Indonesia and Malaysia may resist membership in a 'supplier club', not least because of their prominent role as members of the group of Non-Aligned nations. As a result, Singapore may be wary of breaking with the ASEAN consensus on this question. Given its role as an important supplier of niche markets in military technology, however, Singapore - and perhaps also Indonesia - may be asked to participate in a process of more informal consultation and cooperation with the Wassenaar Arrangement.[28]

It may be some time before any ASEAN member will want to be accepted as a member of the regime. Supplier restraint is still widely seen within South-East Asia as an attempt by Western countries to impose its own political agenda on the region. ASEAN members may not be unhappy that others are restricting the supply of sophisticated hardware to China. But this does not mean that they themselves want to be seen as part of such a regime.

Overall, the immediate scope for supplier restraint making a difference in South-East Asia - with the possible exception of Myanmar - seems to be rather limited. Perhaps the most that the Wassenaar Arrangement can be expected to do in the near future is to provide a means for supplier states to promote greater transparency in their transfers of arms and related technologies to the region, including pre-notification and information on systems outside the UN Register. Whether even these modest steps are taken remains to be seen.

V   Broader peace processes

Processes of security dialogue, confidence-building and mutual restraint are already contributing to regional peace and security, and they could contribute more. But there are limits to their effectiveness. The arms build-up is as much a symptom of deeper tensions as it is a contributor to conflict potential. Peace also requires responses to the broader security problems of the region.

Ultimately, the central security problem of Asia over the next decades is how to manage the region's economic and political modernisation without the horrifying wars that accompanied the same process in Europe. Asia starts with some advantages. By taking advantage of imported technology and expertise, it can achieve much more rapid rates of economic growth than others have done in the past. A transformation that took Europe two hundred years to complete is taking place in Asia in the lifetime of a single generation. From the fruits of this growth, governments can finance investment programmes without reducing living standards. Increasingly, the poorer countries of the region can also benefit directly from the investment and expertise of their more advanced Asian counterparts.

Yet the very pace of the change now under way is itself a source of instability and potential conflict. With hundreds of millions of peasants on the move to overcrowded cities, and levels of education rising rapidly even in the poorest country, every aspect of life is undergoing fundamental change. Expectations of economic betterment and political freedom come up against political structures that, in many cases, have yet to fully adjust to new bases of legitimacy. The rapid depletion of natural resources - forests, fisheries, hydrocarbons, land - should be leading to a shift into less resource-intensive forms of production. But this shift has so far been a slow one, and the combination of economic growth and reckless resource depletion is increasing the vulnerability of many of the region's states to environmental disaster, as well as providing a potent source of conflict. Most of all, perhaps, rapid shifts in the distribution of wealth and power between and within societies add to the potential for political and regional instability.

Into the frantic and confused process of 'modernisation', the governments of the region bring their own aspirations and fears, and their own unsettled scores. Some want to reverse the slights of colonialism, others to restore their nation to what they regard as its rightful place or to complete projects of national unification. The creation of modern 'nation-states', while promoting unity within the state, can also promote tension with others, with national xenophobia often greatest amongst those groups that feel least secure in their own identity. In contrast to Europe, the attempt to create a regional identity cannot call upon a common history or culture in seeking to define what it means to belong to 'Asia' or 'East Asia', far less to the more amorphous 'Asia-Pacific'. The demons of nationalism may appear to have been quelled by the economic miracle of the last two decades, but it is too early to say that they will not return.

Regional resilience

The key to peace in South-East Asia is the development of strong and resilient states: states with a strong basis in national societies, able to respond pragmatically to new challenges, and relying mainly on consent as a means for maintaining authority. Some ASEAN states have been less successful than others in achieving this objective of national resilience (the Indonesian government, in particular, still relies heavily on repression to maintain national unity). But ASEAN governments agree that it is in their common interest to help their neighbours become stronger. The interdependence between the internal politics of neighbours is at the heart of ASEAN's concept of regional resilience. ASEAN states know that domestic pressures can both constrain the external actions of states and, in some circumstances, precipitate policies that will be of concern to others. States are not unitary actors but coalitions of individuals and interests. Indeed it has always been one of the primary tasks of diplomacy - perhaps the oldest form of 'transparency'! - to understand the internal workings of other countries better.

The ASEAN emphasis on the close relationship between internal stability and international security is difficult to reconcile with the dominant, realist, tradition in Western approaches to international relations. But it has much in common with the 'liberal' school of thought that argues that internal politics does matter in determining the prospects for peace and war. American and European analysts, concerned most of all with analysing their own history, have tended to focus their research on the internal/external link on the relationship between democracy and war, with the argument being advanced that democratic governments are far less likely to go to war with each other than are non-democracies.[29] The argument may be overstated to some extent because of coding problems. (Would Germany in 1914 have been coded as a democracy if it had not gone to war?)[30] It may also rely too much on recent European experience, where - both in World War Two and in the Cold War - the distinction between democracies and dictatorships was much clearer than it is in Asia today. Even with these caveats, however, the empirical evidence available suggests that a clear statistical relationship between democracy and peace does exist.

As a consequence of the clear relationship between democracy and peace, however, some analysts have too readily inferred that the converse is also true: that countries that are not democracies are prone to go to war. As a result, the lack of a clear trend towards democratisation in East Asia in recent years (in contrast, for example, to Eastern Europe, Latin America and sub-Saharan Africa) has contributed to a degree of pessimism regarding the long term chances of peace in the region. There has been some progress towards more stable civilian government in Thailand. But the regimes of both Indonesia and Vietnam - the two largest in South-East Asia - seem under no immediate pressure to liberalise, and the prospects for any democratic development in China were dealt a severe blow by the 1989 events in Tianmen Square. Analysts are sceptical that economic interdependence in the absence of democratisation can lead to peace any more than it did in late 19th century Europe.

Such arguments need to be treated with a degree of scepticism. All too often they focus attention solely on democratic forms, rather than on a broader appreciation of the processes and culture that underpin a stable democracy. Moreover, recent empirical research suggests that, while 'mature' democracies may be much less likely to fight each other, states in the transitional phase between dictatorship and democracy may actually be more likely to go to war.[31] Attempts to prescribe democratic forms as a universal panacea, therefore, may be misguided, especially in the absence of the many other elements that go to make up a 'mature' democracy. They may also be over-pessimistic in their implicit assumption that non-democracies are as likely to go to war as they were in the past. In reality, inter-state war has become increasingly uncommon as a means of resolving disputes, not only between democracies but also between the many non-democratic and semi-democratic regimes that still exist.

Yet there are elements of the democracy/peace debate that are of value in considering the prospects for peace in Asia. In particular, the literature suggests that a crucial element in the link between democracy and war-proneness is provided by the extent to which decisions on war preparation and warmaking are subject to broader checks and balances, either within the executive itself or more broadly through the legislature being given a say in key decisions. The dangers of states starting war may thus be particularly acute in one-person dictatorships, where that person is able to overrule or ignore the advice of his most senior colleagues. In such regimes, where personal safety is a primary concern and where paranoia is a precondition for survival, leaders may be more prone to take decisions without access to relevant information and with distorted views of the responses of others. By contrast, leaders who are accountable to a wider group, even if this group is itself 'undemocratic', may be less likely to wage wars of aggression.

A widening of the group with oversight of security policy may thus have a direct impact on the likelihood of war, even in the absence of the full apparatus of 'democracy' as currently conceived in the US or Western Europe. It may also, and perhaps just as importantly, help to reassure others that it will be difficult for potential opponents to launch a surprise attack. The more open a society, the more it will find it difficult to avoid giving other states some degree of warning of an intention to go to war.

In this narrower dimension of political development, the description of South-East Asia as 'non-democratic' needs to be recast. Even in the absence of completely free elections, the market economics of South-East Asia have tended to see the growth of an educated and meritocratic middle class that is increasingly impatient of corruption and authoritarianism. A blanket description of ASEAN regimes as 'soft authoritarian' tends to conceal the variety of their experiences. In fact, most ASEAN members now have electoral mechanisms in place that permit varying degrees of political activity, including the representation of competing parties in parliament. Some (such as Thailand and the Philippines) have a high degree of freedom of expression for the media. A majority of ASEAN members have established, and tested, mechanisms for the peaceful transfer of power from one leader to the next. ASEAN members such as Thailand, Singapore and Malaysia are not as democratic as Sweden or Canada. But it is misleading to classify them as 'dictatorships' as if there was nothing to distinguish them from China, Iraq or Myanmar. Like most of the world's states, their political systems fall somewhere between the two extremes of democracy and dictatorship.

In countries which remain uneasily between these extremes, the promotion of transparency measures may have a particularly important role. Such measures can help to promote peace indirectly, through facilitating greater political accountability for security policy elites. At the same time, the process of gradual democratisation also helps to facilitate the development of greater transparency in the medium to long term.

The process of democratisation in ASEAN is also consistent with the process of rapid market based economic transformation. As Barry Buzan has argued

> 'One advantage of market based political economies is that their very operation generates high levels of transparency across all the sectors that affect security relations. ... The apparent triumph of market over centrally-planned economies in the late twentieth century will be a powerful stimulus to greater transparency, and therefore to the easier achievement of international security.'[32]

Thus, for example, the development of commercialisation makes it increasingly difficult for governments to avoid a degree of transparency in arms procurement. ASEAN states now buy most of their major military equipment from foreign commercial firms which have an ambivalent attitude to transparency. They are sensitive to their potential clients' concerns, and have a vested interest in finding out more about their requirements. They provide assistance in the maintenance and operation of weapon systems, but in the process obtain even more detailed insights into national defence preparations. Not least, they are anxious to publicise the merits of their products and will often be more than willing to advertise their successful sales.

The increasing concentration of regional leaders on economic development is also an important peace-inducing factor. Governments increasingly rely for power, not on their ability to pursue ideological or nationalist projects, but on their ability to make their supporters richer. Even in China, leaders that try to reverse tide of economic development in favour of a return to a more ideological approach are likely to face stiff opposition from those, not least amongst party cadres, who now have an interest in economic growth.

By disturbing old patterns of authority and privilege, the modernisation process can lead to conflict. One of the skills of Asian political leadership, therefore, is to find ways of enlisting traditional power centres in the cause of economic modernisation. It is particularly important to prevent military leaders from being alienated from the process, with all the dangers that this can cause in societies where the military has continuing aspirations to a political role. In many cases, especially in relatively poor countries with large standing armies, the transition is being facilitated by an increased involvement of the military in the civil economy: thus giving armed forces a stake in a new more materialist politics. Thus, for example, a large part of the armed forces of both China and Vietnam now derive much of their income from economic activity. In other cases, the process is facilitated by the acquisition of new and sophisticated weapon systems, which in turn require radical changes in the ways that armed forces operate. This is important, for example, in Thailand, Malaysia and selected 'elite' units in the Chinese armed forces. Yet in parallel with measures of this sort, which give the armed forces a stake in the process of economic and technological development, civilian governments also have a strong interest in reinforcing their own political primacy directly. The more they are successful in achieving this objective, the more secure the region will be.

Constraining military spending

Political leaders in South-East Asia are aware that the continuation of the economic miracle of the last two decades cannot be taken for granted. Singapore's anxiety is well known, since it is likely to become progressively more difficult for it to sustain high rates of economic growth now that it has reached developed world levels of per capita income. But other ASEAN countries also face severe problems in the years ahead. If countries like Thailand and Malaysia are to move into the higher-value products that can sustain growing wage levels, they will need to invest heavily in infrastructure and education. Large current account deficits and growing debt burdens pose a continuing risk of a damaging financial crisis. Corruption at the highest levels of government in some ASEAN states produces severe economic distortions and feeds political unrest. Not least, there is a widespread realisation that, in societies where materialism is more dominant than ever before, economic recession will result in political as well as business casualties.

Given this context, statements that ASEAN countries can easily afford further increases in military spending need to be sharply qualified. Awareness of the opportunity cost of military spending may be the most important factor in persuading regional leaders to pursue restraint in their procurement plans. The recent economic success of East Asia is a result, in large part, of governments that have given overriding priority to economic development over competing goals, and this commitment remains extremely strong. Pressures to build up national military capabilities still face considerable counterbalancing pressures from leaders who know that their own futures depend above all on their ability to deliver the fruits of development at home. The current generation of ASEAN leaders, most notably President Suharto of Indonesia and Prime Minister Mahathir of Malaysia, continues to express its awareness of the potential economic burden of excessive defence spending. If the current arms build-up in the region is to be slowed, the mobilisation of this economic concern will be as crucial a component in a de-escalation process as direct assaults on the political causes of mistrust and arms racing.

Despite recent increases, the proportion of national income spent on defence by ASEAN states is, in most cases, low by world standards. Even in China, where calculation is more difficult, the proportion of GNP spent on the military is much lower than in the past. The rate of growth in defence spending has increased in the early 1990s, and there is a real concern that this build-up could take on an interactive momentum of its own. But, precisely because most of the increase in spending has been used for investment in new arms, it could also be halted quite quickly if decisions were made to divert national resources to other purposes. Confidence-building measures can play a part in persuading national leaders that it is safe to relax their guard in this way. But, in the last analysis, it may be economic factors rather than geo-strategic ones that play the key role in bursting the current bubble of arms build-ups.

VI Conclusion

If countries did not care about the balance of military power and did not fear attack, transparency measures would be irrelevant. Until this happens, however, most states will want to take whatever steps they can to prevent conflict while still preserving their own interests. Transparency and confidence-building measures are not the only, or even the most important, instrument for achieving this objective. They cannot replace the role of the balance of power in preventing war, nor can they substitute for the deeper processes of societal transformation that, it is hoped, will one day make Asia a security community. Yet shedding more light on military forces and military plans can make some contribution to the benign trends in the region, and can perhaps help highlight those that are less benign.

That is why the steps taken since 1993 to establish specific confidence-building measures in the region are of considerable significance. They promise a gradual move towards a cooperative security culture, building on norms already well developed within ASEAN, but also adapting those norms to the new circumstances in which the region now finds itself.

The UN Register is one of the first confidence-building measures that has been introduced into the region during this period. It is therefore important, not only in its own right, but also as an example from which other initiatives - notably the encouragement of annual defence policy statements and the idea of a Regional Register - can draw.

Whether any of these measures prove to be of lasting value remains to be seen. This will depend more on how they are used than on their formal content or structure. CBM's have the potential to contribute to a more cooperative approach to security and to the development and spread of habits of mutual restraint, and considerable progress has been made since 1993. But ASEAN and ARF have a formidable task ahead of them if the processes of confidence-building and dialogue are to match the challenges being thrown up by a rapidly changing region.

Notes

1. Desmond Ball, 'Strategic Culture in the Asia-Pacific Region', *Security Studies*, 3, 1, Autumn 1993, pp. 44-74. For a discussion of the role of pragmatism in the region's economic success, see World Bank, *The East Asian Miracle: Economic growth and public policy*, Oxford University Press, 1994, especially Chapter 7.

2. Kishore Mahbubani, 'The Pacific Impulse', *Survival*, 37, 1, Spring 1995, p. 116.

Notes continued

3.   Shannon Selin, *Asia Pacific Arms Buildups Part Two: Prospects for Control*, Institute of International Relations, University of British Columbia, Working Paper Number 7, November 1994, p. 20.

4.   Janne Nolan, (ed), *Global Engagement: Cooperation and Security in the 21st Century*, Brookings Institution, 1994.

5.   Antonia Handler Chayes and Abram Chayes, 'Regime Architecture: Elements and Principles', in ibid, p. 65.

6.   Antonia Chayes and Abram Chayes, op cit, pp. 81-89. Also see Antonia Chayes and Abram Chayes, 'The UN Register, transparency and cooperative security', in Malcolm Chalmers, Owen Greene, Edward J. Laurance and Herbert Wulf (eds), *Developing the United Nations Register of Conventional Arms*, Bradford Arms Register Studies Number 4, Westview Press, 1994.

7.   Richard Price, 'A Genealogy of the Chemical Weapons Taboo', *International Organisation*, 49, 1, Winter 1995, pp. 73-104.

8.   *Straits Times (Singapore)*, 16 December 1995.

9.   There are some exceptions. In 1992, Gerald Segal suggested that 'it might be possible to cajole states into accepting a UN-sponsored 'military balance' that could be verified by an international agency and subject to challenge inspections'. Gerald Segal, 'Managing New Arms Races in the Asia-Pacific', *The Washington Quarterly*, 15, 3, Summer 1992, p. 97.

10.   Michael Moodie, *The Washington Quarterly*, 13, 1, Winter 1989, p. 190, quoted in Sergey Koulik and Richard Kokoski, *Conventional Arms Control: Perspectives on Verification*, Stockholm International Peace Research Institute/Oxford University Press, 1994, p. 90.

11.   For an argument in support of the continuing relevance of the CFE Treaty after the Cold War, together with a discussion of its applicability in other parts of the world, see Jonathan Dean and Randall Watson Forsberg, 'CFE and Beyond: The Future of Conventional Arms Control', *International Security*, 17, 1, Summer 1992, pp. 76-121.

12.   Paul Dibb, *Towards a New Balance of Power in Asia*, Adelphi Paper Number 295, International Institute for Strategic Studies, Oxford University Press, 1995, p. 93 reports that the number of Chinese combat aircraft has fallen from 6,100 in 1980 to 4,970 in 1995. He projects a decline to around 3000 by 2010.

Notes continued

13.   Barry Posen, 'Crisis Stability and Conventional Arms Control', *Daedalus: Journal of the American Academy of Arts and Sciences*, 120, 1, Winter 1991, pp. 217-232.

14.   Charles Osgood, *An Alternative to War or Surrender*, University of Illinois Press, 1962, pp. 86-87, quoted in Franklin Long, 'Unilateral initiatives', *Bulletin of the Atomic Scientists*, May 1984, p. 50. Also see George W Downs and David M Rocke, 'Tacit Bargaining and Arms Control', *World Politics*, 39, 3, April 1987, pp. 297-325; Amitai Etzioni, *The Hard Way to Peace: A New Strategy*, Collier Books, 1962; Deborah Larson, 'Crisis Prevention and the Austrian State Treaty', *International Organisation*, 41, 1, Winter 1987, pp. 27-61; Herbert Scoville, 'Reciprocal National Restraint: An Alternative Path', *Arms Control Today*, June 1985, pp. 1, 6-8, 12. For a commentary that emphasises the limitations of GRIT, see Alexander George, 'Strategies for Facilitating Cooperation' in Alexander George, Philip Farley and Alexander Dallin (eds), *US-Soviet Security Cooperation: Achievements, Failures, Lessons*, Oxford University Press, 1988, pp. 692-711.

15.   Kenneth Adelman, 'Arms Control With and Without Agreements', *Foreign Affairs*, 63, Winter 1984/85, pp. 259-260. Also see Thomas Schelling, 'What went wrong with arms control?' *Foreign Affairs*, 64, Winter 1985/6, pp. 224-225.

16.   Lew Eng Fee, 'Arms Control in South-East Asia: A review of the debate', *Contemporary South-East Asia*, 10, 3, December 1988, p. 240. For other useful discussions of arms control in the region, see Gerald Segal (eds), *Arms Control in Asia*, Macmillan, 1987, and Ron Huisken, *Limitations of Armaments in South-East Asia: a Proposal*, Canberra Papers on Strategy and Defence Number 16, Australian National University, 1977.

17.   Andrew Mack and Pauline Kerr, 'The evolving security discourse in the Asia-Pacific', *The Washington Quarterly*, 18, 1, Winter 1995, p. 133. Also see Geoffrey Wiseman, 'Common Security in the Asia-Pacific Region', *The Pacific Review*, 5, 1, 1992.

18.   Michael Vatikiotis, 'A Giant Treads Carefully: Indonesia's Foreign Policy in the 1990s', in Robert S. Ross (ed), *East Asia in Transition: Towards a New Regional Order*, M. E. Sharpe, 1995.

19.   Singapore and Malaysia remain in conflict over the Singapore-administered island of Pedra Branca (Pulau Batu Putih). In September

Notes continued

1994, however, the two countries agreed to refer the dispute to independent arbitration.

20. Desmond Ball, *The Political-Security Dimension of Australia and the Asia/Pacific Region*, paper prepared for conference on 'Australia and Indonesia: Diverse Culture, Converging Interests', Jakarta, July 1994, p. 7.

21. Panitan Wattanayagorn, 'ASEAN's arms modernization and arms transfer dependence', *The Pacific Review*, 8, 3, 1995.

22. 'Arms sales to Indonesia defended', *The Guardian*, 22 December 1995.

23. David White, 'Spain may build carrier for China', *Financial Times*, 22 January 1996.

24. 'USN gets Thai request for F/A-18s, AMRAAM, *Jane's Defence Weekly*, 4 November 1995, p. 6.

25. Eric Arnett, 'Military technology: the case of China', in Stockholm International Peace Research Institute, *SIPRI Yearbook 1995*, Oxford University Press, 1995, pp. 367-368.

26. Ronald van de Krol, 'Successor to Cocom agreed', *Financial Times*, 20 December 1995. Also see Theresa Hitchens, 'Export Control Experts Meet to Fill Holes in New Accord', *Defense News*, 15-21 January 1996.

27. Owen Greene, *Developing an effective successor to CoCom*, Saferworld Briefing, September 1995, p. 23.

28. Ibid, p. 24.

29. For example, see Bruce Russett, *Grasping the Democratic Peace*, Princeton University Press, 1993.

30. Ido Oren, 'The Subjectivity of the 'Democratic Peace': Changing US Perceptions of Imperial Germany', *International Security*, 20, 2, Fall 1995, pp. 147-184.

31. Edward D. Mansfield and Jack Snyder, 'Democratization and the Danger of War', *International Security*, 20, 1, Summer 1995, p. 5. The examples of recent conflicts between Serbia and Croatia, and between Armenia and Azerbaijan, are given. In each case, the countries in question had elected their leaders by universal suffrage.

32. Barry Buzan, *People, States and Fear*, 2nd edition, Harvester-Wheatsheaf, 1991, pp. 264-265.

Information provided to the UN Register on imports into Australasia and South-East Asia 1992-1994

(as of 31 December 1995)

Introduction

This Appendix lists all the imports into Australasia and South-East Asia that have been reported to the UN for 1992, 1993 and 1994. It is arranged alphabetically by importing country, and includes data reported by both exporters and importers. The following conventions are used:

1. Data reported by the importing state is reported in plain text.

2. Data reported by the exporting state is indicated by *text in italics* and by a star (*) in the left hand column.

3. Data reported which confirms data reported by a trading partner is indicated by a tick (√) in the left hand column.

4. States were invited by the UN to provide comments on transfers and descriptions of the items involved. The information provided is included in the column 'description/comments'.

5. The column 'description/comments' is also used to include information provided by SIPRI. This is clearly indicated.

The table uses the following abbreviations: tanks = battle tanks; ACV = armoured combat vehicles; artillery = large calibre artillery systems; aircraft = combat aircraft; helos = attack helicopters; MML = missiles and missile launchers. The definitions of each of these categories of armaments covered by the Register (the six noted above plus warships) are provided on page 177.

The Appendix does not include nil returns provided by states.

The sources of the data reported here are:

1. *United Nations Register of Conventional Arms: Report of the Secretary-General,* UN General Assembly Document A/48/344, 11 October 1993, plus: *Addendum 1,* 19 November 1993; *Addendum 2,* 2 February 1994; *Addendum 3,* 23 September 1994; *Corrigendum 1,* 23 February 1994; *Corrigendum 2,* 23 June 1994; *Corrigendum 3,* 16 August 1994.

2. *United Nations Register of Conventional Arms: Report of the Secretary-General,* UN General Assembly Document A/49/352, 1 September 1994, published 13 October 1994, plus: *Addendum 1,* 8 November 1994; *Addendum 2,* 17 November 1994; *Addendum 3,* 19 December 1994; Addendum 4, 8 March 1995; Corrigendum 1, 8 November 1994; *Corrigendum 2,* 3 February 1995.

3. *United Nations Register of Conventional Arms: Report of the Secretary-General,* UN General Assembly Document A/50/547, 31 October 1995, plus *Addendum 1,* 13 November 1995; *Addendum 2,* 14 December 1995.

	Category	From	No.	Year	Description/comments
	AUSTRALIA				
	ACV	Canada	27	1994	ASLAV light armoured vehicle.
*	ACV	Canada	5	1994	*wheeled armoured personnel carrier.*
*	ACV	UK	8	1992	*Obsolete equipment for museums; states of origin Czechoslovakia and US. The Australian reply for 1992 states that: 'Not listed among the imports are one battle tank, one armoured combat vehicle and one large calibre artillery piece. These were imported from Kuwait solely for the purpose of display at the Museum of the School of Armour.'*
*	*Artillery*	UK	2	1994	
√	Artillery	US	1	1994	5-in/54 Mk 45 naval gun, intended for mounting in ANZAC frigate.
√*	*Artillery*	US	1	1994	
√	Aircraft	US	6	1993	F-111 type. Part of a purchase of 15 of these aircraft.
√*	*Aircraft*	US	6	1993	
√	Aircraft	US	9	1994	F-111G, part of total acquisition of 15 over 1993-94.
√*	*Aircraft*	US	9	1994	
*	*Warships*	*Sweden*		1992	*Submarine sections.*

	Category	From	No.	Year	Description/comments
*	*Warships*	*US*	*1*	*1993*	Australia's reply for 1993 notes that it imported 'one DDG-class warship, which was not commissioned into the Royal Australian Navy and never will be, and is now in the process of being dismantled for spares.'
	Warships	US	2	1994	Newport-class Tank Landing Ships. In Australian service, these ships are designated Training and Helicopter Support Ships, named HMAS Manoora and HMAS Kanimbla. It is not absolutely clear whether such ships fall within the definition of a category VI 'warship', but we have decided to include them because we consider that such ships are important components of naval force structure whose transfer should be declared to the Register.
	MML	US	29	1992	Includes imports of Harpoon, Sparrow and Standard missiles and also includes two Mk 13 missile launchers purchased for fitting to the Australian frigates 'Melbourne' and 'Newcastle'. Two of the missiles were delivered in a telemetry (training) configuration.
*	*MML*	*US*	*26*	*1992*	

	Category	From	No.	Year	Description/comments
	MML	US	7	1993	Includes Harpoon, Sparrow and Standard missiles. All were telemetry-training missiles.
*	*MML*	*US*	*106*	*1993*	
	MML	US	46	1994	Standard and Harpoon missiles.
*	*MML*	*US*	*2*	*1994*	

	BRUNEI[1]				
*	*ACV*	*UK*	*6*	*1992*	*Return of equipment after refurbishment.*

	CAMBODIA[2]				
*	*Tanks*	*Czech Republic*	*40*	*1994*	T-55.
*	*Tanks*	*Poland*	*50*	*1994*	T-55A.
*	*ACV*	*Czech Republic*	*26*	*1994*	*APC type OT-64.*

	INDONESIA				
*	*Artillery*	*Slovakia*	*12*	*1993*	
√	Warships	Germany	14	1993	3 Parchim (corvette); 2 Frosch (LST); 9 Condor (mine sweeper).

1　Brunei has not made any submissions of its own to the Register.

2　Cambodia has not made any submissions of its own to the Register.

	Category	From	No.	Year	Description/comments
√*	*Warships*	*Germany*	*14*	*1993*	*3 coastal patrol boats; 2 landing craft, 9 mine sweeper.*
√	Warships	Germany	13	1994	6 Parchim (corvettes); 7 Frosch (LST) demilitarised.
√*	*Warships*	*Germany*	*13*	*1994*	*6 coastal patrol boats; 7 landing craft (demilitarised).*

MALAYSIA

	Category	From	No.	Year	Description/comments
*	*ACV*	*Republic of Korea*	*42*	*1993*	*Infantry Fighting Vehicle K-200. Based on date of departure from Korea.*
	ACV	Republic of Korea	47	1994	IFV K 200, K 281.
*	*ACV*	*Republic of Korea*	*22*	*1994*	*Infantry Fighting Vehicle K-200. Based on date of departure from Korea.*
	Artillery	Belgium	2028	1994	90 mm.
	Artillery	France	15230	1994	81 mm.
	Artillery	France	8260	1994	60 mm.
	Artillery	Italy	1787	1994	105 mm T1 Red.
	Artillery	Italy	1577	1994	105 mm T1 Yellow.
	Artillery	Spain	1024	1994	155 mm HE Low H.
	Artillery	UK	3	1993	155mm into medium guns.
*	*Artillery*	*UK*	*3*	*1994*	
	Aircraft	Russia	18	1994	Mig 29, series 29/29UB .
	Aircraft	UK	28	1993	Hawk aircraft series 100 & 200.
*	*Aircraft*	*UK*	*24*	*1994*	
	Aircraft	US	8	1993	F/A-18D.

	Category	From	No.	Year	Description/comments
	Warships	UK	2	1993	Frigate.
	Warships	US	1	1994	Landing Ship Tank.
	MML	France	16	1993	Exocet MM40. Weapon system for the 2 frigates.
*	*MML*	*France*	*2*	*1994*	
	MML	Italy	36	1993	Torpedoes (Whitehead A 244S MOD). Weapon system for the 2 frigates.
	MML	UK	32	1993	Seawolf missiles. Weapon system for the 2 frigates.
	MML	UK	504	1993	Starburst weapon system.
	MML	US	40	1993	Sidewinder missiles. For use on F/A-18D.
	MML	US	30	1993	Maverick missiles. For use on F/A-18D.
	MML	US	25	1993	Harpoon missiles. For use on F/A-18D.
	MML	US	20	1993	Sparrow missiles. For use on F/A-18D.

MYANMAR[3]

	Category	From	No.	Year	Description/comments
*	*Aircraft*	*China*	*12*	*1993*	(No description included, but SIPRI reports A-5M Fantan and F-7M Airguard transfers).

---

3   Myanmar has not made any submissions of its own to the Register.

	Category	From	No.	Year	Description/comments
	NEW ZEALAND				
√	Aircraft	Italy	6	1992	Aeromacchi MB-339C. New training aircraft, but capable of modification.
√*	Aircraft	Italy	6	1992	MB-339C.
√	Aircraft	Italy	3	1993	MB-339CB. Trainer. Not modified for any combat capability.
√*	Aircraft	Italy	6	1993	MB 339 version C.A.S. and Trainer.
	Warships		1	1994	Military sealift ship.
	PAPUA NEW GUINEA				
*	ACV	UK	1	1992	
	PHILIPPINES				
√	ACV	UK	7	1993	SIMBA armoured fighting vehicle.
√*	ACV	UK	7	1993	
	ACV	UK	13	1994	SIMBA armoured vehicle.
	ACV	US	20	1994	10 V-150 commando; 10 Hummer M1025.
	Artillery	Italy	4	1994	Belly Gun Pod Cal. 50.
	Artillery	US	179	1994	M60C.
	Aircraft	Italy	4	1993	SF-260 TP trainer.
	Aircraft	Italy	24	1994	S-211.
	Aircraft	US	19	1992	OV-10A.

	Category	From	No.	Year	Description/comments
*	*Aircraft*	*US*	*9*	*1992*	
	Aircraft	US	24	1994	OV-10.
	Helicopters	US	33	1994	MG-320.
	Warships	Republic of Korea	12	1993	Patrol boat. State of origin US.
	Warships	US	1	1993	Logistic support vessel.
	MML	US	100	1994	LAC-131.
	MML	US	10680	1994	RX MTR HK 40/56.

SINGAPORE

	Category	From	No.	Year	Description/comments
*	*Tanks*	*US*	*1*	*1992*	
	ACV	US	1	1992	
√	ACV	France	24	1993	(No description included, but SIPRI reports AMX-10 transfer).
√*	*ACV*	*France*	*24*	*1993*	
√	ACV	France	20	1994	
√*	*ACV*	*France*	*20*	*1994*	
	Artillery	France	24	1992	(No description included, but SIPRI reports LG-1 105 mm transfer).
*	*Artillery*	*France*	*26*	*1992*	
	Artillery	France	13	1993	
*	*Artillery*	*France*	*7*	*1993*	
	Aircraft	Jordan	7	1994	(No description included, but SIPRI reports F-5M Tiger II transfer).

	Category	From	No.	Year	Description/comments
*	*Helicopters*	*France*	*8*	*1993*	(No description included, but SIPRI reports AS-555 Fennec transfer, for assembly in Singapore).
	MML	US	1	1992	1 missile. (No other description included, but SIPRI reports: 96 Harpoon missiles, delivered in 1990-91, for 6 Victory class corvettes; 48 Harpoon missiles, delivered in 1988-91, for 6 TNC-45 fast attack craft; 50 Sparrow and 36 AIM-9S Sidewinder air-to-air missiles for F-16C/D).
	MML	US	8	1993	
*	*MML*	*US*	*20*	*1993*	
	MML	US	12	1994	

THAILAND[4]

√	ACV	Germany	18	1993	
√*	*ACV*	*Germany*	*18*	*1993*	*APC Condor.*
	ACV	Germany	18	1994	
*	*ACV*	*US*	*18*	*1992*	(No description included, but SIPRI reports M-113A2 transfer).
	ACV	US	6	1993	
*	*ACV*	*US*	*10*	*1993*	
	ACV	US	26	1994	
*	*Artillery*	*Austria*	*18*	*1992*	*155 mm.*

---

[4] Thailand has not submitted any information for 1992 to the Register.

	Category	From	No.	Year	Description/comments
√	Artillery	US	20	1994	(No description included, but SIPRI reports M109A5 155mm self-propelled gun transfer).
√*	Artillery	US	20	1994	
	Aircraft	Czech Republic	36	1993	(No description included, but SIPRI reports transfer of L-39Z Albatros jet trainer).
*	Aircraft	Czech Republic	8	1993	
	Aircraft	Czech Republic	36	1994	
*	Aircraft	Czech Republic	28	1994	
*	Warships	China	2	1992	(No description included, but SIPRI reports transfer of Jianghu class frigates).
*	Warships	China	1	1994	(No description included, but SIPRI reports transfer of Naresuan class frigates, weapons and electronics to be fitted in Thailand).
	Warships	US	1	1994	HTMS Phuttrayotya Chulalok (USS Knox Class).
*	MML	China	24	1992	(No description included, but SIPRI reports transfer of C-801 Ship-to-Ship missiles for Jianghu class frigates).
	MML	China	90	1993	